Deluded New World

Current Controversies and
Why the Free World Is on Edge

Deluded New World

Current Controversies and
Why the Free World Is on Edge

Charles Pasternak

World Scientific

NEW JERSEY • LONDON • SINGAPORE • BEIJING • SHANGHAI • TAIPEI • CHENNAI

Published by

World Scientific Publishing Europe Ltd.

57 Shelton Street, Covent Garden, London WC2H 9HE

Head office: 5 Toh Tuck Link, Singapore 596224

USA office: 27 Warren Street, Suite 401-402, Hackensack, NJ 07601

Library of Congress Cataloging-in-Publication Data
Names: Pasternak, Charles A. (Charles Alexander) author
Title: Deluded new world : current controversies and why the free world is on edge /
  Charles Pasternak, Oxford International Biomedical Centre, UK.
Description: New Jersey : World Scientific, [2026] | Includes bibliographical references and index.
Identifiers: LCCN 2025027413 | ISBN 9781800618077 hardcover |
  ISBN 9781800618107 paperback | ISBN 9781800618084 ebook |
  ISBN 9781800618091 ebook other
Subjects: LCSH: Social history | Social change
Classification: LCC HN18.3 .P385 2026
LC record available at https://lccn.loc.gov/2025027413

British Library Cataloguing-in-Publication Data
A catalogue record for this book is available from the British Library.

Copyright © 2026 by World Scientific Publishing Europe Ltd.

All rights reserved. This book, or parts thereof, may not be reproduced in any form or by any means, electronic or mechanical, including photocopying, recording or any information storage and retrieval system now known or to be invented, without written permission from the Publisher.

For photocopying of material in this volume, please pay a copying fee through the Copyright Clearance Center, Inc., 222 Rosewood Drive, Danvers, MA 01923, USA. In this case permission to photocopy is not required from the publisher.

For any available supplementary material, please visit
https://www.worldscientific.com/worldscibooks/10.1142/Q0531#t=suppl

Desk Editor: Murali Appadurai

Typeset by Stallion Press
Email: enquiries@stallionpress.com

To all who have suffered, and continue to do so, from trans ideology and other deluded dogma.

About the Author

Charles Pasternak is a British biochemist and the Founding Director of the Oxford International Biomedical Centre, of which he is currently President. He has published over 250 original papers and reviews and is the Founding Editor-in-Chief of *Bioscience Reports*, helming the journal for 28 years. He is also the Editor of *Biosciences 2000* (World Scientific, 1999) and author of eight other books.

Educated at Oxford University, Charles Pasternak spent 15 years on the staff of the Oxford Biochemistry Department, during which time he also held a teaching Fellowship at Worcester College, Oxford. He spent two years as a Post-Doctoral Fellow in the Pharmacology Department of Yale University Medical School and subsequently held an Eleanor Roosevelt Fellowship of the International Union Against Cancer in the Department of Neurosciences at the University of California, San Diego Medical School in La Jolla. In 1976, he was invited to move to St. George's Hospital Medical School, University of London, in order to set up a new Department of Biochemistry, which he subsequently expanded into a larger Department of Cellular and Molecular Sciences as Founder-Chairman. He is currently President of the Oxford International Biomedical Centre, which he founded in 1992.

Charles Pasternak is a tireless promoter of international scientific collaboration. He has been a member of the Executive Committee for a UNESCO initiative on Molecular and Cellular Biology, a member of the

Education Committee of the International Union of Biochemistry and Molecular Biology (IUBMB), a member of the International Advisory Board for the Chulabhorn Research Institute, Bangkok and a member of the Scientific Board of Antenna Technologie, Geneva. In 1979, he founded the Cell Surface Research Fund in order to foster international research links and scientific meetings on various aspects of fundamental and clinical research on the cell surface. He received the degree of Doctor Honoris Causa and the Palade medal from the University of Bucharest in 1993, the honour of Amigo de Venezuela from the Fundacion Venezuela Positiva in 1995 and was elected Foreign Member of the Polish Academy of Arts and Sciences in 2002.

Acknowledgements

I am grateful to (Lord) Nigel Biggar, Khiara Bridges, Carol Bristow, Haruko Fukuda, Iris Gruenebaum, Tim Lott, Robert Plomin, (the late) Aridea Fezzi Price, (Lord) Tony Sewell, Eldred Smith-Gordon, Meirion Thomas and (Lord) Toby Young for information and comments. Kasia Lewis, as always, has been a godsend. To the staff at the London Library, I am indebted for their continuous assistance, and to Robin, Henry and Angus Piercey of Influential Computers in Stoke Row for rescuing me whenever the internet was conspiring against me. I greatly appreciate the suggestions of Shaun Tan Yi Jie, commissioning editor at WSP, and the meticulous editing by Murali Appadurai.

Contents

About the Author   vii

Acknowledgements   ix

Chapter 1. Introduction   1

Chapter 2. Bigotry and Racism   17

Chapter 3. Slavery and Colonialism   33

Chapter 4. Gender and Sex   59

Chapter 5. Political Correctness   95

Chapter 6. Free Speech   135

Chapter 7. Conclusion   157

Chapter 8. Epilogue   167

Glossary   185

Bibliography   187

Index   191

Chapter 1

Introduction

Ideas transmitted by people have criss-crossed the Atlantic for centuries. Following the arrival of English settlers during the 17th century, the religion and culture of Europe was brought to what would become the United States over almost three centuries. Then, societal change began to travel from west to east, like the Gulf Stream. During the 20th century, it brought moving pictures and television, the supermarket and the motel, washing machines and refrigerators, the hamburger and the contraceptive pill, plastic wrapping and the electric toaster. Today, it conveys political correctness, opinions like Black Lives Matter, Critical Race Theory and attitudes towards LGBT (Lesbian, Gay, Bisexual and Trans persons), slavery and colonialism. In this book, I draw attention to the way that these matters are affecting life in the UK and elsewhere.

I grew up at a time without television, personal computers or the internet. People communicated by the written word and telephones were neither smart nor mobile. Commercial air travel was in its infancy, watches merely recorded the time and one's luggage had not yet sprouted wheels. Given my age, I ask the reader to forgive my use of such old-fashioned words as man and woman, female and male.

Controversy and argument are a feature of human behaviour. Debate began to replace rule by a potentate when democracy emerged in the city-states of Greece 2500 years ago. In the agora of Athens, men debated how best to rule their city. Within the home, women could express their views. Democracy would crumble under invasion by Macedonia in the 4th century BCE, but by that time a watered-down version had already been established in Rome where it would last until Augustus's reign in 27 BCE. Thereafter, the concept lay dormant throughout most of the world. Iceland's parliament, the Althing, established in 930, may be the oldest in the world but it was under the control of Norwegian chieftains, who were the island's first settlers. Democracy reappeared to a certain extent in the cantons of Switzerland during the 14th century, and with vigour in America and France during the later years of the eighteenth. It is what defines the Free World.

Today, over half of the 195 the nations of the world – but no more – are administered by freely elected governments. 'The survival of democracy', Aldous Huxley wrote, 'depends on the ability of large numbers of peoples to make realistic choices in the light of adequate information. A dictatorship, on the other hand, maintains itself by censoring or distorting the facts, and by appealing, not to reason, not to enlightened self-interest, but to passion and prejudice ... present in the unconscious depths of every human mind' [1]. The title for this book has been adapted from Huxley's earlier work, *Brave New World*. Huxley, in his turn, took the title from Shakespeare. In *The Tempest*, Miranda, meeting people for the first time, says 'O Brave new world that has such people in it'. *Brave New World* is fiction; *Deluded New World* is fact. Huxley wrote for amusement; this book is a warning.

Politicians and their adherents argue amongst themselves about achieving a more effective government than the previous one (generally not an arduous aim), but political differences between people are not what this book is about. Instead, it addresses controversies that have arisen during the opening decades of the 21st century. These amplify and extend the thrust of Helen Joyce's excellent *Trans. When Ideology Meets Reality*, published in 2021. Their range may be illustrated by reports that appeared in a British newspaper on just one day in 2023 [2]: 'Canada has lost its moral bearings and is testing woke ideology to destruction'; 'The lone professor speaking truth to the "decolonising" mob'; 'Free societies can't survive the elevation of feelings into facts'; 'British "dead white guys" and the King dropped as school names by Canadian state'; 'Gladstone statue under shroud as church investigates slavery link'; 'Women-only student group triumphs in trans dispute'; 'Concern for Muslim pupils over Church's gay blessings';

Introduction

'Scottish discus champion fears for children over Sturgeon's trans policy on school sport'; 'Sorry, Nicola, it turns out we're all "Terfs" now'; 'Outcry as academics liken feminist conference to "enabling eugenics"'.

Such a potpourri of topics – as well as their origins and outcomes – is what this book is about. I began writing it in 2023. Since then, some of the controversies are slowly being resolved. But most, such as transgender issues, children's education, political correctness, free speech and cancel culture remain. A flavour of the issues follows. Most of the controversies described here are being debated in Western democracies. Few people in the autocracies of China or Russia, Iran or Afghanistan – not to mention North Korea – are prepared to put forward views that run counter to their rulers' tenets. Voicing a provocative view in Cambridge (England or Massachusetts) won't land you in trouble with the police. Doing so in Beijing or Moscow, Tehran or Kabul might well. This encapsulates the difference between life in a free society and one in a dictatorship. This broad-brush conclusion, of course, hides variations of policy in regard to specific issues by different Western countries. Within the European Union, for example, Hungary defied the Commission and angered most member states by passing a law banning homosexual and transgender propaganda aimed at under eighteen-year-olds in 2021. Homosexuality itself, though, is legal and discrimination on grounds of sexual orientation is forbidden. Same-sex partnerships (though not marriage) have been recognised since 2009. A similar situation exists in Poland, which was heavily criticised by ILGA-Europe (International Lesbian, Gay, Bisexual, Trans and Intersex Association) [3] in 2022 on account of certain legal challenges faced by LGBT persons. Homosexuality has been legal in Poland since 1932, and employers are forbidden from discriminating on the basis of sexual orientation.

In the United States, too, there is a huge variation in attitude towards the LGBT issue. Each state has its own range of policies. The most liberal are mainly along the west coast (Washington, Oregon and California, as well as Nevada) and in the northeast (Maine, Vermont, New York, Massachusetts, Rhode Island, Connecticut, New Jersey and the District of Columbia). The least liberal are largely in the South (Oklahoma, Arkansas, Tennessee, South Carolina, Louisiana, Mississippi and Alabama) [4].

There is considerable overlap between those states and those that restrict education on racism, sexism, and other 'divisive issues'. Unsurprisingly, the latter are all in Republican-dominated states [5]. The number of same-sex households, which are largely between females, is one of the highest in DC (that envelops the sophisticated Washington elite): over 4% of the population by 2015, with 80% supporting same-sex marriage [6]. In the USA as a whole, around a million households consisted of same-sex partners in 2019. In Alabama, a typical southern state in regard to this issue, on the other hand, matters could be moving backwards [7].

Across the rest of the free world, homosexuality was still being criminalised in 69 countries a few years ago. Muslim countries are the most vociferous. Others are in Sub-Saharan Africa, where religiously conservative Christians among the lawmakers maintain their opposition to homosexuals and others leading an unconventional life. Such attitudes have been retained by those who now inhabit some of the Caribbean islands such as Antigua and Barbuda, Barbados, Dominica, Grenada, Guyana, Jamaica and St Lucia [8]. Yet the opposition from global pressure groups like the UN Human Rights Council and Amnesty International is slowly changing attitudes. In 2014, the World Bank postponed a loan to Uganda on account of its anti-gay law. Disapproval from such quarters will surely exert a gradual effect elsewhere.

Ousting Kathleen Stock

None of the topics discussed here is particularly new. Many have existed for more than two millennia and have been controversial for much of that time. What distinguishes the 21st century from previous ones is that participants in the debate can now be forced out of their jobs. This is what happened to Kathleen Stock, professor of philosophy at the University of Sussex in the UK. In 2020, she wrote *Material Girls. Why Reality Matters for Feminism*, published during the following year [9]. In this book, Stock sets out very clearly the difference between Gender Identity – a subjective description of oneself first raised by Simone de Beauvoir in her 1949 book on *The Second Sex* – and natal sex, which is a biological reality of only two kinds. Yes, I am aware of rare anomalies, such as a female (XX chromosomes and normal ovaries) born with an enlarged vagina that resembles a penis, also of the extremely uncommon (less than 0.001% of the population) condition of hermaphroditism (ovotesticular syndrome) in which someone has both ovarian and testicular tissue. The rare event of a person born without arms (amelia; several cases resulting from the insufficiently trialled administration of thalidomide to pregnant mothers in order to ease morning sickness sixty years ago) or with one ear (anotia) does not exclude the statement that 'humans have two arms and two ears'. To add 'in 99.9% of cases' every time a physical attribute is mentioned jeopardises normal speech and script.

Stock points to the anomaly that since 2016 violent trans-women (see Glossary) have been placed in female prisons and muscular trans-women allowed to compete in the women's sections of various sports. Throughout, she acknowledges the right of any one to identify with a gender of their choosing. Nevertheless, in October 2021, a group of students describing themselves as queer, trans and non-binary accused her 'of espousing a bastardised version of radical feminism that excludes and endangers trans people' and asked for her to be sacked. The Vice-Chancellor strongly supported Stock's right to express her views and pointed out that the university had 'legal and moral duties to ensure people can speak freely'. The local branch of the University and College Union on the other hand criticised the Vice-Chancellor. Its delegates backed the students and those staff members who agreed with them. 'Institutional transphobia' was not to be tolerated at the university, they decided. Tempers flared. Police recommended that Professor Stock install CCTV at her home and be protected by a bodyguard on campus. By the end of the month, Stock had had enough and resigned. The academic career, spanning nearly twenty years, of Kathleen Stock OBE [10] was over.

Denigrating W E Gladstone

Another difference between this century and previous ones lies in attitudes towards such topics as slavery. No one today would argue against the fact this has been a particularly evil practice of humankind, from the earliest 'civilisations' across the globe onwards. Today's virtue-signalling guardians of correct behaviour go further. The reputation of any historical figure deemed to have been associated with slavery is to be reassessed in a negative manner. The four times Liberal Prime Minister of the UK during the 19th century, W E Gladstone, provides a good example. He opposed the slave trade and supported emancipation in 1833. As a man of progressive principles, Gladstone in 1870 introduced schooling for all children between 5 and 11 years of age in England and Wales. The following year, his government legalised trade unions. Not surprisingly Liverpool – the city of Gladstone's birth – honoured him in a number of ways. The University, for example, named its halls of residence after him. But because Gladstone's father had been the owner of large plantations in Guyana and Jamaica, students campaigned to have the son's name removed. In 2021, the University capitulated.

Other examples of the names of well-known figures and philanthropists being removed will be found in Chapter 3. But is historiography really being served when we ignore the attitudes that existed in a previous age and interpret the actions of people at such times in terms of opinions that have come to prevail centuries later? For the last five thousand years, women have been second-class citizens throughout most of the world (see, for example, [11]). A Roman Briton visiting England in the 19th century would have been amazed by smoke-belching trains carrying people between cities that contained houses of three or more storeys, beautiful parks and wide streets lit at night. But that a married woman could not own property, make a will or sue for divorce would have been of no surprise. Material innovation has for long outstripped changes in attitude – whether towards females, or subjugated people, or believers in a divergent religion, or anyone of different complexion. Queen Victoria's Poet Laureate Alfred Tennyson made a somewhat related point with 'Knowledge comes, but wisdom lingers' [12].

Climate change

One of the most important controversies throughout the world concerns climate change. Over the 4 billion years since our planet formed, the surface temperature has oscillated between warm and cold periods. For the last 150 years, it has gradually been getting warmer. But already in the 18th century, Scottish philosopher David Hume postulated that 'human activity was responsible for causing the planet to warm' [13]. In contrast, eminent French naturalist George-Louis Leclerc held that the earth had been getting colder since its creation and would keep on doing so; 'ultimately little would stop an inevitable freeze' [14]. It may be apt that Leclerc was also the Comte de Buffon.

We now know that Hume's view was correct. Though he could not have known it, the recent rise in temperature is the direct result of burning fossil fuels for energy. This releases more carbon dioxide into the atmosphere than can be absorbed by forests and the oceans. That gases in the atmosphere trap heat generated on earth – the so-called greenhouse effect – was first suggested by the French polymath Joseph Fourier in the 1820s [15]. The current temperature is 1.1°C above pre-industrial levels, and rising. This means that extreme weather events – storms and floods, severe heat and droughts – will increase to make life exceedingly unpleasant for many. Melting ice in the polar regions could result in sea levels rising by as much as a metre by the end of this century, thereby inundating islands such as the Maldives. London could see areas along the Thames as far inland as Fulham and Chelsea being flooded at high tide. But already within the next ten years, cities like Amsterdam, Bangkok, Kolkata (formerly Calcutta), New Orleans and Venice could be partially under water. The Dutch have been building effective barriers against the sea since the 13th century, and flood gates in the Venetian lagoon may yet save that city. So, there is hope that novel technology may counter nature in this regard. One reason for the rise in global temperature is that much of the world's natural forests – that absorb carbon dioxide – are being lost to logging and replacement by industry and palm oil trees. Greening urban areas would help to restrict temperature rises (and reverse the loss of biodiversity). The Dutch, as well as the Japanese, are again at the forefront here (see [16]). The Dutch are also generating islands by dredging mud and sand from the floor of a lake [17]. Not only is the water quality of the lake improved but the new land created could play a beneficial role, as mentioned earlier.

Arguments between countries, their entrepreneurs and their bureaucrats, about how to curb global warming and attain 'net zero' (the situation in which emission of greenhouse gases no longer exceeds their absorption) by 2050, continue to seethe. In order to achieve this goal, the average global temperature should not exceed 1.5°C [18] above the level in 1850 (which stayed constant for the following 80 years). 196 nations, meeting in Paris in 2015, signed up to this objective. Despite good words, and yearly conferences on the topic in different parts of the world, the target is unlikely to be met. Perhaps the fact that most of the 40,000 delegates to the 2021 meeting in Glasgow COP 26 (Conference of the Parties) arrived by greenhouse gas-emitting aeroplanes has something to do with it. Two years later, 9,000 eco-warriors travelled to Doha (COP 28) in the United Arab Emirates (UAE). Yet discussion of how net zero can be achieved through phasing out fossil fuels was left to the very end of the conference (despite the fact that 'the science is clear' [19]) – hardly surprising given that the UAE is one of the world's largest oil producers. In 2024, the COP 29 climate conference was held in Baku, the capital of Azerbaijan. An astonishing 67,000 delegates are reported to have attended, many arriving by private jet. The UN has rightly demanded that future COP meetings be reformed and shrunk. This, as science columnist Matt Ridley has pointed out, is unlikely. 'The beauty of the COP process is that it can go on forever because it never makes a difference. It is, in a word, sustainable. Carbon dioxide emissions keep breaking records. Gas, coal and oil still supply 82 per cent of the energy the world uses. These meetings have gone on for nearly one third of a century already; they are an institution complete with traditions and ceremonies; people have spent entire careers attending them. The last thing they need is for somebody to solve the problem' [20].

Nor are actions like Just Stop Oil or Extinction Rebellion in the UK much help. Blocking roads or gluing themselves to roads and motorways at peak travel time, they claim to save the planet by stopping the flow of gas-emitting motor vehicles. Instead, one such action prevented a motorist from reaching his dying father. When Extinction Rebellion's co-founder Roger Hallam was asked about these activities, he replied that he would block an ambulance carrying a dying patient in order to get their message across [21], a bold statement considering that the UK contributes just 1% to global greenhouse gas emissions. (The highest emitter is China at close to 30%; it is currently building two new coal-fired power plants every week. India is not far behind, with Bangladesh, Cambodia, Indonesia, Japan, Pakistan, Philippines, South Korea and Vietnam continuing to construct such plants to produce electricity [22].) Hallam has since been jailed for conspiring to block traffic in connection with the Just Stop Oil campaign on the M25 in November 2022.

Although climate change, like politics, is not a topic that features in the rest of this book, I mention it because the following item, too, belongs to the 21st and no preceding century: 'Cows will get flatulence blockers so UK can hit net zero goal' [23]. Methane, which cows and other ruminants expel through their breath and flatulence, is 25 times more effective as a greenhouse gas than carbon dioxide. (New Zealand's Labour government is planning to tax livestock-emitting methane; but merely switching to seaweed-based livestock feed would reduce methane emissions significantly [24].) Its release into the atmosphere – due mainly to human activities such as landfills, waste water treatment, coal mining, in addition to emission by ruminants – has more than doubled over the last two centuries and now accounts for 20% of greenhouse gas emissions. Like generating infertile *Anopheles* mosquitoes in order to minimise the spread of malaria, producing 5 billion insects that carry the bacterium *Wolbachia* in order to prevent the insects from carrying the dengue virus [25] or vaccinating condors to halt the spread of bird flu [26], eliminating bad breath among cattle and sheep is very much a 21st-century enterprise.

Religion

An issue that has come up for argument in the 21st century concerns religion. The oldest examples of venerating the dead by burial in order to preserve their bodies from wild animals go back to the middle of the stone age. Near Mount Carmel in Israel, forty covered graves – some containing skeletons identified as *H sapiens*, others as *H neanderthalensis* – have been dated to 130,000 to 100,000 years ago [27]. In a cave near the coast of

Southeast Kenya, the skeletal remains of a 2- to 3-year-old child (*H sapiens*) have recently been unearthed in a grave and dated to be around 78,000 years old [28]. Apart from such indications of a possible belief in an afterlife, we do not know what the earliest humans thought about the world about them. As civilisations emerged many millennia later, in Asia, North Africa, Mesoamerica, South America and eventually Europe, the notion of some sort of creator god appears in the earliest documented religions.

In Sumeria, that character was known as Enki. Within the Hindu religion, Brama and Shiva are the main figures to whom the creation of humanity is ascribed. In Pharaonic Egypt, the god most closely associated with creation was probably the sun god Ra, later fused with Amun as Amun-Ra. The oldest civilisation in Mesoamerica, that of the Olmec, revered several gods but none was particularly associated with creation. The Maya, whose empire stretched across what is today Southeast Mexico and its neighbours, ascribed their creation to the feathered serpent Q'uq'umatz. The Inca, who lived along the west coast of South America, considered the god Inti as the creator of humankind. For the Aztecs, it was the deities known as Huitzilopochtli and his brother Quetzalcoatl. The ancient Greeks believed that the god Chaos ruled the emptiness that preceded life on earth. The god Zeus (known as Jupiter by the Romans) then gave life to humanity. The Abrahamic religions of Judaism, Christianity and Islam recognise only one deity to whom they ascribe the creation of life.

Unsurprisingly, all the gods I have just mentioned were depicted and referred to as males. (Only in 'Old Europe' was a female creator of life revered. Archaeologist Marija Gimbutas has unearthed hundreds of figurines depicting a 'fertility' or 'mother' goddess, in an area roughly corresponding to the Balkans, which have been dated to around 6500 – 3500 BCE [29].) Prior to the establishment of agriculture, humans lived in families and small groups, probably controlled by a male leader. As the population increased dramatically following the emergence of farming, the leader became a ruler and eventually a king. On his death, he was venerated as a god. Such an explanation for the concept of a male deity is part of psychologist Julian Jaynes's theory of the nature of consciousness [30].

With the rise of political correctness in speech and script in the 21st century, the (former) Archbishop of Canterbury, Head of the Anglican Church, and some of his bishops recommend that a commission should consider making the Christian God gender neutral (a proposal considered by some clerics previously from time to time). The Archbishop of York, second most senior cleric in the Church of England, agrees: 'It is problematic'. For whom? For a possible 1% of boys abused by their father [31]. So, will the Lord's Prayer now begin 'Our non-gendered parent who art in heaven ... ?' [32]. Whether the Pope and the Catholic community will follow this proposal is unlikely. We may yet witness a rift not seen since 1534. But creation deities, whether female or male, are really no longer necessary since science has shown how Mother Earth was created four billion years in the past and how we evolved on it through many ancestors less than a million years ago. On the other hand, many people are curious – a very human characteristic – as to where the miniscule bundle of sub-atomic particles that exploded in the 'Big Bang' 13.8 billion years ago and formed the solar system came from in the first place. Is there a Creator of the Universe whose deity unites all faiths on earth and beyond?

Agriculture

The most successful idea that humankind has come up with was put into practice ten thousand years ago in Anatolia and perhaps also in Papua New Guinea [33]. It had occurred to some groups that instead of gathering grains and berries and having to move on when supplies became exhausted, they could try to propagate these by planting their seeds instead. The practice of agriculture emerged at different times in seven further locations, all quite independently of each other: in China, other parts of Asia, Africa, Mesoamerica and South America [34]. Was this idea inspired by women? The task of foraging has often been assumed to have been carried out largely by women, while men hunted. Recent evidence suggests that this is an oversimplification. First, because it appears that women joined in the hunt for large animals [35]. Second, because 'osteological analysis ...

reveals upper-body strength at levels that would have surpassed today's female athletes. Musculoskeletal stress levels in both men and women suggest that there was a sharing of labour ... leading some to suggest that separate gender roles did not emerge until around 3000 BCE' [36]. To what extent either sex contributed to the earliest agricultural practices is therefore irrelevant. What is remarkable is that at each of the eight locations where agriculture was born, individuals of extraordinary curiosity and intellect inspired others to embark on entirely novel practices. These have fed the world since then, and can continue to do so provided population growth and destruction of the environment are checked. Nevertheless, the 21st century saw a technology to produce nutritious food in a laboratory emerge [37].

During the first few decades of the 21st century, then, some unexpected propositions and practices have diffused across the free world. The former threaten – among other things – the freedom to express oneself by speech and the written word, which is taken for granted in any democracy. Their successful dissemination is due to the support by certain 'establishment' figures: university professors – vice-chancellors even – school teachers, heads of artistic institutions, politicians, bureaucrats, business leaders and so on. Yet some of these are not among the most enlightened characters. In the land that produced Benjamin Franklin, John Adams and Thomas Jefferson, it is surprising to find a university professor who thinks that the first three letters of *history* refer to the male pronoun (the French *histoire* and the Italian *storia* are in fact feminine). When I first read about *herstory*, I assumed it was a joke, though I now realise that it has been used by feminist organisations since the 1970s.

The civil service, the armed forces, the National Health Service, the fire service, construction companies, banks, supermarkets [38], law firms, local government, universities and other institutions spend time and money on Equity, Diversity and Inclusion (EDI; a triple oxymoron, surely) courses. But is such training, prescribed by EDI warriors, really the way to solve some of the societal changes thrown up by altered attitudes during 21st century? Most humans are empathetic towards those in problematic situations. Kindness is not a quality easily taught.

Bigotry is part of human nature and racism persists in pockets (Chapter 2). The evil of slavery that was endemic across the world for ten millennia has largely died out, while colonialism is being reassessed (Chapter 3). Women are being denied their own space by some and challenged on the sports field by others; children are encouraged to reconsider their gender in the school room, not in the home. Ideologues consider sex not to be binary (Chapter 4). The views of militant students are allowed to trump those of the faculty. The writings of past authors are being edited to conform with current dogma. History is being assessed in the light of 21st-century opinions without regard to the culture at the time (Chapter 5). Freedom of speech is under attack (Chapter 6) but the free world has not fallen off the edge yet (Chapter 7). A far greater threat exists from the autocracies outside the free world. It is for that reason that I have added an epilogue (Chapter 8).

The second half of the previous century witnessed two societal changes of note: the acceptance of homosexuality and the abolition of smoking in public spaces. But to think that adopting the controversial measures documented here will likewise benefit future generations is a delusion.

As a biologist, I am aware of the difference between innate and cultural dispositions, and I have no doubts that sex is binary. Having been an Oxford 'don' for more than a decade, the foibles of students and faculty are not unknown to me. As a former member of international committees like IUBMB [39] and a UNESCO initiative on Molecular and Cellular Biology, I appreciate that cultural and social change sweeps westward from America to Europe via Britain. That background is what emboldened me to write this book.

Notes

1. Huxley, 1959, p 73.
2. *The Sunday Telegraph*, 5 February 2023. Many of the articles cited in the pages that follow are from the *Daily Telegraph* or *Sunday Telegraph*. They are largely without political implications and are likely to have been printed also in any other British newspaper such as the *Guardian, Daily Mail, Times* or *Sunday Times*. Only after July 2024 when Labour entered government did certain topics adopt a political slant.
3. https://www.google.com/search?q=ilga+europe&oq=ilga+europe&aqs=chrome..69i57j0i512j0i455i512j0i51212j0i455i51215.9577j0j15&sourceid=chrome&ie=UTF-8.
4. https://www.lgbtmap.org/equality-maps.
5. https://www.google.com/search?q=Censorship+of+school+curricula+in+the+United+States&oq=Censorship+of+school+curricula+in+the+United+States&aqs=chrome.0.69i59j0i22i30j0i390i65014j69i60.1155j0j15&sourceid=chrome&ie=UTF-8.
6. https://en.wikipedia.org/wiki/LGBT_rights_in_the_District_of_Columbia.
7. For gay couples in Alabama, it's 'one step forward, two steps back,' say women who sued for marriage equality: https://www.al.com/life/2022/07/for-gay-couples-in-alabama-its-one-step-forward-two-steps-back-say-women-who-sued-for-marriage-equality.html.
8. see, for example, https://www.bbc.co.uk/news/world-43822234 and https://commonslibrary.parliament.uk/research-briefings/cbp-9436/.
9. Stock, 2021.
10. https://en.wikipedia.org/wiki/Kathleen_Stock.
11. Pasternak, 2022.
12. from 'Locksley Hall', 1835.
13. Frankopan, p 449.
14. *ibid* p 452.
15. *ibid* p 499.
16. https://www.facebook.com/davies.white.landscape.architects/videos/i-am-david-attenborough-and-im-93-this-is-my-witness-statement-there-is-a-tremen/738293350351952/.

17. Aisling Irwin: Can the Netherlands' artificial islands lead the way to rewilding the planet? *Nature* **616**: 644–648, 2023.
18. Comment: Approaching 1.5°C: how will we know we've reached this crucial warming mark? *Nature* **624**: 33–35, 2023.
19. COP 28: the science is clear – fossil fuels must go. *Nature* **624**: 225, 2013.
20. Matt Ridley: 'It's high time to end this ludicrous COP jamboree – but just won't die' *Sunday Telegraph* 17 November 2024.
21. https://www.independent.co.uk/tv/climate/i-would-block-ambulance-with-dying-patient-onboard-says-xr-founder-roger-hallam-b2185727.html.
22. Andrew Neil, *Daily Mail* 7 October 2023.
23. *Sunday Telegraph* 2 April 2023.
24. Emma Gatton: 'Cows have greener burps on seaweed diet' *Sunday Telegraph* 30 June 2024.
25. Mariana Lenharo: Massive mosquito factory in Brazil aims to halt dengue. *Nature* **616**: 637–638, 2023.
26. Max Kozlov: United States to vaccinate birds against avian flu for first time. *Nature* **618**: 220–221, 2023.
27. https://www.cambridge.org/core/books/abs/african-genesis/oldest-burials-and-their-significance/1B10F74654E37D2BC17D34C79E819134.
28. *Nature* **593**: 95, 2021.
29. Marija Gimbutas: *Goddesses and Gods of Old Europe, 6500 – 3500 BC: Myths and Cult Images* (London: Thames and Hudson, 1982).
30. Jaynes, Julian: *The Origin of Consciousness in the Breakdown of the Bicameral Mind* (Boston: Houghton Miflin, 1976).
31. *Sunday Telegraph*, 30 July 2023.
32. https://www.dailymail.co.uk/news/article-11722729/God-non-gendered-Church-England-services.html.
33. Gideon Ladizinsky: *Plant Evolution Under Domestication* (Dordrecht: Springer, 1998).
34. Marcel Mazoyer and Laurence Roudart: *A History of World Agriculture* (tr James H Membrez; London: Earthscan, 2003).
35. Maya Wei-Haas: Prehistoric female hunter discovery upends gender role assumptions. *National Geographic* 4 November 2020).
36. Frankopan, p 64.

37. Jeffrey L Fox: Test tube meat on the menu? *Nature Biotechnology* **27**: 873, 2009.
38. https://www.walkgrove.co.uk/case-studies/john-lewis-equality-diversity-and-inclusion/.
39. International Union of Biochemistry and Molecular Biology.

Chapter 2

Bigotry and Racism

We divide the inhabited world into five continents – Europe, Asia, Africa, Australia and the Americas. But Europe and Asia are not separate land masses. They are one, arbitrarily separated by the Ural Mountains. Until the completion of the Suez Canal in 1869, Africa was attached to Eurasia by a sliver of land. The peoples living within the continents are not as distinct as generally perceived. Europeans and northern Indians (Indo-Europeans) are more closely related to each other than the latter are to Chinese. North Africans are nearer to Arabs than to the Bantu of sub-Saharan Africa. Geographical proximity and ethnic origin are not necessarily related. In this chapter, I examine the origin of racism and its relevance to the theme of *Deluded New World*.

Bias

We tend to assess a stranger in a positive or negative way as a result of instinct. This has survival value, but of course we can be wrong in our judgement. This applies especially if the stranger looks different from us. According to Susan Fiske, professor of psychology at Princeton University, prejudices are emotional biases that can lead to discrimination [1]. Bias is not always negative. As behavioural scientist Pragya Agarwal points out, 'a parent's bias that their child is the smartest, cleverest, most beautiful is an evolutionary response, designed to trigger parental love and care' [2].

The evidence that bias is shaped by our genes depends on the observation that children with Williams syndrome (WS), a rare condition in which some 26 genes on the long arm of chromosome seven have been deleted, show none of the fear of strangers that others experience. In short, they lack the cerebral capacity to discern 'them' from 'us'. A study of 20 children with WS carried out by neurologist David Amodio at New York University came to the conclusion that those with WS 'show no racial bias and did not develop negative attitudes about other ethnic groups. They did show patterns of gender stereotyping found in other children, but their responses were significantly less stereotype-consistent for racial attitudes' [3].

You don't need to be a child with WS to not feel anxiety when with someone of a different ethnicity. I am probably typical of most white persons living in Europe, in that I am involuntarily aware of a 'difference' (no more) when in the company of an ethnically dissimilar individual. But when I am in Rwanda, where everybody is of another ethnicity, that 'difference' is absent. The explorer Wilfred Thesiger, who spent much of his life among the tribes of Arabia and Central Africa, considered that 'colour prejudice is something I have never felt. Aesthetically, I regard white as the least attractive colour for skin' [4].

Race

The word 'race' is derived from the Old French *'rasse'*. It entered the English language during the 16th century to mean 'a group of people belonging to the same family and descended from a common ancestor' [5]. 'Family', of course, has so many meanings that this doesn't take us very far, but 'descended from a common ancestor' has clear implications. Since we now accept that all humans alive today are descended from a common ancestor (*Homo sapiens*) that emerged in Africa around 300,000 years ago, it follows that there is only one race: the human race. According to science writer Rina Bliss, all humans are – by certain criteria – genetically 99.9% the same (Rina Bliss: *What's Real About Race?* W W Norton, 2025). Within it, groups of people have different characteristics, such as skin colour. This depends on where the group's ancestors lived. If in a tropical location, such as northern or sub-Saharan Africa, their skin would be pigmented in lighter or darker shades of black. Such colouration, due to the protective effects of melanin in the skin, is the result of an evolutionary adaptation to bright sunlight, which is deleterious, leading to skin cancer. Australian Aborigines presumably became dark-skinned only after they left Southeast Asia 50,000 years ago. Most black Ethiopians are genetically less related to dark-skinned Bantu speakers than to Armenians or other light-skinned people [6].

As the sociologist Pierre van den Berghe put it in 1987, ' "Races" are social constructs corresponding to no biological reality' [7]. So, how do we describe the people of different colours and other dissimilarities across the world? A decade earlier, in his magisterial book *Race*, biologist John Baker used the words 'ethnic taxa' [8] to refer to human groups defined by him as Europids, Australids, Sanids (Bushmen) and Negrids (Negroes); surprisingly, he included 'Jews' and 'Celts' as separate ethnic taxa. For want of a better phrase, I shall use 'ethnic groups' to refer to the various sub-species of the human race. Within each ethnic group there is a vast person-to-person variation that exceeds any differences between one and another ethnic group. A quality such as intellect, for example, extends from retarded to genius, with most people falling somewhere in between. A similar person-to-person diversity in qualities such as aggression or empathy and cheerfulness or despondency is found within every group of humans. None is in any way related to physical appearance, such as pigmentation of the skin. All ethnic groupings tend to favour their own over their neighbours. Ethnocentrism, which inspired Richard Dawkins' formulation of the 'selfish gene' in 1976, is key to the evolution of humans and other animals as described by Charles Darwin in the *Origin of Species* in 1859.

Racism

The words 'racism' and 'racist' have been retained to describe antagonism towards a particular ethnic group. Black Africans ('Negrids' in Baker's terminology) have been targets since their first appearance in Europe during Graeco-Roman times. Yet the external features of a person bear no relation to what is going on within their body. As mentioned, skin colour – black, brown, or white – is no more related to an individual's physical ability, character or cognitive function than is the colour of their eyes or hair, or height or weight. Charles Darwin was prescient when he remarked that 'the same state of mind is expressed throughout the world with remarkable uniformity; and this fact is, in itself, interesting as evidence of the close similarity in ... mental disposition of all the races of mankind' [9]. Aristotle's 'environmental determinism' [10] led him to consider the Greeks as superior to all others due to certain innate qualities acquired on account of the climate in which they lived. These qualities were passed on to their progeny (provided they married other Greeks). Their neighbours from the east or south lacked these characteristics and were thus born to be subjects of the Greeks. The Romans adopted these ideas, though they naturally assumed themselves to be superior to the Hellenic people.

According to classicist Mary Lefkovitz, 'Although the Greeks knew the Egyptians to be what we now call "people of colour", they did not think less or more of them (or any other Africans) on that account'. For the Greeks, the 'salient fact was that these other people were foreigners'. The Greeks distinguished themselves from all foreigners, and foreigners were regarded as '*barbaroi*', people who speak unintelligibly [11]. For the Greeks, 'culture was a far more important factor in human behaviour than skin colour or other "racial" characteristics' [12].

The attitude of the ancients towards the Jews varied between different cultures and changed with time. The Greeks ignored them. 'As far as we know, the Greeks lived happily in their classical age without recognising the existence of the Jews' [13]. Caesar was favourably inclined towards Jews, as was Emperor Augustus. Claudius, on the other hand, expelled the Jews from Rome. Historian Benjamin Isaac sums up such attitudes as follows: 'Roman views of other peoples practicing their ancestral religion, such as the Jews, varied from admiration to highly critical and could contain elements of prejudice or proto-racism. There was, however, no doubt as regards their legitimacy, while Christianity was definitely regarded as an illegitimate religion without proper historical roots' [14] (until it became the official religion in 380 AD under Emperor Theodosius).

Europeans have long considered those different in appearance from themselves, such as Black Africans, as being inferior in certain characteristics, of which intellectual ability is one. The number of black people in ancient Rome was significant (the same as that in 18th-century Britain): between 0.3% and 0.4% of the population. Some of the latter, such as property owner John London, led a considerably better life than many poor whites [15]. According to author Lloyd Thompson, 'We do not know much about the ancients' attitude because the loves and lives of humble couples (of whatever colour) held no interest for Roman writers' [16]. A dissenting voice against the assumption of black inferiority was heard during the 13th century. The Islamic scholar Ibn Khallikan is said to have described a Negro Caliph who reigned in Baghdad during the 9th century as 'a man of great merit and a perfect scholar', while a contemporary poet commented that 'blackness of skin cannot degrade an ingenious mind, or lessen the worth of the scholar or the wit' [17].

By the time of the Age of Enlightenment, such views were not uncommon. Thus, the 18th-century visionary William Blake 'shares with the author of a 3rd c Romano-Egyptian epitaph the urge to describe a black man as possessor of a white soul despite his somatic blackness'. A century later, the French writer Victor Hugo expressed a similar view, namely that 'all souls are white in God's sight' [18]. Such views are, of course, in a sense correct (and their authors can be forgiven for assuming that white is the default colour in view of the prevailing attitudes at the time of their writing). As Benjamin Isaac points out, the French philosopher Claude-Adrien Helvétius 'firmly denies any correlation between physical and mental characteristics' [19]. Other enlightened figures, such as Charles-Louis de Secondat (Baron de Montesquieu), Francis Hutcheson, Adam Smith, Edmund Burke and James Beattie (but not David Hume), argued along similar lines. Beattie sums up their views: '... all the inhabitants of this globe, who have reason, speech, and erect figure, must be considered as one great family, and as informed with souls of the same order, whatever slight variations may appear in their bodies' [20].

On the other hand, Thomas Jefferson, who owned some 600 slaves during his lifetime, wrote (perhaps to justify this fact) along more conventional lines. He considered that 'black people require less sleep, are superficial and transient in their emotions as compared with whites, and much inferior in reasoning, though not in memory' [21]. As recently as 2002, the educational psychologist Arthur Jensen came to the conclusion that black Americans differed, on average, by as much as 12 IQ points from white Americans of the same class [22]. Support for this conclusion is difficult to sustain [23]. During her 2021 interview with Oprah Winfrey, Meghan, Duchess of Sussex, suggested that a member of the royal family had wondered about the colour of her forthcoming child. And why not? People often speculate about what features, such as colour of eyes or hair, their new relative will have. Skin colour is in the same category. By implying that dark skin might be something to be ashamed of, and Oprah's feigned horror, the two ladies contributed to a continuance of racial prejudice.

The USA

Bigotry against black people has been a feature of American society for centuries. African slaves may have been emancipated in 1863, but discrimination against African Americans endured for well over a century and continues to exist in pockets today. As recently as 2019, the average white family in America 'had seven times the wealth of the average black family' [24]. On my first visit to the US, by boat, in the late 1950s, one of the passengers sharing my cabin struck up a conversation with me. In his southern American drawl, he informed me about African Americans in words that no editor would consider printable. When I subsequently travelled across the country, I was surprised to find three lavatories at Greyhound bus stations: 'men', 'women' and 'colored'. The internationally acclaimed singer Josephine Baker (vilified by Nazi propaganda minister Josef Goebbels for being 'black, female, exotic and very sexy – worse still she was a tonic for French morale'; he might well have added 'and a member of the (British) Secret Intelligence Service' [25]) was welcomed at top hotels in Paris, where her body now resides in the Panthéon [26] and London, but in

New York City she was forced to stay at the seedy Theresa Hotel in Harlem [27]. A (half-)African American may have been elected president in 2008, but in 2020, George Floyd was 'accidentally' murdered by a member of the Minneapolis Police Department. A year later, another black man, Tyre Nichols, was allegedly assaulted and beaten by five officers of the Memphis Police Department in Tennessee. He was hospitalised and died three days later. The fact that the officers were themselves black indicates the lawlessness of certain police forces.

When the film *Guess Who's Coming to Dinner*, in which an African American proposes to a white American girl, was released in 1967, it caused a sensation. Years later, its leading man, Sidney Poitier, was asked about his success as a black actor: 'You could ask me many questions about many positive and wonderful things that are happening in this country, but we gather here to pay court to sensationalism. We gather here to pay court to negativism … you ask me one-dimensional questions that fall continually within the "negro-ness" of my life. I am artist, man, American, contemporary, I am an awful lot of things, so I wish you would pay me the respect due (to me)' [28]. What can account for the enduring disparagement of, and animosity towards, African Americans? I believe it may be related to a feeling of guilt for past errors, which subsequently expresses itself – counterintuitively – as aggression. One of the founders of Critical Race Theory (CRT), US lawyer Derrick Bell, considers that racism is not an aberration but a normalised feature of American society [29] – except for those who espouse the Quaker way of life (which also forbade its members to own slaves).

According to the *Encyclopaedia Britannica* (2021), CRT is 'an intellectual and social movement and loosely organized framework of legal analysis based on the premise that race is not a natural, biologically grounded feature of physically distinct subgroups of human beings but a socially constructed (culturally invented) category that is used to oppress and exploit people of colour'. Anthropologist Khiara Bridges considers it an 'analytical toolset for interrogating the relationship between law and racial inequality' [30]. Kimberlé Crenshaw, also a lawyer and contributor to CRT, has pointed out that African American women suffer double discrimination – first on account of their ethnicity and second because of their gender – and that anti-discrimination laws should take this fact into account [31]. African American women in academia are particularly disadvantaged. As one such lady points out, 'I know only too well how often we are asked to prove ourselves – we must work twice as hard to get half as much, yet our imperfections are seldom overlooked. In 2022, only 1.9% of the 189,362 full professors at US institutions were Black women' [32]. (On the other hand, black African women live on average nine years longer than white men in the UK [33].)

Such conclusions, of course, conflict with the fact that skin colour and mental qualities are unrelated. Treating coloured ethnic minorities in the predominantly white societies of America and Europe differentially is unwarranted and leads to feelings of victimhood and exclusion. In order to achieve equality and inclusion, colour blindness is surely the right approach. In his 1963 'I have a dream' speech, Martin Luther King Jr. proclaimed, 'I have a dream that my four little children will one day live in a nation where they will not be judged by the color of their skin but by the content of their character'. Colour blindness continued to be advocated by the likes of social philosopher Thomas Sowell and attorney William Bradford Reynolds (US Assistant Attorney General for the Civil Rights Division in the 1980s). No less a person than Supreme Court Justice Clarence Thomas has spoken out in defence of a 'colorblind Constitution' [34]. CRT may have its adherents, but it will not lead to a fairer society. Readers may note that most white children are by nature colourblind. They become colour-conscious (unless indoctrinated by their parents or neighbours) only when they enter pre-school. Such observations are supported by neurologist Eva Telzer's research at the University of North Carolina at Chapel Hill. She concludes that differential perception of ethnicity is not innate but develops around adolescence in an area of the brain known as the amygdala [35].

Antisemitism has been a feature of American society since General Ulysses S. Grant tried to expel Jews from Tennessee, Kentucky and Mississippi during the Civil War. President Lincoln prevented this, but Jews have, in a way, been second-class citizens since then. Discrimination is expressed mainly by restriction to certain associations, such as private clubs. When Senator Barry Goldwater, the Republican contender for the US Presidency in 1963, was denied membership at a nearby golf club, he wondered whether 'perhaps I may be allowed to play 9 holes as I'm only half-Jewish'. The British novelist Zadie Smith summed up racism within the US by suggesting that 'race in America is what class is in Britain'. Fortunately, both are dying out, the latter faster than the former.

Elsewhere

Yet discrimination against particular ethnic groups continues to be a worldwide problem. While not as overt as the kind of racism in the US mentioned above, 'there is racism in society, and we universities are not free of it', according to Isolde Karle, vice-rector for diversity, inclusion and talent development at Ruhr University Bochum. Journalist Hristio Boytchev considers that it is 'a strikingly male-dominated academe (that) perpetuates racist, sexist and classist dynamics' [36]. Germany may be particularly sensitive to accusations of racism for historical reasons, but prejudice against ethnic minorities – whether in academia or any other sphere – is widespread. Few make it into higher education in the first place. In the UK, for example, 'Black people make up 4% of the country's working-age population, and 8% of its science undergraduates, yet just 0.6% of its science professors. In all academic fields, just 160 of the United Kingdom's 22,855 professors are Black (among those, just one-quarter are women)' [37]. Despite such a depressing statistic, I do not believe that appointing professors by any criterion other than merit provides a solution. The fact that there are twice as many Black science undergraduates as expected from demographic data shows that, over time, such anomalies will disappear.

The conflict between Hamas and Israel (see Chapter 8) has led to an increase in anti-Semitic racism in Britain, the US and elsewhere. Israel's determination to flush Hamas out of Gaza, where the terrorist group steals foreign-donated supplies and funding intended for Palestinians, as well as using the latter as human shields, has led to unavoidable deaths (greatly exaggerated by Hamas-run and other agencies, including the UN).

Pro-Palestinian marches with a strong anti-Semitic flavour and other incidents became a feature during 2024. Whistleblowers and others have accused some of the media, such as *The Guardian* and the BBC, of 'Israel bashing' on a daily basis [38]. Anti-Semitism is particularly high in universities. The Community Security Trust (CST) recorded nine assaults in 2023–2024, compared to one the previous year; 17 cases of damage to Jewish property, up from four the previous year; as well as a threat to rape and kill the wife of a member of the Israeli Defence Force on his way to carry out reservist training in Israel [39].

Thus, many consider that overt racism of one sort or another continues to be a problem in the UK. In response, the government set up the Commission on Race and Ethnic Disparities, which reported in 2021. For its chairman, Prime Minister Boris Johnson chose not a well-tried bureaucrat like Lord Scarman, who had chaired the enquiry into the Brixton race riots in 1980. In an inspirational moment, he asked someone from a completely different background to head the Commission: he appointed Tony Sewell.

Cleveland Anthony Sewell was born in the London Borough of Brixton in 1959, of Jamaican parents who had emigrated to Britain in the 1950s. In the early 1960s, the family moved to neighbouring Penge, where young Tony went to primary school. He failed his 11 plus exam and was therefore denied a place at a decent grammar school. Instead, he was enrolled at the failing Kentwood Secondary Modern School (later a comprehensive school). The school was two-thirds white and one-third African-Caribbean. He hated every minute there. On the other hand, he loved going to the local Anglican church with his brother and sister every Sunday, followed by Sunday School. Here, he found an education that suited his tastes. There were discussions on predestination and grace (he was only 14). He participated in intellectually demanding Bible conferences and was taken on holidays by some of the church elders.

At 16, Tony was accepted to work on Saturdays and during the holidays at the local library. He enjoyed the role of librarian, as he was able to borrow as many books as he wanted, as well as classical and other music. Such self-education resulted in his acceptance to read English literature at the University of Essex, the only black student in his class. He was on excellent terms with his teachers, with whom he was able to discuss topics such as the role of knowledge in *Hamlet* over Sunday dinner, largely at his own instigation.

Sewell's determination to succeed is surely inherited from his mother. Mrs. Sewell worked in a factory close to their home, making small electronic components. The only black woman there, she bossed her 50 white male workmates about without an ounce of fear. When she went shopping at the local open market, she always obtained the best cuts of meat and the freshest vegetables and fruits. The reality of the racism at the time she simply ignored. If anyone proved to be his own man, it was her son Tony.

Tony Sewell has carved out a most successful life for himself. Following his degree at Essex and a doctorate at Nottingham University, he lectured at the University of Kingston and later at the University of Leeds. He served as an international consultant in education for the World Bank and the Commonwealth Secretariat, and he worked for the Justice Board for England and Wales. In 2022, Sewell was created a life peer and is now the Lord Sewell of Sanderstead. He has every reason to be proud of his achievements. But I fancy that if asked which of his appointments has had the most impact on life in Britain, he would refer to the fact that every one of the 24 recommendations made by the Commission on Race and Ethnic Disparities (see the following) under his chairmanship has been adopted.

The main conclusions of the Commission were that 'there are indeed disparities for many groups relating to education, employment, crime and health – but the majority of these did not originate from racism' 'though racism does still exist': the Report found that there are historic issues of trust, which remain real and important – but that things are improving, particularly in education and employment [40]. Not unexpectedly, politicians (including the present prime minister of the UK) and others (such as the UN Human Rights Council) criticised this conclusion. Yet, as Sewell has pointed out, 'In 2019 the average GCSE attainment score of eight for black African pupils was above that of white British pupils. 66.9% of black African young people had progressed to higher education by the age of 19. ... Among the under-30s who are employed, there are no significant pay gaps for any ethnic minority group' [41].

Sewell also alluded to the fact that black Caribbean families were more likely to be single-parent than black African families. In response to criticism regarding the membership of the committee, he drew attention to the fact that 'the Commission was established with 10 of us drawn from a variety of fields spanning science, education, economics, broadcasting, medicine, and policing. And, with one exception, all from ethnic minority backgrounds' [42].

To suggestions that some black ethnic minorities are being let down by the NHS, Sewell points out that 'for many key health outcomes, including life expectancy, overall mortality, and many of the leading causes of mortality in the UK, ethnic minority groups have better outcomes than the white population. This evidence clearly suggests that ethnicity (or racism) is not the major driver of health inequalities in the UK but deprivation, geography, and different exposure to key risk factors' [43].

Summary of the recommendations of the Commission on Race and Ethnic Disparities [44]:

Build Trust
Recommendation 1: Challenge racist and discriminatory actions.
Recommendation 2: Review the Care Quality Commission's (CQC) inspection process.
Recommendation 3: Improve the transparency and use of artificial intelligence.
Recommendation 4: Bridge divides and create partnerships between the police and communities.
Recommendation 5: Improve training to provide police officers with practical skills to interact with communities.

Promote Fairness
Recommendation 6: Replicate the factors of educational success for all communities.
Recommendation 7: Invest in proven interventions through better targeted funding.
Recommendation 8: Advance fairness in the workplace.
Recommendation 9: Investigate what causes existing ethnic pay disparities.
Recommendation 10: Improve understanding of the ethnicity pay gap in NHS England.
Recommendation 11: Establish an Office for Health Disparities.
Recommendation 12: Prevent harm, reduce crime and divert young people away from the criminal justice system.
Recommendation 13: Build social and cultural capital – enrichment for all.
Recommendation 14: Increase legitimacy and accountability of stop and search through body-worn video.

Create Agency
Recommendation 15: Empower pupils to make more informed choices to fulfil their future potential.
Recommendation 16: Open up access to apprenticeships.
Recommendation 17: Encourage innovation.

Recommendation 18: Improve safety and support for children at risk.
Recommendation 19: Undertake a 'support for families' review.

Achieve Inclusivity
Recommendation 20: Making of modern Britain: teach an inclusive curriculum.
Recommendation 21: Create police workforces that represent the communities they serve.
Recommendation 22: Equip the police service to serve the needs of their local communities.
Recommendation 23: Use data in a responsible and informed way.
Recommendation 24: Disaggregate the term 'BAME' (Black, Asian and Minority Ethnic).

You can't say they weren't trying.

Education

Sewell is right to point to social, rather than innate, differences to explain the disparity between the achievements among various ethnic groups. In regard to what is actually being taught, today's ideologues consider that we have not yet gone far enough in ridding the curriculum of 'racist' – implying Eurocentric – attitudes (more on this in Chapter 5 on Political Correctness). Should we not go further to 'decolonise the curriculum'? The former president of the National Association of Schoolmasters Union of Women Teachers (NASUWT), Michelle Codrington-Rogers, certainly thinks so: 'All subjects need to ensure that there is inclusivity in their teaching. That there is black visibility in design and technology, modern foreign languages, science and English, music and geography, art and maths, computer science and citizenship, food technology and drama, and all subjects have a responsibility to change the narrative that black people only have a history of enslavement and colonisation' [45]. Indeed, though how some of her aspirations are to be achieved is not clear.

The Ministry of Defence (MoD), a department within the Civil Service, has been making research on the 'Psychosis of Whiteness' available to managers running the mandatory Operation Teamwork. The definition of whiteness as a 'Eurocentric worldview that produces the privileges of white skin ...' has led one of its civilian employees to claim that this suggests white people are 'psychotic, cannot be reasoned with and must be destroyed'. The man sued the government for racial discrimination and harassment, pointing out that such views represent 'Left-wing and Marxist political ideology'. Unsurprisingly, he lost his case [46]. Denigrating white people does not by itself foster better relations with other ethnic groups.

On the contrary, as columnist Zoe Strimpel reminds us, 'Children need to understand past racism, not be shielded from it'. So, the decision by the Welsh exam board to remove books that focus on 'very derogatory, negative depictions of black people' from the GCSE syllabus is counter-productive. One of these is John Steinbeck's 1937 classic, *Of Mice and Men*. Another is Harper Lee's 1960 novel, *To Kill a Mockingbird*. The first contains racial slurs; the second actually 'exposes the hideous ways in which anti-black racism could play out and induces intense empathy and anger'. There is surely much for teenage children to learn from both books [47].

Others adopt a different strategy. Nigerian-born British author Atinuke asserts, in a children's book, *Brilliant Black History*, that Stonehenge was built by Black people. Along these lines, the Book Trust claims that 'Britain was a black country for more than 7,000 years before white people came' [48]. Do such myths really help to ease racial tensions?

Notes

1. Agarwal (2020), p 37.
2. *ibid*, p 13.
3. *ibid*, p 67 *et seq.*
4. Thesiger (1987), p 167.
5. *Oxford English Dictionary* (Oxford University Press; latest edition 2024).
6. James F Wilson *et al.*: Population genetic structure of variable drug response. *Nature Genetics* **29**: 265–269 (2001).
7. van den Berghe (1981), p 2.
8. Baker (1974), p 185.
9. Charles Darwin: *The Expression of the Emotions in Man and Animals* (London: John Murray, 1872).
10. Isaac (2004), p 108.
11. M Lefkovitz: *Not Out of Africa: How 'Afrocentrism' Became an Excuse to Teach Myth as History* (New York: Basic Books, 1996), pp 13–14.

12. *ibid*, p 9.
13. Arnaldo Momigliano: *Alien Wisdom. The Limits of Hellenization* (Cambridge University Press, 1975).
14. Isaac (2004), p 491.
15. Inaya Folarin Iman: Britain's black history has never just been a story of oppression, *Daily Telegraph* (25 October 2024).
16. Thompson (1989), p 108.
17. Blyden (1967), p 16.
18. both from Thompson (1989), p 11.
19. Isaac (2004), p 12.
20. James Beattie: *Elements of Moral Science* (1817) quoted in Roger Anstey: *The Atlantic Slave Trade and British Abolition 1760–1810* (London: Macmillan Press Ltd., 1975), p 112.
21. Isaac (2004), p 106.
22. Frank Miele: *Intelligence, Race and Genetics. Conversations with Arthur R Jensen* (Boulder, Colorado and Oxford: Westview Press, 2002), p 180.
23. Pasternak (2018), pp 29–46.
24. Whitehouse (2022), p 181.
25. Spicer (2024), p 152.
26. *ibid*, p 362.
27. Talbot (2016), p 342.
28. quoted by Sewell (2024), p 9.
29. Derrick A Bell: *The Permanence of Racism* (New York: Basic Books, 1992).
30. Khiara Bridges: *Critical Race Theory: A Primer* (St Paul MN: Foundation Press, 2019), p 7.
31. Kimberlé W Chrenshaw: Demarginalizing the intersection of race and sex: A black feminist critique of antidiscrimination doctrine, feminist theory and antiracist politics. *University of Chicago Legal Forum* (1 January 1989).
32. Malika Jeffries-EL *et al.*: Black women on the academic tightrope: Four scholars weigh in, *Nature* **634**: 542–544 (2024).
33. Tony Sewell: The NHS is not "systemically racist" against ethnic minorities, *Daily Telegraph* (23 October 2024). https://www.nbcnews.com/politics/supreme-court/colorblind-constitution-supreme-court-wrangles-future-race-law-rcna90661.
34. https://www.nbcnews.com/politics/supreme-court/colorblind-constitution-supreme-court-wrangles-future-race-law-rcna90661.

35. Agarwal (2020), p 93 *et seq.*
36. Hristio Boytchef: *Nature* **616**: 22–24 (2023).
37. Elizabeth Gibney: *Nature* **612**: 390–395 (2022).
38. Patrick Sawyer: Anti-Semitism at BBC "normal" after Oct 7, *Sunday Telegraph* (1 December 2024).
39. Janet Eastham: Anti-Semitic abuse at British universities reaches a record high, *Sunday Telegraph* (8 December 2024).
40. Sewell (2024), p 6.
41. *ibid*, p 7.
42. https://www.gov.uk/government/organisations/commission-on-race-and-ethnic-disparities.
43. Tony Sewell: The NHS is not "systemically racist" against ethnic minorities, *Daily Telegraph* (23 October 2024).
44. see Sewell (2024), p 244.
45. Furedi (2024), p 189.
46. Telegraph Reporters: MoD civil servant sues over "attack on white people" in diversity course, *Daily Telegraph* (10 July 2023).
47. Zoe Strimpel: *Sunday Telegraph* (Features 29 December 2024).
48. Furedi (2024), p 147.

Chapter 3

Slavery and Colonialism

These two subjects are not directly related. It is only today's guardians of virtue who link the two. America had slavery without colonialism, Britain had colonialism without slavery. A 19th-century Sunday school song is not so wide of the mark:

> '[Britain's] rule of empire is to *save*
> She gives the Bible, and she frees the slave!' [1].

The last five words are probably based on Britain's attempts, through the Royal Navy, to disrupt the Atlantic slave trade in the early 19th century. Britain abolished the slave trade in 1807 and spent the next 60 years trying to prevent the other European nations from continuing the hideous trade. The Royal Navy's West Africa Squadron may have rescued some 200,000 African men, women and children – at a cost of 1–2% of government expenditure – but ten times as many continued to be transported during this time. Those who were rescued and brought to places like Freetown in Sierra Leone could start a new life. Some were quite successful. William Crowther, bound for Brazil, eventually became the first Anglican bishop in West Africa [2].

According to anthropologist Pierre van den Berghe [3], slavery goes back some 10,000 years to the birth of agriculture. Certainly, the earliest 'civilisations' [4] that emerged in Mesopotamia, Egypt, along the Indus valley and in China all condoned slavery. As did primitive cultures in Sub-Saharan Africa like the Nok (in today's Nigeria) and the 'Five Civilized Tribes' (Cherokee, Chickasaw, Choctaw, Creek and Seminole) in the southeast of North America. So the origin of slavery can hardly be laid at the door of 'white' European males. It did not appear on European soil until the classical age of Greece and Rome.

Colonialism, on the other hand, is a product of European nationhood: Spain and Portugal (in Central and South America from the 16th century); Britain (in North America from the 16th century; India and parts of Africa from the 19th century); Denmark (Greenland from the 18th century); the Netherlands (Indonesia from the end of the 18th century); France (in North Africa from the 19th century); Germany (in parts of West and East Africa from the 19th century); and Belgium (in West Africa from the beginning of the 20th century).

Slavery

Jean-Jacques Rousseau's view about the morality of slavery was clear. 'So, from whatever aspect we regard the question, the right of slavery is null and void. not only as being illegitimate, but also because it is absurd and meaningless. The words *slave* and *right* contradict each other, and are mutually exclusive. It will always be equally foolish for a man to say to a man or to a people: "I make with you a convention wholly at your expense and wholly to my advantage; I shall keep it as long as I like, and you will keep it as long as I like"' [5].

The word slave probably comes from Slav, the people of Eastern Europe who were enslaved by invading Muslims in the 9th century. But as mentioned earlier, the origin of slavery itself can be traced back much further, to the emergence of cities in Mesopotamia (present-day Iraq). As these grew into states, such as Sumer, conflict between different city-states led to open warfare. Prisoners captured during such skirmishes often became enslaved by the winners. In ancient Egypt, as elsewhere, prisoners of war ended up as slaves. But the distinction between slave and servant was blurred. Females sometimes received payments or other benefits. Men did not, but were instead granted an even greater reward: entrance to the afterlife. What is clear is that the Great Pyramids of Giza were built by free men, not slaves.

Slavery Across the World

By classical times, slavery had become so extensive that during Athens' most innovative period, slaves made up some 50% of the population. Thus, only 25% (that is, free males) were able to participate in democratic resolutions. In Rome, the percentage of slaves was less, reaching 30% only during the early years of the empire. Within a few hundred years, it had declined to less than 10% [6]. Moreover, the prospects for a slave were brighter in Rome than in Athens. Under the empire, those who achieved freedom (manumission) were also granted Roman citizenship. Slavery in China goes back to the short-lived but highly influential Qin Dynasty (221–206 BCE) [7]. As in Pharaonic Egypt, the distinction between a slave and an indentured peasant was often minimal. Although the number of slaves within the population in China was much smaller than that in classical Athens or Rome, the practice continued not for centuries but for two millennia. Only during the first decade of the 20th century was slavery officially annulled. But the region that many people nowadays associate most closely with the misery of slavery was actually that which also gave a few an opportunity to rise to a position of eminence and power: Sub-Saharan Africa.

Africa

In the kingdom of Cayor (1549–1879; today's Senegal), slaves constituted the backbone of the army and 'were commanded by one of their own, the infantry general, who was a pseudo-prince in that he might rule over a fief inhabited by freedmen' [8]. The racial tolerance of Islam (in its early days) enabled Malik Sarwar, an Ethiopian slave who ended up in Northern India, to be appointed wazir (provincial governor) by the Sultan of Delhi in 1394. Sarwar proved himself to be an able militarist by subjugating neighbouring territories and, in effect, founding the Sharqi Dynasty as Sultan of Jaunpur. He adopted another former slave (Sarwar himself was a eunuch) who succeeded him in 1399. Another Ethiopian slave who was able to distinguish himself was Shambu, born around 1550. He was passed from owner to owner (one of whom named him Ambar) and was eventually employed by the Sultan of Bijapur in Southwest India. He became an independent ruler in Kirkee (near Pune), where he was able to indulge his talents. 'With a passion for planned civic development and embellishment, he furnished his capital with wide roads, canals, drains, public gardens, and buildings. ... Ambar was certainly not the last Habshi [Abyssinian] to leave a mark on Indian history, though he remained the most notable' [9].

The Arab Slave Trade

It was in Sub-Saharan Africa that the most extensive trade in slaves developed, though during Egypt's New Kingdom period (16th–11th century BCE), Nubian slaves were already being taken north into the land of the Pharaohs. The Arabs who began to arrive in Africa in the 7th century CE brought with them the new religion of Islam. This had two consequences: the growth of a minority of well-educated scholars and the development of the slave trade. In the mid-14th century, intrepid traveller Ibn Battuta [10] witnessed the long caravans of enslaved men, women and their children, joined by iron rings around their necks, being marched barefoot, diseased and starving, northwards a thousand miles or more from the empire of Mali across the Sahara to slave markets along the Mediterranean coast. From there, many victims were transported further to Constantinople and other European cities.

From Central Africa, men, women and children were snatched from their homes (their villages razed to the ground as a warning to others not to resist) by Arabs, sometimes accompanied by Africans themselves. The captives were assembled in the slave market of Ujiji, on the eastern shore of Lake Tanganyika. A catholic missionary described the scene in 1888. The market was 'crowded with slaves, joined by cords or chains in long lines, and with others revealing signs of starvation ... Nearby was a cemetery where the dying as well as the dead were left for the hyenas' [11]. Here, the Scottish explorer David Livingstone (whose aim to bring Christianity, civilisation and commerce to Sub-Saharan Africa fell largely on deaf ears) watched the caravans pass his dwelling. 'The price paid for every living slave was at least ten dead' [12]. The slave route then ran southeastwards towards Kilwa on the coast and the island of Zanzibar just beyond. These unfortunates were destined to be shipped to Arabia and across the ocean all the way to Persia and the Indian sub-continent.

The Arab slave trade, that accounted for well over 11 million dispossessed victims, lasted over a millennium – well into the 20th century. In Saudi Arabia, slavery was not abolished until 1962.

The Atlantic Slave Trade

Along the Gulf of Guinea, from present-day Senegal down to Angola, in the southwest of Sub-Saharan Africa, local chiefs found a lucrative market for the slaves in their possession. From the 16th century onwards, European traders began to arrive in their ships, eager to trade humans for weapons and other merchandise. The victims were shipped to the Caribbean islands, to Brazil and to the south of North America, where the owners of cotton, sugar and tobacco plantations were eager to expand their workforce. The Atlantic slave trade had begun. The responsibility for exporting the victims – as opposed to the callous treatment on the slave ships and the subsequent brutality on the plantations – can clearly be laid at the door of the exporting nations. Ghana, formerly the Gold Coast and a major exporter of slaves, indeed apologised in 2006 and repeated this with a formal delegation to Kansas City in 2022 [13]. But other countries have remained silent.

Conditions aboard the slave ships were horrendous. Over 10% died from dysentery, fever, smallpox and eye diseases due to overcrowding and poor ventilation below deck [14]. 'The men were packed together below deck and were secured by leg irons. The space was so cramped they were forced to crouch or lie down. Women and children were kept in separate quarters, sometimes on deck, allowing them limited freedom of movement, but this also exposed them to violence and sexual abuse from the crew' [15]. The stench from sweat, vomit, urine and excrement below deck must have been horrendous. There was worse. In 1781, Luke Collingwood, captain of the *Zong*, overloaded his ship and took a wrong course. Water was running short and disease was breaking out. His reaction?

130 victims – still shackled – were thrown overboard. Collingwood was not charged with murder, but the owners of the *Zong* claimed insurance for loss of merchandise [16].

'Never can so much misery be found condensed into so small a space common as in a slave ship' stated the indefatigable anti-slavery campaigner and Member of Parliament William Wilberforce. Having achieved the abolition of the slave trade in Britain in 1807, he continued to campaign against fierce opposition for the end of slavery throughout the British Empire. The Act for the Abolition of Slavery itself was passed in August 1833, but Wilberforce was unable to celebrate. He had died just one month earlier.

The number of slaves transported between 1500 and 1850 has been estimated at almost 14 million [17], somewhat more than those caught up in the Arab slave trade. The sheer inhumanity of the Atlantic slave trade over three centuries bears comparison only with the murder of more than 6 million Jews and others by the Nazis during World War II.

Today's Views About Slavery

Anyone who was connected with slavery is to be condemned and any memorials to them removed. The history of slavery is to be rewritten with a sensitivity that ignores attitudes relevant at the time. The descendants of anyone connected with slavery should apologise for the sins of their forefathers and make appropriate reparations. According to the moral philosopher Onora O'Neill, 'claims to compensation have to show that continuing loss or harm resulted from past injury. This is all too often impossible where harms have been caused by ancient or distant wrongs ... Is everybody who descends (in part) from those who were once enslaved or colonised still being harmed by those now ancient and distant misdeeds? Can we offer a clear enough account of the causation of current harms to tell us where compensation is owed? Can we show who ought to do the compensating? [18]. Or as Tony Sewell, himself of African Caribbean origin, put it in a slightly different context, 'We must acknowledge the suffering of our parents and grandparents, but not be burdened with their trauma. Rather,

Slavery and Colonialism

inspired by their example of resilience and fortitude, we must create our own drive and agency in order to move forward' [19].

Despite such qualifications, the journalist Laura Trevelyan, whose family owned some 1,000 slaves in Grenada during the 19th century, has decided to pay more than £100,000 in reparation and has presented a letter of apology to Grenadians signed by her and her relatives [20]. She has done more. She quit her job at the BBC and launched a campaign called 'Heirs of Slavery' to encourage others to follow in her footsteps. Some are doing just that [21]. Along similar lines, the Joseph Rowntree Charitable Trust, which has already apologised for using cocoa produced through slavery in Portuguese West Africa for its chocolate products, has now committed to 'Examining, confronting, and critiquing our own colonial and capitalist history and not assuming a position of moral superiority as a grant-maker' [22].

The great reforming prime minister of the 19th century, William Gladstone, who called slavery the 'foulest crime', is under a cloud. Why? Because, as mentioned in Chapter 1, his father owned plantations in the Caribbean. Now, ecclesiastical authorities, no less, are concerned about the suitability of a bronze bust of William Gladstone that had been erected in 2013 outside Our Lady, Star of the Sea church in Seaforth, Liverpool, to mark the bicentenary of the politician's life there. The bust has been temporarily removed [23].

The Duke of Wellington is regarded as a national hero for saving Britain from defeat by Napoleon at Waterloo in 1815. His support for the abolition of slavery in 1833 is now considered by the Welsh government's Anti-Racist Action Plan to have been insufficiently robust. Together with Admiral Nelson, whose defeat of the French navy at Trafalgar in 1805 prevented an invasion of Britain, their achievements are considered to be merely those of 'powerful, older, able-bodied white men' that perpetuate 'racist colonial myths about white superiority'. Statues erected in their honour are regarded as potentially offensive and their retention should be 're-evaluated' [24].

The British monarchy stands accused of links to slavery (and has agreed to open its archives). After his restoration in 1660, Charles II and his brother, the Duke of York (later James II), set up the Royal African Company. Its initial aim was the exploitation of gold that had been found along the Gambia River in West Africa, but it rapidly became associated with the export of human beings enslaved by their African masters and sold to European traders. The company stopped trading in slaves in 1731 when it reverted to commerce in gold and ivory. Nevertheless, George III (born seven years later), while he opposed slavery, which he considered morally wrong, was implicated in the slave trade insofar as 'he did nothing to hasten its abolition' [25]. He did, however, give 'his royal approbation' to Sir Guy Carleton's decision on 6 May 1783 to refuse George Washington's request for slaves freed by the British to be returned to servitude under the colonists. 'Carleton instead issued 3,000 freedom certificates to help protect the runaway slaves still in New York against the slave catchers still rife in the city' [26].

The Anglican Church, too, is charged with abetting slavery through its investment, early in the 18th century, in the South Sea Company, which transported 34,000 slaves from Africa to the New World. Its response is to spend a billion pounds on virtue-signalling projects like investing in 'black-led businesses' (rather than upgrading some of its decaying buildings or initiating measures to halt the decline in church attendance by disillusioned members of its faith) (see [27] for more).

Eric Williams, the writer and first prime minister of Trinidad and Tobago, was among those who considered that the Industrial Revolution and capitalism in Britain were funded by the slave trade [28]. But others disagree. The political economist Kristian Niemietz, for example, writes that 'Historical interest in the slave trade rested on its obvious immorality, not its economic importance. The business formed a relatively small share of the Atlantic trade of any European power. Its direct contribution to the economic growth of any nation was trivial' [29]. Slavery fuelled, not funded, the Industrial Revolution insofar as it provided 70% of the cotton that was turned into clothes in the factories of Manchester and exported across the world. It was the owners of slave plantations who became prosperous, largely through the cultivation of sugar in Jamaica and cotton in the American South. Their wealth increased further after the abolition of slavery in British territories in 1834, for they received generous compensation from the government for every person liberated. An owner of 415 slaves, for example, received more than £20,000, the equivalent of £17 million today [30]. The newly emancipated, who had suffered the horror of transportation across the Atlantic and had then been worked to the point of death, received nothing.

'Capitalism not slavery made Britain rich' stated journalist and politician Daniel Hannan. '... vast sums (were) devoted to stamping out slavery, calculated by Chaim Kaufmann and Robert Pape as 1.8% annually of GDP between 1808 and 1867, the most expensive foreign policy in human history. ... What we are seeing is not a debate about history, but an argument about contemporary politics. Critics want to convince us that Britain became rich through exploitation rather than, as was actually the case, through private property, free contracts and independent courts. ... The easiest way to demonstrate the negative correlation between capitalism and slavery is to look at the places where human bondage is most prevalent today – in order, North Korea, Eritrea, Burundi, the Central African Republic and Mauretania' [31].

Androcentrism – man's assumed superiority over women – is roughly contemporaneous with slavery. It too began to emerge with pastoralism 10,000 years ago and became entrenched 5,000 years later with the establishment of urban life [32]. Both petered out between the middle of the 19th and 20th centuries. And both, I believe, are largely *cultural* (the cerebral ability of males and females may well be different [33], but that doesn't excuse male suppression of females over the centuries), whereas an attitude like bigotry – leading to racism – is mainly *innate*.

The iniquity of slavery has finally ended. Would that the same could be said of warfare and the brutal treatment of innocent people by malevolent dictators.

Colonialism

At the height of the British Empire in 1919, by which time Britain had acquired Germany's African colonies, the size of its colonies exceeded that of the motherland (315,000 km^2) by more than 30:1. Until 1953, the figure for Denmark (43,000 km²) was 50:1, as was that of the Netherlands (42,000 km²) prior to 1949. So, you don't have to be a large country to own huge colonies. You don't have to be a country at all to own a colonial outpost. The Greek city-state of Miletus on the western coast of Anatolia – home to philosophers like Thales and Anaximander during the 7th and 6th centuries BCE – possessed colonies as far away as Massalia (Marseilles) on the Mediterranean and Naukratis on the lower Nile, south of Alexandria.

India

An often-cited criticism of colonialism concerns the presence of the British in India between 1600 and 1947. Although the East India Company was essentially a commercial venture, exporting goods like spices, tea, cotton, silk and other products to Britain, it also fielded an army of enlisted natives and was involved in the eastern slave trade. So far as the latter is concerned, the Company subsequently initiated the Indian Slavery Act of 1843, which outlawed economic transactions based on slavery. The Indian Penal Code of 1860 abolished slavery entirely. It meant that exporting slaves to India was no longer an option for the Arab slavers. Another little-known but benign venture inaugurated by the East India Company was its support of science in Britain. This has recently been documented by Jessica Ratcliff in her *Monopolizing Knowledge: The East India Company and Britain's Second Scientific Revolution* (Cambridge University Press, 2025).

In May of 1857, in the garrison town of Meerut, northeast of Delhi, a group of sepoys (Indian soldiers in the company's army) rebelled against their British officers and perpetrated acts of extreme violence against British families in general (with consequential reprisals). The main reasons were changes in the sepoys' terms of service and their pensions. The introduction of the new Enfield rifle in 1853 was a particular cause of resentment – its paper cartridges (that had to be bitten to release the powder that, when ignited, propelled the bullet) were coated in animal fat, both of pigs and cows. The former was offensive to Muslims, the latter to Hindus. The mutiny spread across India and was not resolved until the following year, when the British granted amnesty to all sepoys who had not committed murder. The East India Company was dissolved in 1874, and the British government took possession of the entire subcontinent apart, from the princely states.

According to Bengali-born Tirthankar Roy, professor at the London School of Economics, 'Many Indians, because they did not trust other Indians, wanted the British to secure power. They preferred British rule over indigenous alternatives and helped the Company form a state ... the empire emerged mainly from alliances. It emerged from lands "ceded" to the Company by Indian friends, rather than lands it "conquered" ... The Company came to rule India because many Indians wanted it to rule India' [34].

On the other hand, ethicist (Lord) Nigel Biggar points out that 'The claim that India had been a prosperous society, which British exploitation impoverished, circulated throughout academic and political circles from 1900 onward, especially in the Indian National Congress, and has found recent expression in Shashi Tharoor's 2016 *Inglorious Empire: What the British Did to India*. The British, so the argument goes, destroyed much of the native peasant textile industry and prevented the development of manufacturing industry, in order to benefit British traders and manufacturers. In addition, they drained India's resources by making it pay for British military expenses, the salaries of British officials, and the interest due on British loans and investments. In sum, the charge against the Raj is that its "combined effect was to condemn India to perpetual poverty as a nation forced to remain a primary producing country that was bled of the surplus which might have provided investment for modernisation"' [35].

Tirthankar Roy disputes this. 'Without the 18th century transformation of Bombay, Calcutta, and Madras, without the emerging trades in cotton and grain, without the extension of [East India] Company power inland, without Indian businesses migrating to the port cities, without the enterprise of the private traders in indigo or opium, and without the institutional consequences of Indo-European trade, it would be hard to explain the emergence of a 19th century economic system in India that was modern in two senses, in enabling the prospect of one of the most impressive episodes of industrialization outside Europe, and in establishing India as a trading power in a globalising world' [36]. So far as economic benefit to Britain is concerned, 'the average person in Britain got little or nothing out of the British Empire. Yet Queen Victoria loved becoming an Empress and Disraeli loved making her one, and so imperial India was born [37]. Already in 1776, the philosopher Adam Smith had written that 'under the present system of management ... Great Britain derives nothing but loss from the dominion which she assumes over her colonies' [38].

An incident that cast shame on Britain occurred on Sunday 13 April 1919. Nigel Biggar describes what happened: 'At about 5 pm ... General Reginald Dyer marched 50 Gurkha and Indian (Baluch and Pathan) soldiers armed with rifles ... into a walled park ... in Amritsar in the Punjab. There he found a large crowd of civilians ... although he could not have known it, they were mostly unarmed and numbered about 25,000 – and without warning, ordered his troops to fire on them. The shooting continued for between six and fifteen minutes, after which, without tending to the wounded, Dyer withdrew his men. They left behind them ... at least 379 dead and approximately 1,200 wounded. ... In March 1920 the government of India rejected Dyer's claim that he had been faced with an insurrection and severely censored him for not promulgating the prohibition of assemblies more widely, not issuing a warning before opening fire and not ceasing fire when the crowd had begun to disperse. It rejected Dyer's justification of prolonged firing as intending to intimidate law-breakers because it "greatly exceeded the necessity of the occasion", and concluded: "We can arrive at no conclusion other than at Jallianwala Bagh General Dyer acted beyond the necessity of the case, beyond what any reasonable man could have thought to be necessary, and that he did not act with as much humanity as the case permitted"' [39].

A century earlier, during the First Anglo-Afghan War (1838–1842), a British force of 20,000 men – the Army of the Indus – had invaded the Emirate of Kabul in order to reinstate its ruler Shah Shujah, who had been living in exile in Ludhiana (a hundred miles southeast of Amritsar as it happens). Few Afghans were happy to see their king returned and fought bitterly against the invaders. But British superiority won the day. This caused one observer to express in his memoir opinions that preceded those made by Shashi Tharoor by 180 years. 'British executive government has riveted the shackles of slavery upon the whole agricultural population of British India' and has inflicted 'famines, discontent, disaffection, rebellion, financial distress, fall of prices, reduced revenues, crime abounding ... might against rights, cultivation declining, total absence of internal improvement, no public works, no roads, no canals, no dissemination of knowledge or improvements in education. We see here the consequences of a military despotism; a government imposed upon millions, and sustained by the sword, without a philanthropic motive; originating in cupidity, nourished and developed by tyrannous force, sealed in blood' [40]. Who was this person?

No savant at the end of the age of enlightenment, to be sure. Josiah Harlan, born in 1799, was an American Quaker from Chester County, Pennsylvania. He was shrewd and highly successful in his one aspiration: self-promotion. During his wanderings through the Punjab and Afghanistan, he became the friend and confidant of the two most powerful men (and mutual enemies) in the region: Maharaja Ranjit Singh, ruler of the Punjab, and Dost Mohammad Khan, emir of Kabul. For over a decade, he oscillated successfully in the service of one or the other, advising and raising armies first for one, and then for the other. He was also the self-appointed Prince of Ghor and inspiration for Rudyard Kipling's *The Man who would be King*. It is for these reasons that I include his views about colonial Britain.

The construction of the railways was a major project promoted by the British. In the 1880s, the railway system covered 10,822 miles; by 1922, 37,266 miles; and by 1947, 45,000 miles [41]. And not just railways. Medical education with associated hospitals was high on the British Empire's list of priorities. Madras Medical College (in today's Chennai) was founded in 1835, as was the Medical College of Bengal (in today's Kolkata). In 1845, a large donation by Sir Jamsetjee Jeejebhoy enabled the establishment of the Grant Medical College (named after Sir Robert Grant, Governor of Bombay) in today's Mumbai.

As historian Andrew Roberts has pointed out, Britain gave India a 'mass education system, irrigation projects, law and order, English as its first national lingua franca, universities, newspapers, standardised units of exchange, telegraphic communications, an uncorrupt legal system, medical advances, and the abolition of the widespread practice of burning widows alive on their husbands' funeral pyres' [42].

In July 2005, Prime Minister Manmohan Singh was awarded an honorary degree by the University of Oxford. His remarks at the ceremony illustrate what the leading Indian of his day thought about the presence of the British in India. After admitting to certain economic grievances, he stressed that 'India's experience with Britain had its beneficial consequences too. Our notions of the rule of law, of a Constitutional government, of a free press, of a professional civil service, of modern universities and research laboratories have all been fashioned in the crucible where an age-old civilisation of India met the dominant Empire of the day. These are all elements which we still value and cherish. Our judiciary, our legal system, our bureaucracy and our police are all great institutions, derived from British-Indian administration and they have served our country exceedingly well. ...' [43]. And I recall participating in a scientific conference in Bangalore in the early 1990s at which the chairman began by 'thanking Charles Pasternak and the other British participants for helping Indian scientists to achieve international recognition.'

Egypt

Britain's interest in Egypt (then a virtually independent country within the Ottoman Empire) dates to the construction of the Suez Canal, completed in 1869. The canal was owned by the Egyptian government, but France and Britain exercised financial control through their investment in its construction. In 1882, a British force invaded Egypt from Alexandria, ostensibly in support of the Khedive, Mohamed Tewfik Pasha, the de facto ruler of Egypt. The exact reasons for the invasion are debated to this day, but the attempted coup by Ahmed Urabi, an officer in the Egyptian army, against the Khedive surely played a part.

The colonial administrator Evelyn Baring (later Lord Cromer) had been appointed Controller-General of Egypt to sort out that country's economic woes (being a member of the banking family – to which Egypt was indebted – made him an obvious choice). Following the British invasion in 1882, Baring was appointed Consul-General of Egypt. He saw no reason to make Egypt a British protectorate or for Britain to remain in Egypt any longer than necessary. 'I do not see what the Egyptians, considered as a nation, have done to forfeit their right to self-government. There remains nothing in the area of fiscal reform that can't be done by Egyptians themselves' [44].

Moreover, 'He must be blind who see not what the English have wrought in Egypt: the gates of justice stand open to the poor; the streams flowing through the land are not stopped at the order of the strong; the poor man is lifted up and the rich man pulled down; the hand of the oppressor and the briber is struck when outstretched' [45].

Another Egyptian, Professor Afaf Lutfi Al-Sayyid Marsot, agrees. 'Financial policy ... – low taxation, efficient fiscal administration, careful expenditure on remunerative public works, and minimum interference in the internal and external traffic of goods – ... had by 1890 brought prosperity to the country'. She goes on to point out that 'Although Cromer has turned Egypt into a British dependency in all but name, yet materially and in the best colonial tradition, he has given the Egyptians much ... In spite of all its shortcomings, British rule in Egypt was benevolent ... British justice in Egypt was at least better than the justice meted out by the Khedive' [46].

South Africa

At the other end of the continent, British interests were on the rise, but the first colonists in Southern Africa were not British. They were Dutch. In 1652, the Dutch East India Company, which had been using the Cape of Good Hope as a port to refuel with supplies on the sea voyage to the East Indies, decided to establish a colony in order to provide the Company with a permanent base. (The Portuguese had been the first to land here but decided to exploit the interior of Southwest Africa instead.) The immigrants were mainly Dutch Calvinists accompanied by some Germans, Scandinavians and French Huguenots, who had left their homeland to escape the religious oppression sweeping across Catholic Europe. They moved north and east into the interior, to take up the farming of cattle, as the native Khoi – whom they displaced – were doing. They became known as Boers (farmers), also referred to as Afrikaners.

The British arrived at the Cape in 1795 in order to gain control of this important staging post to the East Indies. They ceded their newly acquired colony to the Dutch in 1802 but took it back four years later when the latter became vassals of the French under Napoleon. The attitude of the Boers and of the British towards the native population differed. The former imposed a colour bar and restrictive pass laws. The latter abolished both. They also replaced Dutch with English as the administrative language and substituted the British pound sterling for the Dutch rix-dollar. By 1836, the Boers had had enough. They chose to leave the territory and set out on what has become known as the Great Trek. They moved northwards into what is now the Northern Cape, then across the Orange River into what became known as the Orange Free State, and east into present-day Natal.

In 1866, a farmer's boy living in the village of Kimberley in today's Northern Cape Province found a pebble on the bank of the Orange River. It proved to be a 21-carat diamond. More even larger diamonds were soon discovered, and the British promptly annexed the area. Over the next 40 years, some 13,600,000 carats of diamonds would be unearthed – with no more than picks and shovels – from this huge mine. It cost the lives of more than a thousand workers, mainly native labour – 200 in a single day – due to accidents of one sort or another. By 1888, the mine – the largest diamond mine in the world – was being operated by De Beers Consolidated Mines, which a British entrepreneur named Cecil Rhodes had founded.

Rhodes was considered a racist and brutal employer of native labour. In 2015, a movement that came to be known as Rhodes Must Fall succeeded in having his bronze statue removed from the campus of the University of Cape Town. The campaign swiftly moved to Oriel College in Oxford, which Rhodes had attended during the 1870s. The aim, led by students of the college with some senior support, is to remove a small bust of Rhodes that looks down on Oxford's High Street. The protest is ongoing as I write. Are the accusations against him justified?

Cecil John Rhodes, born in 1853, was a somewhat sickly and unprepossessing vicar's son. His father thought the South African climate would do him good, and when Cecil was just seventeen years of age, sent him to join an older brother, Herbert, on the latter's small cotton farm near Pietermaritzburg in Natal. The discovery of diamonds at Kimberley led the brothers to try their luck in the rapidly developing mine there. Within a month or so, Cecil was making a good profit finding diamonds, acquiring concessions and investing his income in various projects. He could now fulfil his dream of going to Oxford. He managed to be accepted to read for a pass degree at Oriel College. He stayed for just one term before returning to Kimberly in order to resume the life of a diamond prospector. By 1876, he had amassed a small fortune. Over the next five years, he would sporadically travel between Kimberley and Oxford in order to notch up the nine terms of residence required to qualify for a pass degree. When in Oxford, he enjoyed himself carousing with the Bullingdon Club (of which Oscar Wilde was a member), playing polo and becoming master of the Drag Hunt. He finally took his degree in 1881 after which he left Oxford for good.

Rhodes now devoted himself full time to life in South Africa. He entered the Cape Parliament aged just 27. Within nine years, he was prime minister. His policy was to prevent native Africans from owning property and to restrict their rights to vote in elections, and he succeeded (though he later changed his mind, arguing that he 'always differentiated between the raw barbarians and the civilised natives' and that he supported 'equal rights to every civilised man south of the Zambesi' [47]). He was an ardent imperialist and dreamt of establishing a railway link, across British possessions, from the Cape to Cairo. We're still waiting for this to happen. His ambition to make a fortune – which he would use not for his own pleasure but to help others – was more successful. The scholarships that bear his name were set up to enable over a hundred graduates of exceptional talent from English-speaking countries – plus Germany – to study for a year at Oxford with all fees paid. The restrictions regarding the country of origin have now been relaxed. So far as 'racial' background is concerned, Rhodes was very clear that the scholarships should be open to all.

In 1889, the British South Africa Company (BSAC), with Rhodes as its leading light, received a Royal Charter. Its aims were to acquire and exploit the land north of the Limpopo River known as Mashonaland or Shonaland. Rhodes and a column of men marched into the territory in 1890, expecting to find rumoured deposits of gold. They did not, and considered annexing the land to the east (present-day Mozambique) that had been occupied by the Portuguese for the last four centuries. But this proved not to contain the precious metal either. Mashonaland may have been devoid of gold, but it contained valuable deposits of chromium and manganese. It also proved to be excellent agricultural land. Until Robert Mugabe expropriated the farms owned by European settlers, Rhodesia, as it came to be known, was the breadbasket of Africa.

By 1895, Rhodes's largest source of income was from Consolidated Gold Fields, an enterprise based on mining in the Transvaal. This was deep in Boer territory, under the rule of President Paul Kruger. Annexation of the Transvaal would give Rhodes not only better control of his investment but would add valuable territory to the British Empire. Together with his surgeon-turned-political colleague Leander Starr Jameson, Rhodes plotted in London – with the connivance of the British government – to stage a planned insurrection against Afrikaner rule in the Transvaal. It would be complemented by an invading force from the west in Bechuanaland (present-day Botswana). The enterprise, which has become known as the Jameson Raid, proved an utter disaster. Rhodes had to resign from the premiership of the Cape Parliament and his directorship of the British South African Company. The Jameson Raid was Rhodes's only failure. It was also his last initiative. He died, by now in poor health, in 1902, aged just 48 years of age.

So far as the accusations against Rhodes are concerned, there is 'no disputing the magnitude of his personality and its impact on the world. He was greatly hated and greatly loved'. He has been compared to Oliver Cromwell in that regard, as well as in his determination to achieve his vision. But the writer G K Chesterton disagrees. 'What was wrong with Rhodes was not that, like Cromwell … he made huge mistakes, nor even that he committed great crimes. It was that he committed these crimes … in order to spread certain ideas … but Rhodes had no principles whatever to give to the world'. The author Robert Rotberg is more measured in his analysis of Rhodes's character. 'He was boyish, sentimental, and shy; cynical, ruthless, impatient, and vindictive' [48].

In 1894, Rhodes opined as follows: 'Now, I say the natives are children. They are just emerging from barbarism. They have human minds … we ought to do something for the minds that the Almighty has given them. I do not believe that they are different from ourselves' [49]. Referring to the African natives as children would today be considered offensive, demeaning and politically incorrect. Not so during the second half of the 19th century. The main point is that if Rhodes was using children as an analogy for the primitive conditions in Sub-Saharan Africa, then in one sense I believe he was correct.

Let me digress. If one takes a hundred or a thousand persons and analyses their capacity for original thought, the values fall on a bell-shaped curve – dullards to the left and geniuses to the right with most of us somewhere in the middle. In any population, there will be some with the *potential* for innovative actions. As evolutionary biologist Stephen Jay

Gould has pointed out, 'I am, somehow, less interested in the weight and convolutions of Einstein's brain than in the near certainty that people of equal talent have lived and died in cotton fields and sweatshops' [50]. But the ambience, the atmosphere and the culture have to be right for people to be able to achieve their potential.

This was so for men during the 5th–3rd centuries BCE in the Athenian world, and again in Europe during the Age of Enlightenment of the 17th and 18th centuries. The difference is that Rhodes (and many others) thought that the uncivilised could be *taught* intellectual skills, whereas the range of those skills is the same in all humans. It is the opportunity to *express* those skills productively that depends on the right conditions. But by implying that the human mind is universal, Rhodes was stating what we now know to be true.

Elsewhere in Africa

By the turn of the 20th century, most of Africa had been colonised. Only two countries remained independent: Liberia, the newly created nation for freed American slaves on the Atlantic coast, and Ethiopia, the birthplace of humanity in the Horn of Africa. The British and the French had the largest share, followed by Germany, Belgium, Portugal, Spain and Italy. In one case at least, there was good reason for colonisation. The British annexed Nyasaland (today's Malawi) because in 1888 they had been asked by missionaries to rid the area around Lake Nyasa of marauding Arab slave traders. 'Imperialism was the only antidote to the East African slave trade' [51].

In India, the British had built schools, hospitals and medical centres largely for the benefit of the local population. In Africa, the situation was different. The colonists occupied the land and built the necessary infrastructure. The quality depended on the recipients. In Kenya, during the 1950s, for example, the colonial government spent $180 a year on the education of each white child, $65 on each Asian child and $5 on each African child [52].

The French educational system was the best in that 'texts and courses (were) designed to fit native needs' [53]. The Germans had little regard for the education of their African subjects. In German East Africa, barely 1% of the population was catered for. In German West Africa, it was even worse. The number of students attending the one 'upper school' in the country was 12 [54]. No wonder. Had not the Prussian Chancellor Otto von Bismarck in 1868 predicted that 'The supposed benefits of colonies for the trade and industry of the mother country are, for the most part, illusory' [55]? He was proved right. By 1912, Germany was spending 87.4 million Reichsmark a year on its colonies (mostly in Africa) and receiving 63.9 million in return [56].

Overall, the French and the British spent the most on their colonies, the Belgians and Portuguese the least. In the Belgian Congo (today's Democratic Republic of the Congo), the government abrogated its responsibility for the education of youth by passing this over to the various missionary groups – Catholic and Protestant – that had been set up. In Guinea-Bissau (not to be confused with its neighbour Guinea to the southeast – both on the Atlantic coast), three hundred years of Portuguese rule produced little benefit to the native population. In 1974, the illiteracy rate was 97% and the country could boast of just fourteen university graduates. So far as infrastructure is concerned, the colonists had managed to build just 265 miles of paved road in a country the size of Belgium [57].

Independence from their former rulers came to Sub-Saharan Africa during the second half of the 20th century. You might have thought that life improved for everyone. Not so. Apart from Botswana, which benefited from enlightened leadership, things got worse. I have attempted to show how this happened in a book published a few years ago [58]. Botswana, formerly Bechuanaland, once described as a 'basket case', bucked the trend. Why? Because it was led by an honest and enlightened man, Seretse Khama [59]. Elsewhere, things got worse.

The Nigerian author Chinua Achebe illustrates the decline with a few well-chosen examples. 'One had a great deal of confidence and faith in the British system that we had grown up in, a confidence and faith in British institutions. One trusted that things would get where they were sent; postal theft, tampering, or loss of documents were unheard of. Today (in Nigeria), one would not even contemplate sending off materials of importance so readily, either abroad or even locally, by mail' [60]. Conditions began to deteriorate a mere 2 years after Nigeria's independence in 1962. 'Before (under colonial rule), justice may have been fierce but it could not be bought or sold ... Now all that has changed' [61].

I can vouch for the sense of decay in Nigeria. In 1988, I spent a week at the University of Ibadan as an external examiner in biochemistry. Founded as a college in 1948, it is the oldest academic institution in Nigeria. Like the town in which it is situated, the university suffers from frequent outages of electricity and the water supply. Yet the area is close to a rainforest. When the dean of the medical school, Prof David Sebag-Montefiore (brother of a former Bishop of Birmingham), showed me round the town's hospital, I was dismayed at the squalor. On arrival, I had been informed that I would not be seeing any students, for the university had closed on account of certain disciplinary problems. My host, a kindly gentleman, suggested that I might like to spend a day at the nearby International Institute of Tropical Agriculture. It could not have been more of a contrast. The laboratories were clean and air-conditioned (the institute is situated next to a river which supplies it with fresh water and electricity). Half the staff are Nigerian. The reason for the conditions in Ibadan town, university and hospital, I was told, is simply the inefficiency and corruption among the region's politicians.

The discovery of oil during the 1950s should have made Nigeria one of the richest countries in Africa. Political corruption (even before independence) has had the opposite effect. 'The people of the delta are poor; they are less likely to go to a school, see a doctor, than those almost anywhere else in Nigeria. The people cannot farm or fish ... the waters are slicked with oil, and the air is choked with fumes ... Next to a Chevron platform for pumping oil to ships offshore I saw a row of unadorned huts in the sand: the village (had) no electricity, no school or clinic, no running water, and no bridge to connect it to anywhere. Yet this place made Nigerian soldiers and politicians wealthy ...' [62]. It was not colonialism that ruined Nigeria. It was the calibre of the politicians, some appointed even before independence, that held the country back [63].

Britain granted its colonies independence during the second half of the 20th century. Today, the USA, under President Trump is aiming to acquire Greenland and the Panama Canal (again). Britain under Sir Keir Starmer, on the other hand, is negotiating [64,65] to hand the Chagos Islands to Mauritius (more than 2,000 km away and under Chinese influence). In order to retain Diego Garcia (the largest of the Chagos Islands – which hosts a joint UK–US military base), it is offering Mauritius some £100 million a year for the privilege of renting its own territory. Needless to say, the Chagossians, of whom there are only some 10,000 worldwide since their expulsion from Diego Garcia during the 1970s, have not been consulted in regard to these negotiations.

None of the European countries derived much income from their colonies. In the case of Belgium, the Congo 'Free' State was administered as a private company whose owner, King Leopold II, made a small fortune from it. Colonialism was never an altruistic project. In a few instances, the colonised and their countries actually benefitted through infrastructure installed by the colonisers.

Yet members of The Key, an organisation that purports to give 'Trusted advice and resources that you can rely on' to school teachers, consider that the British Empire resembled Nazi Germany in terms of the commitment of "atrocities"' [66]. They are clearly ignorant of the colonial events over the last 400 years that I have described. Of European history between 1933 and 1945, they seem totally unaware. Nevertheless, The Key currently provides 'teaching resources' to over 100,000 school leaders [67]. It is such instances that lead me to conclude that we are living in a deluded world.

Notes

1. Quoted by Christopher Harding in his review of Lawrence James's *The Lion and the Dragon* in the *Sunday Telegraph* of 6 August 2023.
2. Rex Niven; *Nine Great Africans* (London: G Bell and Sons, 1964), pp 130–148.

3. van den Berghe, p 117.
4. I use the term in its original sense of 'a society made up of cities' rather than that of 'a society that is culturally superior to one of uncouth barbarians'. I do not consider slavery to be cultured in any way.
5. J J Rousseau: *Le Contrat Social* (book I, chap IV), quoted in Anstey, p 120.
6. https://study.com/academy/lesson/slavery-in-ancient-history.html#:~:text=Male%20slaves%20worked%20in%20agriculture,them%20more%20time%20to%20pay.
7. *ibid*.
8. Diop, p 3 *et seq*.
9. Segal, p 75 *et seq*.
10. Ross E Dunn: *The adventures of Ibn Battuta: A Muslim traveller of the fourteenth century* (Beckenham, Kent: Croom Helm, 1986).
11. Segal, p 157.
12. *ibid*, p 159.
13. https://www.binnews.com/content/2022-09-26-ghana-to-formally-apologize-for-its-role-in-transatlantic-slave-trade/.
14. https://www.hull.ac.uk/work-with-us/more/media-centre/news/2020/sailors-were-appalled-by-conditions-on-slave-ships#:~:text=The%20terrible%20conditions%20for%20those,and%20poor%20ventilation%20below%20deck.
15. https://www.blackhistorymonth.org.uk/article/section/history-of-slavery/life-on-board-slave-ships/.
16. Frankopan, p 366.
17. van den Berghe, p 125.
18. O'Neill, Onora: 'Rights to Compensation', in *Justice across Boundaries: Whose Obligations?* (Cambridge: Cambridge University Press, 2016), p 51.
19. Sewell, p 3.
20. Harry de Quetteville, *Daily Telegraph*, 16 March, 2023: Laura Trevelyan: 'This is history in the making. This is Britain's reckoning with its colonial past'.
21. Craig Simpson: *Daily Telegraph* 9 September 2023.
22. Hayley Dixon: 'Rowntree heirs vow to face up to colonial past' *Daily Telegraph* 3 August 2024.
23. Craig Simpson: *Sunday Telegraph*, 5 February 2023.

24. Craig Simpson: *Sunday Telegraph*, 12 March, 2023.
25. Roberts, p 499.
26. *ibid*, p 446.
27. Daniel Hannan: 'The Church of England is replacing its Christian nature in a fit of woke frenzy' *Sunday Telegraph* 10 March 2024.
28. Eric Williams: *Capitalism and Slavery* (Richmond, VA: University of North Carolina Press, 1944).
29. Niemietz, p 33.
30. *The Independent*, 8 August 2014.
31. Daniel Hannan: *Daily Telegraph* 8 April 2023.
32. Pasternak 2022, pp 11–27 and pp 28–49.
33. Sarah Knapton: 'Men and women's brains do work differently, scientists discover for first time' *Daily Telegraph* 19 February 2024.
34. Roy, Tirthankar: *An Economic History of India, 1707–1857* (2nd ed, London: Routledge, 2021) pp 4–5.
35. Fieldhouse, D K: *West and the Third World* (Oxford: Blackwell, 1999), p 35; quoted by Biggar 2023, p 166.
36. Roy, Tirthankar: *An Economic History of India, 1707–1875* (2nd ed, London: Routledge, 2021) p 176.
37. Niemietz, p 18.
38. *ibid*, p 13.
39. Biggar, 2023, pp 226 and 229.
40. Macintyre, p 280.
41. Lalvani, Kartar. *The Making of India: The Untold Story of British Enterprise* (London: Bloomsbury, 2016) pp 161, 199, 222.
42. Andrew Roberts, reviewing Walter Reid's *Fighting Retreat: Churchill and India* in the *Daily Telegraph* 6 January 2024.
43. from Biggar, 2023, p 283.
44. Roger Owen: *Lord Cromer: Victorian Imperialist, Edwardian Proconsul* (Oxford: Oxford University Press, 2004), p 177.
45. Storrs, Ronald: *Orientations* (London: Nicholson and Watson, 1939), p 89.
46. Afaf Lutfi Al-Sayyid, Afaf Lutfi: *Egypt and Cromer: A Study in Anglo-Egyptian Relations* (London: John Murray, 1968), pp 128, 196, 202.
47. Rotberg, p 618.
48. *ibid*, pp 8 and 9.

49. Vindex. *Cecil Rhodes, his Political Life and Speeches, 1881-1900* (London; Chapman and Hall, 1900) pp 383, 388.
50. Science aid. Donors and African governments must invest in advanced science and maths education. *Nature* **491**: 159–160, 2012.
51. Pakenham, p 413.
52. Lamb, p 156.
53. Vaillant, Janet G: *Black, French and African. A life of Léopold Sédar Senghor* (Cambridge MA: Harvard University Press, 1990) p 50.
54. Wolfgang Mehnert: *Education Policy* in Stoecker, Helmuth (ed): *German Imperialism in Africa. From the Beginnings until the Second World War* (trans. Zöllner, London: C Hurst & Co, 1986) p 221.
55. Niemietz, p v.
56. *ibid*, p 49.
57. Lamb, p 5.
58. Pasternak 2018.
59. *ibid*, pp 183–195.
60. Achebe, Chinua: *There Was a Country: A Personal History of Biafra* (NY: Penguin, 2012), p 36.
61. Quoted in Ezemwa-Ohaeto: *Chinua Achebe: A Biography* (Oxford: James Currey, 1997), p 88.
62. Peter Cunliffe-Jones: *My Nigeria. Five Decades of Independence* (New York, NY: Palgrave Macmillan, 2010), p 35.
63. Pasternak 2018, pp 263–271.
64. Greg Heffer: *Daily Mail* 8 January 2025.
65. Samaan Lateef: 'Indian Ocean country claims £9bn deal for air base is not enough' *Sunday Telegraph* 12 January 2025.
66. Craig Simpson: 'Present British Empire like Nazis to pupils, guide insists' *Daily Telegraph* 13 July 2024.
67. https://schoolleaders.thekeysupport.com/.

Chapter 4

Gender and Sex

When Princess Elizabeth acceded to the throne as Queen Elizabeth II on the death of her father in 1952, her husband, Prince Philip, realised that henceforth he would be required to walk one step behind his wife. 'I'm no more than a b----y amoeba', he muttered. It was a jocular analogy. For Prince Philip, like his predecessor a century earlier, Prince Albert, proved a highly influential yet loyal innovator (Duke of Edinburgh Awards and Great Exhibition of 1851, respectively). Like Albert, Philip was an intelligent man with – in his case – a wonderful sense of humour. Prince Philip fathered four healthy children (Albert managed nine). But an amoeba is a sexless single-celled organism that perpetuates itself through simple cell division. Sex – designated male or female – evolved some two billion years ago [1] and now accounts for the reproduction of most of the inhabitants of this planet: animals (including humans), plants and fungi.

The Cambridge Dictionary defines gender as 'a group of people in a society who share particular qualities or ways of behaving which that society associates with being male, female, or another identity'. It is not a defined feature of human beings but a way of looking at oneself. It is a social quality, not a physical one. Biological sex, on the other hand, is a physical state of being. That is how gender and sex are generally viewed today, and it is how I employ them in this book. A recent article in the scientific journal *Nature* confirms my usage. It defines sex as referring to 'differences between females and males caused by biological factors, whereas gender refers to differences caused by social factors, including gender roles, expectations and identity' [2].

Changing Gender

As far as transitioning (male to female and *vice versa*) is concerned, we should remember that the type of chromosomes within a person's cells don't change with time. Someone born with XX or XY will remain so for the rest of their life. Hence, referring to them as female or male, simple words that have been in use since the advent of speech, is perfectly logical. However, I appreciate that the promoters of trans ideology don't accept this fact of nature. Nor, it seems, does a pharmaceutical company as experienced as AstraZeneca or an organisation as respected as the BBC. The former has been criticised over a training manual, admittedly produced by AZPride, the staff group for LGBT+ employees, that asserts sex to be non-binary [3]. The latter's Executive Complaints Unit considers that a remark made by one of its presenters, to the effect that a trans-woman is a man, 'gave the impression of endorsing one viewpoint in a highly controversial area' [4]. To realists, there's nothing controversial about this.

A birth male may change his gender. He may have been given puberty blockers as a child. He can take feminising hormones (oestrogen) which will change his voice and appearance; he can cut off his penis, or have it surgically turned inside-out to become a pretend vagina; he can have breast implants. But the cells in his body – from brain to toe – will continue to contain an X and a Y chromosome until his death. Whether male or female, a person can no more change their sex than the colour of their eyes. Changing gender can be achieved by a simple document or an alteration in one's passport.

The number of transgender persons in the world today is not insignificant. In the UK, for example, some 250,000 people (0.4% of the population) consider themselves to be of the opposite gender to that in which they were born (birth sex). Many suffer from the condition known as gender dysphoria. Until 30 years ago, little was known about this affliction. Then, in 1995, a group of researchers at the Institute for Brain Research in Amsterdam published an intriguing result [5]. They examined the brains of six recently dead transgender individuals, as well as a number of normal 'controls'. What they found was that the volume of part of the hypothalamus – which is larger in men than in women – corresponded to the gender not the birth sex of the individual. This suggests that changes in the brain of transgender persons happen before birth. The study has been repeated several times, but the results have been inconsistent. More research needs to be done, and this is happening. In 1991, there was one neuroimaging study of transgender participants. In 2024, there were 83 [6].

Gender dysphoria leads to depression and anxiety, for which psychotherapy is of some help, but others go further. The American Academy of Pediatrics considers that the only ethical treatment for gender dysphoric children is 'gender affirmation'. This is a debatable view. First, because it is based on poorly conducted research [7]. Second, because of the hazards involved in gender-reversing procedures. Treating children with puberty blockers can lead to a number of medical complications [8]. Many youngsters subsequently wish that they had never taken this step (or had not been encouraged by their elders who should have known better). The same applies to hormonal therapy, which has its own hazards. For girls (and women), these lead to 'higher risks of cardiovascular problems, including high blood pressure, heart attacks and stroke, dementia in later life, liver problems, diabetes and joint problems'. In the case of boys (and men), 'low testosterone is known to cause fatigue, brittle bones and high cholesterol levels in biological males, and taking oestrogen is likely to raise their risk of some cancers, including breast cancer' [9].

Women in their twenties who had transgendered earlier (now transmen) have been found to suffer very unpleasant urinary and bowel symptoms like incontinence not normally seen before menopause. The cause appears to be related to the testosterone they had received as part of the transgendering process [10]. It has recently been shown that females have stronger immune responses than males, and that this is due to their hormonal status. So, giving women, who have transgendered to men, testosterone therapy – often for the rest of their lives – has a negative effect on their ability to fight infections [11].

Kathleen Stock (see Chapter 1) is aware that 'From the mouths of doctors we find risky experimental surgeries recommended for minors, and a relative disregard for complications that in any other branch of medicine would be treated as unacceptable'. 'Perhaps the most shocking revelation', according to files emanating from the World Professional Association for Transgender Health, is a clinician prepared to recommend a radical double mastectomy for a 16-year-old girl already suffering from liver cancer, despite believing – along with the girl's surgeon and oncologist – that the cancer is probably due to the cross-sex hormones she had been prescribed. Highly debilitating side effects of surgeries and hormone treatments in young patients – including pelvic inflammatory disease, vaginal atrophy, incontinence, excruciating pain, and an increased rate of abnormal smear tests – appear to raise only vague disquiet at most [12].

The good news, at least for the UK, is that its Health Secretary Wes Streeting intends to make the ban on giving children puberty blockers in private clinics (the NHS no longer performs such treatment) – initiated by his predecessor Victoria Atkins – permanent [13]. Despite his motive being to 'protect children from the irreversible effects of these drugs, which may include infertility, anorgasmia, osteoporosis and an impact on brain development', he has received 'hysterical vitriol' and been accused of 'having blood on his hands' by those 'who cheer on the sterilisation and mutilation of young (mainly female) bodies' [14]. However – perhaps under pressure – he has allowed an NHS trial involving puberty blockers for children to go ahead [15].

Cass report

A new review by Dame Hilary Cass, whose report in 2022 contributed to the closure of the Tavistock transgender clinic, warns that 'many schools have been allowing pupils to change gender without their parents' knowledge, despite government guidance to the contrary' and that 'children may experience "psychological" repercussions as a result of being allowed to change their name and pronoun to the gender of their choosing' [16]. Of course, it has been worse than that. One father, whose son was ordering Chinese-made hormones off the internet, obviously welcomed the Cass report. 'One of the reasons we have got into this situation over the past 10 years is the NHS and Tavistock legitimising all these ideas. We need to push back, and treat children and young adults by thinking about what's going on in their minds, rather than medicalising it' [17].

Columnist Charles Moore points out that 'The trans debate – moral, medical, social, scientific, political – will now be based on much better information. ... Dr Cass's conclusion is that the provision of puberty blockers – and other aspects of gender identity treatment – has been rushed forward on dangerously thin evidence. She speaks of "a failure to reliably collect even the most basic data and information"' [18]. We're lucky in the UK to have had this sensible review. In Germany (following some other countries), the Bundestag has passed a law that will enable children from the age of 14 onwards to change gender without any medical assessment simply by going to a register office [19].

The fightback against Dr Cass's measured review has begun. As might be anticipated, Scotland, governed by the deluded SNP (Scottish National Party) is first off the mark. Far from accepting her conclusions, a charity called LGBT Youth Scotland is encouraging schools to set up LGBT clubs and 'sexual orientation alliance groups'. Primary schools will appoint children and some teachers as LGBT champions. Their task? To question children as young as four – most of whom will not yet have learned to read – whether they are gay, lesbian or trans [20]. Such are the priorities of the Scottish educational system, once the envy of the rest of the UK. (Might Scotland's obsession with trans ideology be related to the wearing of the kilt by some of its menfolk?) The LGBT charity Stonewall has so far not criticised the Cass review outright. Its Scottish branch (Stonewall Scotland), however, had earlier urged schools to shred the governmental advice they had received regarding the dangers of puberty blockers [21]. After more than 30 years of being supported by businesses in exchange for their staff, Stonewall is losing its prestige [22]. Promoting puberty blockers is finally being recognised to be incompatible with a charitable status.

A study of gender dysphoric children in the 1970s and 1980s – before treatment with drugs or surgery became fashionable – showed that many grew up as homosexuals, and no longer wished to identify as members of a different gender. Others decided to change gender for reasons unrelated to any medical condition [23]. As Dr Hilary Cass's review pointed out,

'Exploration of identity is a completely natural process during childhood and adolescence and rarely requires clinical input. However, over the past 5–10 years the number of children and young people being referred for NHS support around their gender identity has increased rapidly' [24]. Since homosexuality is much more common than gender change (and does not involve risky medical interventions), I shall devote the next section to this topic before returning to the consequences of gender realignment for the rest of this chapter.

Homosexuality

Homosexual, derived from the Greek (*homo* = same), refers to affinity – sexual or merely platonic – between a male or female and someone of the same sex. In contrast, heterosexual (Gk *hetero* = other) describes the more usual affinity between a male or female and a person of the opposite sex. According to author Michael Young, the word homosexual entered common usage only in the late 19th century [25]. It provides a more inclusive rendering of this condition than the biblical 'sodomy' that was used from the 11th century onwards [26].

During classical times, in the Greek city-state of Sparta, male homosexuality between an adult and a youth was commonplace. The youngster would generally develop heterosexual relationships in adulthood, having benefitted from the knowledge and discernment imparted by his elder partner. It has been suggested that such a relationship may have been of evolutionary benefit.

Female homosexuality may be less common than that between males, though, as mentioned in Chapter 1, all-female households are now on the rise in the USA. During Spartan times, there lived on the Aegean island of Lesbos a famed poetess named Sappho. She also ran a girls' school and is said to have had several homosexual partners. As a result, the words sapphic and lesbian have come to describe female homosexual relationships. Sappho appears to have borne a daughter and to have died by throwing herself off a rock for the love of a ferryman. So, she was probably bisexual, which applies to many of today's homosexuals. In fact, the ability of homosexuals to procreate is one of the reasons why a potential 'homosexual' genetic element has not been eliminated over time. The other reason, of course, is that such elements are passed on by one's kin [27].

Thus, many homosexual men are actually bisexual, generally producing offspring at an early stage of their lives. The same is true of female homosexuals (lesbians). Many are emotionally bisexual throughout their lives. A good example is that of the writer Vita Sackville-West, married to the bisexual Harold Nicolson (see in the following). Their tempestuous relationship is well described by their son Nigel Nicolson in *Portrait of a Marriage* (1973). Another well-known bisexual was the man who brought Scottish blood into the English monarchy at Queen Elizabeth's death in 1603: James VI of Scotland and I of England.

James Stuart (born 1566) was the only child of Mary Queen of Scots and Lord Darnley. But there was a rumour that he was the son of Mary's secretary (and lover) David Riccio (murdered by Darnley), and that James was aware of this. After Darnley's murder (suspected to have been carried out by Mary and the Earl of Bothwell, whom she subsequently married), Mary was forced to abdicate and leave Scotland in favour of James, aged 13 months. He was brought up by the Earl and Countess of Mar, who engaged a learned tutor for him. As a result, James spoke Latin, Greek, French and a little Italian. He wrote poetry throughout his life and has been considered 'one of the most learned and intellectually curious men ever to sit on any throne' [28].

James was attracted to young men throughout his life. His first relationship was probably at age 14 with his cousin Esmé Stuart, Lord d'Aubigny, the Duke of Lennox, who, according to Antonia Fraser, 'awakened James's sexuality' [29]. His greatest *amour* seems to have been George Villiers, whom he subsequently made Duke of Buckingham (later in his life, he would dispense titles not out of love but for cash). The reason for deeming James to have been bisexual is that at the age of 23, he married the 15-year-old Princess Anne of Denmark, with whom he fathered seven children (one being the future Charles I; most of the others died in infancy).

Despite his obvious homosexuality, James proved a good ruler. He ended the war with Spain and started no new conflicts. Undeterred by the failed gunpowder plot of 1605, he tried to keep the peace between Protestants and Catholics, appointing several of the latter to major offices. He sponsored a new translation of the bible, known as the King James Authorised Version, which was easier for the multitudes to read. He ruled Scotland as efficiently as he did England, entirely from his base in the latter country. Criticism of his authority was limited to vague and indirect references to Edward II and Piers Gaveston.

The nature of sexual relations between James and his enamoured gentlemen has been much debated. In his book *Basilikon Doron*, James refers to sodomy as one of the 'horrible crimes that yee are bound in conscience never to forgive'. And a letter from Buckingham to James states that 'there is this difference betwixt that noble hand and heart, one may surfeit by the one, but not by the other, and sooner by yours than his own' [30]. So, it is quite possible that intercourse was limited to masturbation and did not involve anal penetration. Either way, the Courtiers of the Bedchamber frequently observed the king in bed with another man without comment.

Four hundred years ago, 'sodomy' was considered a sin and a crime (in the 12th century, sodomites had been burnt at the stake [31]). Not much has changed with time. Only during the 20th century was the latter aspect dropped in most non-Islamic countries. Today, politicians in the USA and Britain no longer need to hide their homosexuality from the electorate on whom their career depends.

An example of a female homosexual who was bisexual is that of the writer Vita Sackville-West, married to the bisexual Harold Nicolson.

Vita was born on 9 March 1892 in the grandest house in the country. The building alone covers more than six acres. Knole had been given to Vita's ancestor, Thomas Sackville, by his cousin Queen Elizabeth I. But for how long Vita would live there was not clear. The reason concerns a dispute as to whether Vita's mother Victoria – who had married Lionel, the 3rd Lord Sackville (Vita's father) – was legitimate or not. If not, her brother Henry would claim ownership of Knole. The uncertainty arose because it was not established whether Victoria's mother, a Spanish dancer called Pepita, had been married to Victoria's father, the 2nd Lord Sackville or merely been his mistress. It was finally settled in February 1910. Vita and her parents, who had been living in Hill Street in Mayfair during the years of uncertainty, could return to Knole, secure in the knowledge that the house and the thousand-acre park belonged to Lionel.

From an early age, Vita adored her father Lionel ('Dada') more than her mother Victoria ('Bonne Mama; B.M.'), who was the dominant parent. Lionel suffered as much as Vita from Victoria's overbearing nature. Insofar as such a situation – the opposite of an Oedipus complex – may be said to typify a future female homosexual, it certainly applied to Vita.

By the age of 12, she was writing ballads, plays and historical novels – all inspired by the olden days at Knole. Between 1906 and 1908 (aged 14–16), she wrote three plays in French, as well as winning a prize for completing a limerick. Vita's first published work was *Poems of West and East*. It had been accepted by Bodley Head in 1914 but was not printed until 1917 on account of the war. Her mother immediately bought 100 copies to distribute to friends and bookshops. It was a kind gesture, but unnecessary because the book was well reviewed in the *Morning Post*. Vita's professional career as a writer had been launched.

During the dispute about the ownership of Knole, Vita was living with her parents in London. At 13 years of age, she attended a small day school off Park Lane where her fellow students included Rosamund Grosvenor and Violet Keppel, whom she had met the previous year. Both girls would become more than just good friends. Of the former, she would write in her diary, 'I love her so much' [32]. With Violet, she went much further. In 1918, already a mother of two, she would spend a night with Violet as man (dressed accordingly) and wife in a boarding house in Orpington.

Vita had been courted by a number of men, including Orazio Pucci, an Italian nobleman whose passion for her was not reciprocated, Henry Lascelles (later Earl Harewood), whom she thought dull, and also Patrick Shaw-Stewart (Fellow of All Souls Oxford), whose cleverness was well known. In 1910, Vita was introduced to the man who would dominate the rest of her life. Harold Nicolson, 6 years older than Vita and slightly shorter, was an up-and-coming diplomat currently serving as an attaché in the Madrid embassy. They met at a dinner party in London to which her parents had taken her. Vita liked what she saw. Emboldened, she took the initiative and invited Harold to Knole. Here, he witnessed a charity production of a Shakespeare masque in the park. Vita played Portia, for which Ellen Terry, who took part alongside the likes of Venetia Stanley and Mrs Winston Churchill, lent Vita her Portia costume.

Harold was even more stricken with Vita. They met occasionally at social events and corresponded frequently. Harold's declarations of love were sometimes met with ambivalence, though by early 1913, she wrote in her diary, 'These days I think so much about Harold that I can't sleep. I've got a mad longing to see him again, and I can't let him go out of my life. I shall marry him' [33]. She did so on 1 October of that year in the chapel at Knole. The ceremony was conducted by the Bishop of Rochester, with Rosamund Grosvenor as one of the bridesmaids. The honeymoon began in Florence, from where they travelled to Cairo to spend 10 days at the British Agency with Lord Kitchener, on their way to their final destination in Constantinople, where Harold was Third Secretary. By Christmas, she was pregnant. The result was a boy, Ben. Another boy, Nigel, would be born two and a half years later. Sexual relations, but not affection, between Vita and Harold declined.

In 1917, an event occurred that might have ended their marriage, but didn't. Harold discovered that he was infected with a venereal disease and rightly felt that he had to tell Vita. She accepted his affairs with young homosexual men, went to a doctor and received appropriate treatment. A greater threat was Vita's increasingly close liaison with Violet, whom Harold, naturally enough, hated. But he continued to put up with the situation. Violet's engagement and subsequent marriage in 1919 to World War 1 hero Denys Trefusis did nothing to change matters. On the contrary, having spent four months earlier that year with Violet in France, Vita was now actively pursuing her. During Violet's honeymoon with Denys in Paris, Vita arrived and took Violet to a small hotel where 'she made love to her' [34].

Yet Harold and Vita's marriage bloomed. They had bought Long Barn, a good-sized house of considerable antiquity near Knole, and were now indulging in their favourite pastime – that would continue to the end of their days – of planning and cultivating a garden. Vita was also happy at her literary success. Her first novel, *Heritage*, was well received, with positive reviews in papers such as the *Sunday Times*, *Manchester Guardian* and *Birmingham Post*: it sold over 1400 copies in its first year.

At the end of 1922, Vita met Virginia Woolf, 10 years her senior. By the following year, Vita began to fall under Virginia's spell, but a dinner at which Vita and Harold met the Bloomsbury group (Virginia and Leonard Woolf, Duncan Grant, Clive Bell and Lytton Strachey) was not a success. On the other hand, Vita's new friendship with Virginia finally severed the bond that had attracted Vita to Violet Keppel a decade earlier. Vita reassured a concerned Harold that 'one's love for Virginia is a very different thing: a mental thing, a spiritual thing if you like, an intellectual thing …' [35] (though she had twice gone to bed with her). So far as the relative quality of their writing was concerned, Vita was under no illusion. 'I don't know whether to be dejected or encouraged when I read the works of Virginia Woolf. Dejected because I shall never be able to write like that, or encouraged because somebody can' [36].

Yet there were compensations for Vita. In 1927, she received the Hawthornden Prize for 'imaginative literature'. Ten years later, her *Pepita*, based on her exotic Spanish grandmother and now published by the Woolfs' Hogarth Press, sold 10,000 copies in the first 2 months. In 1933, during a successful lecture tour in the USA undertaken with Harold, Vita had been lionised wherever she went.

In 1930, the Nicolsons decided to give up Long Barn. A friend of Vita's mentioned that a property twenty miles away, called Sissinghurst Castle, was for sale. When Vita and Harold visited it the next day, they found an uninhabitable ruin. All that remained was a single tower and some outbuildings set on seven acres of muddy wilderness. But Vita saw that the grounds had potential for an extensive garden. Since she would be paying for the property, she did not hesitate to purchase it. Designing beds and paths, as well as renovating the buildings, gave her joy for years to come. She would select every flower, shrub and tree to be planted and became a knowledgeable horticulturist, writing weekly articles, lecturing and delivering talks at the BBC. Within two decades, visitors to Sissinghurst were contributing £1,400 a year, at one shilling a time, to its upkeep. In 1955, Vita was awarded the Royal Horticultural Society's Veitch Memorial Medal.

Gender and Sex

The war had brought Violet from France (relations were not renewed) and German aircraft over Sissinghurst (the house was spared potential damage). For many of the following years, Vita and Harold were together only during the weekends (Monday or Tuesday to Friday Harold spent in his Albany apartment). During the winter, Vita and Harold took long cruises into the sunshine of the southern regions. Returning from South America in 1962, Vita felt extremely unwell. A hysterectomy was advised, and she was found to be harbouring a cancer. On the second of June, back at Sissinghurst, she succumbed. Her last words were to Glen (her golden retriever). Following her wishes, Vita's ashes are preserved in the family crypt at Withyham.

Vita was both transvestite and lesbian. She had passionate affairs with at least six other women, as well as with some men, during her lifetime. These were against a background of loving and lasting affection for Harold. She derived as much pleasure from tending a garden she had designed with him as from writing novels, plays and poetry. Her early success in that regard, as well as her aristocratic heritage, caused her to become personally acquainted with the world's leading literary and intellectual figures [37].

How does homosexuality arise? Sigmund Freud thought he had the answer. First, all humans are essentially bisexual. At certain stages of our development, from suckling baby to adulthood, the homosexual side predominates; at other stages, the heterosexual side prevails. Both are affected by what Freud called our 'libido'. Before we enter adolescence, the Oedipus complex asserts itself. (Recall Sophocles's play about King Oedipus, who unknowingly kills his father and marries his mother). According to Freud, males are in love with their mother because she has sustained them through the nutrients emanating from her breast, but they are aware that incest is taboo, so they seek another woman for affection, which means antagonising their father. Depending on the relative influence of the homosexual versus the heterosexual drive throughout development, one or the other eventually prevails. I appreciate that this summary gives the reader no more than a hint of Freud's hypothesis. It is more fully presented by the Canadian philosopher Michael Ruse [38]. It should be noted that this says nothing specific about female homosexuality.

The response to Freud's views has been mixed. Philosopher Roger Scruton dismissed Freud's hypothesis as his 'ability to proclaim speculative nonsense in the tone of voice appropriate to meticulous science' [39]. Peter Medawar, the 'father of transplantation' and Nobel Laureate in Medicine, considered Freud's psychoanalytical theory to be 'akin to a dinosaur or zeppelin in the history of ideas, a vast structure of radically unsound design and with no posterity' [40]. Michael Ruse is more generous. 'Freud's theories are not pseudo-science. ... Freud's views on homosexuality may well draw our attention to some interesting facts about the early lives of (male) homosexuals' [41].

Homosexuality is considerably more common than gender change. The American sexologist Alfred Kinsey carried out a survey of 6,000 American males during the 1940s. He found that more than 30% of adults had had some homosexual contact to the point of orgasm. This result naturally surprised many. But it is probably an overestimate, as much of Kinsey's survey was carried out in San Francisco, a city notorious for the large number of male homosexuals within its population. Kinsey also surveyed 6,000 females and found the prevalence of homosexuality to be roughly half that for males [42].

Today, homosexuality is simply part of normal life, and many homosexual couples may have merely a platonic not a sexual relationship with each other. For example, when watching the BBC's weekly *Gardeners' World*, I notice that several of the amateur gardeners whose creations are presented are in quiet homosexual (some male, others female) associations – all without the drama of the Vita–Harold affair mentioned earlier. I am not implying that this is any kind of statistic. Overall, some 3% of the population in the UK may be homosexual. Most people probably prefer to live with another person – homosexual or heterosexual – rather than alone.

Like other human traits, homosexuality results from a mix of inherited [43] and environmental influences. A recent study points to certain genetic loci that may be involved [44]. That homosexuality is partly innate also receives support from observations on our nearest relative, the chimpanzee. The primatologist Frans de Waal has studied the behaviour of the bonobo or pygmy chimpanzee. These animals live in a matriarchal society of bisexual individuals in which homosexual encounters, especially between females but also between males, are rife [45]. Homosexual encounters have been observed in all great apes, and beyond: in bats, American bison, dolphins, elephants, giraffes, marmots, lions, sheep and spotted hyenas. Same-sex affinities and parenting among same-sex pairs occur not just in mammals but also in birds like black swans, albatrosses, ibises and penguins. And in reptiles like lizards and tortoises. Even in invertebrates like insects and arachnids [46]. So, aspects of homosexual behaviour have ancestry going back hundreds of millions of years.

You might think that the decriminalisation of homosexuality in Britain during the last century (1967 for England and Wales, 1980 for Scotland and 1982 for Northern Ireland) ended much interest in the issue. Not so. In 2024, Birmingham City University advertised for research students to undertake a 3-year project (funded to the tune of £30,000 per year by the Arts and Humanities Research Council) on 'The Europe That Gay Porn Built, 1945–2000' [47].

Changing Gender (cont.)

Expressing a gender other than one's sex (at birth) has been going on across the world for millennia. From the ancient Romans who were able to show their true colour in public during the annual Saturnalia festival of dancing and drinking in the streets, to the lower class Hijra sect in India who have been recognised as a 'third gender' for more than 500 years, to the Sworn Virgins (trans-men) of the Balkans since the 15th century, to the Mukhannathun (today's Khanith) who have lived in Arabia in a third-gender role for over a millennium, to trans societies in Africa, Oceana and the Americas. Until the advent of hormonal treatment and surgical removal of breasts and sexual organs during the latter half of the 20th century, gender change involved little more than cross dressing (transvestism); in the case of men, this was sometimes accompanied by castration.

Returning to ancient Rome, the early 3rd-century CE emperor, Marcus Aurelius Antoninus, better known as Elagabalus, is an example of a specific person who may have suffered from some kind of gender dysphoria. He became emperor at the age of 14. Elagabalus was a precocious youth and is said to have displayed many feminine characteristics that included asking to be called 'my lady' rather than 'my lord'. He married four women, as well as a male chariot driver, said to have been his lover. Homosexuality and bisexuality may have contributed to his behaviour: particular aspects of human nature are not easily defined by a single word. Elagabalus changed the main god from Jupiter to Elagabal and meddled in other religious affairs. His life was cut short at the age of 18 by the Praetorian Guard, who considered his behaviour scandalous and a disgrace to Rome. His demise was not heroic. He was allegedly pushed into Rome's sewer, whence he drifted into the Tiber together with the city's human waste. Elagabalus's biographers have not minced their words. Edward Gibbon, author of the classic *History of the Decline and Fall of the Roman Empire*, considered him to have 'abandoned himself to the grossest pleasures with ungoverned fury', while a contemporary historian writes that 'Elagabalus was not a tyrant, but he was an incompetent, probably the least able emperor Rome had ever had' [48].

As mentioned, people change gender for reasons other than dysphoria. In previous times, a man might pretend to be a woman and dress accordingly in order to avoid military service (though it is not clear how they would have passed a medical examination). Conversely, some women have tried to live as a man, frustrated by their lack of opportunity in a world dominated by men. James Barry is a good example.

Born Margaret Anne Bulkley around 1789 in Ireland, James Barry managed to enter Edinburgh University Medical School and gain a degree in medicine. He then enrolled in the army (presumably without a medical examination) as a surgeon and served in South Africa for the next ten years. He proved to be most skilful at his job and performed the first recorded caesarean operation in the British Empire. Mother and child both survived. In 1857, he was promoted to Inspector General in charge of military hospitals with the rank of Brigadier General. Like his contemporary Florence Nightingale, with whom he crossed paths, he argued for proper sanitation and better food for soldiers and prisoners alike. He died from dysentery in 1865. Only when being washed prior to burial was his true gender revealed [49].

James Barry may have been preceded 1,500 years ago by an Anglo-Saxon in Kent. Several graves in the village of Buckland (now part of Dover) dated to the 7th century have been found to contain either feminine or masculine grave goods 'which appear to be at odds with the sex of the person buried' according to James Davison, a tutor of medieval history at Liverpool University. 'One burial contains the remains of a person designated as "possibly female" who died aged 35 and was buried with a number of typically masculine artefacts. These include a sword, a spearhead, fragments of a decorated shield and fragments of a belt buckle, which suggest it was a warrior's grave' [50].

Not content with such an example of possible transgendering in Kent, the Denbighshire council in Wales decided to invent their own example with no less a person than the legendary King Arthur. In order to include the warrior king on its timeline of LGBTQ+ history, the council maintains that he once dressed in female clothes in order to sneak into a dance to meet a girl of interest to him. None of the stories about Arthur have ever suggested that he was homosexual, bisexual or transgender. This does not stop the Welsh government's LGBT Action Plan to 'improve the representation of LGBTQ+ communities in the heritage and culture of Wales' from including the fabled Arthur. Other – real in this case – personages suggested to have been transgender include Joan of Arc (naturally), Queen Elizabeth I and Alfred Lord Tennyson (for obscure reasons). According to Fiona McAnena at the human rights charity Sex Matters, 'We've reached a new level of desperation when a legend about King Arthur dressing in women's clothes qualifies for entry on a local government's LGBTQ history timeline. ... To claim that a person in "opposite sex" clothes is part of LGBTQ is confusing nonsense' [51].

In contrast to some violent males to be described shortly, there are many cases where men have transitioned with quiet dignity. Jan Morris, born James Morris in 1926, is a good example.

Morris was a notable writer, publishing a history of Britain and acclaimed portraits of cities such as Oxford, Venice, Trieste, Hong Kong and New York City. Morris received a traditional education – Lancing and Christ Church, Oxford – followed by military service in the 9th Queen's Royal Lancers. In 1953, Morris was appointed journalist to the Mount Everest expedition led by Colonel John Hunt and was able, from 22,000 ft, to report the successful ascent by Hillary and Tenzing in time for Elizabeth II's coronation on 2 June. During the 1960s, Morris had decided to change gender and in 1972 underwent reassignment surgery in Morocco. In 1949, Morris had married Elizabeth Tuckniss, with whom five children were produced. Despite divorcing after her gender change, Morris, now Jan, remained friends with Elizabeth for the rest of her life. Indeed, Jan and Elizabeth entered into a civil partnership in 2008 and lived happily together in Morris's beloved Wales until her death in 2020. An autobiography of Morris's extraordinary but exemplary life was published in 1974 [52].

Gender recognition reform (Scotland) bill

In March 2022, Nicola Sturgeon, Scotland's First Minister, introduced a Bill by which the age at which a person can change their legal gender was reduced from 18 to 16 years. It also removed the requirement for a medical diagnosis of gender dysphoria. The waiting time was cut from 2 years to 6 months. Adolescents would now be able to legally change gender (without their parents' knowledge or consent). In December 2022, the Scottish parliament passed the Bill by 86 votes to 59. But the UK government made an order to prevent the Bill from proceeding to royal assent, so it failed. Humza Yousaf, Sturgeon's short-lived successor as First Minister, tried (unsuccessfully) to resurrect the Bill with one amendment: the age at which consent could be granted was further reduced to a mere 11 years. The consequences of such hare-brained (with apologies to *Lepus europaeus*) proposals soon became apparent.

They probably inspired the likes of Adam Bryson, a married man who was committed for rape in 2016 and again in 2019, to legally change gender to become Isla Bryson the following year. In 2023, Bryson was convicted of the two rapes and sent to a women's prison to await sentence. This caused outrage and Bryson was transferred to a male prison and eventually sentenced to eight years in prison on two charges of rape. Andrew Burns, charged with stalking a 13-year-old girl, was being held in the male Low Moss prison in Glasgow, where he violently attacked a prison guard. Burns decided to become Tiffany Scott in order to be sent to a female prison. The transfer was approved. It was rescinded only after an indignant public pointed to the lunacy of sending a violent sex offender to a female prison. Another man encouraged by Nicola Sturgeon's Bill is Andrew Miller. Dressed in female clothes, he enticed a school girl (who clearly thought Miller was a woman) into his car. He took her to his home where he subjected her to hours of 'sexual torment'. She managed to escape Miller's clutches only by calling the police while he was asleep. Miller was subsequently jailed for 20 years [53].

It had been happening outside Scotland, too. In 2022, transgender Karen White was on remand in a women's prison near Wakefield in

England for multiple rapes against women. There, White allegedly went on to assault at least four inmates before being transferred to a male prison. Between 2016 and 2019, six out of seven sexual assaults carried out in women's prisons were committed by former males [54]. But no more. The Ministry of Justice has since decreed that trans-women will no longer be housed in female prisons if they have male genitalia or have committed a sexual offence. So, Lexi-Rose Crawford (born Dominic Risden), who had invited a friend into her house to play video games but instead went on to rape her, was sentenced to serve 9 years in a male prison. (During the trial, it emerged that Crawford had previously been convicted of forcing a 15-year-old into oral sex and sexual intercourse [55].)

The number of trans-women accused of rape is not insignificant. According to the Crown Prosecution Service in the UK, 1.5% of those suspected of committing rape (some 260 persona) have been referred to by the police as 'female' since 2019, though the law states that rape can only be committed by a biological male [56], which of course trans-women are. And 'more than 70% of transgender prisoners in British jails are serving sentences for sex offences and violent crimes ... including rape, forcing under-age children into having sex, grievous bodily harm and robbery ... five (out of 149 transgender women)' were still in female jails in 2024 [57].

Among transgender offenders are Maddison Wilson, a 37-year-old trans-woman only recently in court charged with sexual offences against young children (a boy as well as two under-13 girls) more than a decade ago [58], and 25-year-old Bex McCullgh, a trans-woman, given an 8-year sentence for inciting a young boy to engage in sexual activity [59]. They join the likes of Adam (Isla) Bryson, Andrew Burns (Tiffany Scott), Andrew Miller, Karen White, Dominic Risden (Lexi-Rose Crawford), and other trans-women mentioned earlier, all of whom have committed serious sexual offences. I am not aware of any trans-man accused of criminal behaviour. And, of course, a trans-woman like Jan Morris or Bruce Jenner (see below) is no threat to anyone. Most trans-women who commit sexual offences against females presumably decide to become transgender for reasons other than gender dysphoria. The same is true of trans-women who try to compete in female sports, a practice that President Trump intends to ban in the USA. Genuine dysphoria – feeling that one is in the wrong body – is unlikely to occur in a birth male who lusts after a birth female.

Trans and other issues in schools

The results of Scotland's radical approach to sexuality have been felt in schools as well as in prisons. At Boroughmuir High School, Edinburgh's top state school, 11-year-olds are being told they are 'queer' if they do not yet know their sexual orientation. Staff at Wick High in Caithness have been told to refrain from using words like mother, brother or sister as it might upset some trans pupils. Naturally, parents are worried about such trends, but there is little they can do. Often, they are not even aware of what is going on because of the Scottish government's advice to schools: parents need not be informed if their child is changing gender at school. [60].

Elsewhere, parents are equally concerned about the content of sex education being received by their offspring. At Queen Elizabeth II High School in Peel on the Isle of Man, for example, 11-year-olds are being taught about oral and anal sex as well as gender-change operations. When a drag queen who had been invited to address the children told the youngsters that there are 73 genders, one young stalwart ventured to proffer the number as two. The visitor told the boy that he had upset her and sent him out of the room (he was subsequently denied his midday meal as a punishment) [61]. At this point, even the school realised that they had overstepped the mark and the drag queen was not invited back. Are 11-year-olds really ready for the rigours of adult life? The Department for Education in the UK is reviewing this very issue. It needs to. By March of 2023, nearly half of all secondary schools in the UK were enabling children to change gender without parental consent [62]. In the USA, incidentally, transgender drag queens like Martha P Johnson and Sylvia Rivera, both of whom have worked as prostitutes, are being promoted as 'inspirational mums' by the CBeebies website to children *under six* [63].

Transgender issues in schools are no less common in England than in Scotland. At Rye College, a Church of England school in East Sussex, children in year 8 (12- to 13-year-olds) learn in 'life education' that there are three biological sexes 'because you can be born with male and female body parts or hormones'. The teacher responsible for this opinion (who apparently does not understand the difference between sex and gender, about the latter of which she has even stranger views) reprimanded one of her pupils because she had criticised a fellow student for claiming that she was a cat. The offending girl had said, 'How can you identify as a cat when you're a girl?' (another girl in the class was recording the interchange). The teacher responded with 'how dare you – you've just really upset someone' by 'questioning their identity'. She went on to say that she would report this to senior staff and pointed out that 'you need to have a proper conversation about diversity and inclusion'. A spokesman for Rye College said, 'We are committed to offering our pupils an inclusive education. Teachers endeavour to ensure that pupils' views are listened to and encourage them to ask questions and engage in discussion' [64]. This appears not to apply to someone challenging a teacher.

A primary school teacher in Nottinghamshire was dismissed because she refused to address an 8-year-old girl, who had decided that she was a boy, by her preferred forename. She was concerned about the girl's welfare after the school accepted the girl's decision and told her to use the boys' toilets and dressing rooms. The teacher took her disquiet to the school's governors and the local authority. Neither took any action apart from a warning that her welfare concerns could constitute 'an act of direct discrimination'. She now works in a sandwich shop [65].

Parents are unaware (and can do little about it) of what their children are being taught at school. At Thurston Primary School in Suffolk, nine-year-olds have been shown a BBC Bitesize video of a boy getting an erection and ejaculating. The mother of an autistic eleven-year-old only found out that his class was being taught about multiple genders and sex changes when he brought his exercise book home. Now, 'all he has talked about is masturbation'. Journalist Celia Walden is rightly disturbed when a letter from the head teacher to concerned parents claims that the school is 'only following' the national curriculum for Personal, Social, Health and Economic Education (PSHE): no such curriculum exists. Walden considers that 'This warped experiment in schools is creating an entire generation afraid of sex' [66].

It gets worse. At Genesis Pre School in Hull, 4-year-olds have been shown pictures from a book entitled *Grandad's Pride* that features partially naked men in bondage gear. A staff member, responding to parents' concerns, replied that 'the children would not understand the erotic and sexualised depictions'. So, what is the point of showing them? One couple promptly removed their child from the school [67].

The fight back against exposing young children to inappropriate remarks and dubious opinions has begun. Youngsters between 7 and 11 years of age are to participate in a session in Oxford organised by the Centre for Tutorial Teaching. This promotes rigorous intellectual debate among small groups of students. The event is being held in honour of Member of Parliament Sir David Amess, who was murdered by an Islamist terrorist in 2021. Amess had been due to host an online session of the Children's Parliament shortly after he died. The organisers' aim is to 'teach children to challenge and debate the views of people they do not agree with, rather than denying their right to hold their views' [68], which is surely an abrogation of free speech.

Related Topics

Now, a railway company has joined the fray. The Great Western Railway (GWR) in England has taken it upon itself to block the website of a gender-critical group called Sex Matters from the wi-fi network that it supplies for the benefit of its customers. Best-selling author Helen Joyce asks, 'Why does GWR classify a human rights organisation as so dangerous that travellers have to be protected from accessing its website? Sex Matters stands up for women's single-sex spaces, child safeguarding and freedom of belief and speech. What is there to object to about that?' [69].

Trans-women in sport

A much wider problem – with international implications – concerns sport. In 2022, in a women's 500-yard freestyle swimming final at an NCAA (National Collegiate Athletic Association) event in Atlanta, Lia Thomas, a competent though not outstanding swimmer from the University of Pennsylvania, beat three-time US national champion and Olympic silver medallist Emma Weyant from the University of Virginia into second place by more than a second and a half. This caused surprise among some, anger among others. The reason? The latter knew that Lia, at 6 feet 3 inches tall, had been born William and had changed gender only a few years earlier. Until then, he had been ranked about 500 in men's events. Although Lia had been undergoing hormone replacement therapy (HRT) to reduce her testosterone, she had passed puberty as a fully fledged male. Transitioning at around 20 years of age, Lia was well into the range (18–24 years old) at which muscle strength peaks. It is unlikely that relatively short HRT would have reduced Lia's muscle strength to that typical of a woman of similar age. Since then, World Aquatics, swimming's governing body, has restricted transgender athletes from competing in elite women's swimming competitions. Lia appealed against this decision, but her case has been dismissed by the Court of Arbitration of Sport [70].

So, should a trans-woman be allowed to compete in women's events at all? Transgender athletes have been allowed by the International Olympic Committee to compete in women's events since 2004, but there have been no disputed medals so far (see the following). The Lia Thomas episode, however, caused Sebastian Coe, president of the World Athletics Council, to rule in 2023 that 'the right of those born women to compete fairly trumps the desire to be included in elite sport of those who have gone through male puberty but run or jump as women' [71].

But trans-women are still competing in the women's category of ice hockey competitions, a fact condemned by Lord Clifton of Wrottersley, chairman of Ice Hockey UK [72]. In the USA, trans-women over 14 years of age must have undergone at least one year of testosterone suppression therapy to be allowed to compete in women's ice hockey events (though that is unlikely to have brought their muscle mass down to equate with that of a typical cis-woman).

You might have thought that the one sport from which trans-women should be excluded is boxing. Not so. Despite the fact that biological males punch on average 2.6 harder than females on account of their shoulder width and biceps strength, Algerian Imane Khelif, previously barred from fighting in women's events for failing a testosterone test in India the previous year, was allowed to compete in the women's welterweight competition at the 2024 Paris Olympics. Within 46 seconds, Khelif had landed such blows on Italian Angela Carini that she feared for her life and left the ring. Yet the International Olympic Committee (IOC) was aware that Khelif was biologically male as a result of a DNA test [73]. Every Olympic contest involves a certain measure of muscular strength, which is why, from the inception of the modern games in 1896, women and men have competed in separate sections. (This is in contrast to the case for competitions like bridge or chess, or for examinations in school or university.) When confronted with the Khelif scandal, the IOC official responded that Khelif's passport showed the owner to be female. Shame on the IOC.

Of course, it is not only in elite events that cis-women suffer through competition from trans-women. 'Trans ideology is now a growing threat to female grassroots sport. Fourteen million women and girls are regularly active in England – and most of us are not professional athletes. According to many national governing bodies, those of us within grassroots sport are not important enough to warrant safe and fair play. Instead, we must "be kind" and "inclusive" – and allow men who identify as women to steal our records, medals and opportunities' [74].

It's not just about athletics. Trans-women who had muscled (literally) their way into women's fly-fishing and other angling competitions have now been disbarred [75].

What could be more persuasive than a trans-woman telling other trans-women not to compete in women's sports? That is exactly what Bruce Jenner, US gold winner for decathlon at the 1976 Olympics, has done. Born a boy in 1950, it was not until 2015 that Jenner decided to transition from Bruce to Caitlyn. Unlike many trans-women, Jenner accepts that his sex has not changed. 'Let me explain – I am biologically male ... There's nothing I can do to change that. If you believe in gender dysphoria, and I think most people do realise it's not a disease, it's a mental condition, just like some people are left-handed and some people are right-handed, it's kind of the way you're born and I've dealt with it my entire life. I consider myself a trans-person, I am still genetically male. I changed all of my ID right down to my birth certificate so technically yes, I am female, but on the other hand I know I'm not'. Jenner believes in keeping female sports for those born female. and opposes the so-called 'radical gender ideology' [76]. Likewise, Debbie Hayton, born a boy in 1968 who underwent gender reassignment surgery in 2016, wears a T-shirt that proclaims 'Trans Women Are Men. Get Over It!'. Debbie, a teacher and trade unionist, was accused of hate speech and was hounded out of the Teachers Union LGBT committee [77]. In a memoir [78], she tells her remarkable story, surpassed only by that of Jake and Hannah Graf (see the following).

Changing one's mind

Many of those who have undergone gender realignment have come to regret their decision. Some had been pressured by doctors – with parents unsure of the consequences – before they realised that they had made a mistake. But detransitioning leads to negative clinical consequences. Chloe Cole, a girl from California, was only fifteen when she was persuaded by doctors that changing to a boy would make her happier. She was given puberty blockers, underwent a double mastectomy and received testosterone injections. At nineteen, she realised she had made a huge mistake and regretted the fact that, as a result of the transitioning treatment, she is unlikely to be able to have children in the future. She suffers from urinary tract infections and moisture leaking from the grafts that had been inserted after her double mastectomy – quite apart from the psychological toll she has endured. But Chloe is tough, becoming a *cause célèbre* in a campaign to make gender realignment below the age of eighteen illegal in the USA. In this, Chloe has considerable Republican support [79]. The number of adolescents who have transgendered in the USA is significant. Around 1.5%

of 13- to 17-year-olds have undergone gender realignment in one or other direction. In the UK, the number is thirtyfold less. Of those, only a small fraction has undergone detransitioning: some 64 patients between 2010 and 2020, according to the (now disgraced) Tavistock Clinic.

Ritchie Herron is a 37-year-old civil servant. Six years ago, he considered transitioning to a woman, using the NHS. He told the therapist at a gender clinic that he 'cannot see myself as a man with another man, but I can see myself as a woman with a man'. 'That is because you are trans', the therapist replied, and encouraged him to undergo gender realignment with oestrogen therapy and vaginoplasty. The surgery was complicated, and he lost almost three pints of blood. On recovery, he immediately realised that he had made a 'monumental mistake'. He now suffers from incontinence, skin problems and numbness around his entire crotch area – not to mention psychological problems. All he wants is to return to his original gender, but he admits that it's going to be difficult because of his lack of testosterone over the past 10 years. Although it is possible to partially reverse vaginoplasty, Herron wants no more 'experimental surgery' [80]. My reason for recounting these two instances of gender-realigned persons wishing to detransition is to point out how careful one should be before undergoing gender change involving serious clinical interventions. In contrast, becoming homosexual in early life but changing back later on – perhaps starting a family – is easy.

Views on trans-persons

Objecting to the use of the feminine article to describe a trans-woman is not allowed, as illustrated by the following event. In court for murder of a man by hitting him over the head with a vodka bottle and then pushing him into a river where he drowned, the defendant, a trans-woman called Scarlet Blake was throughout referred to as a woman by the judge and other officials. This is because judges have been told to respect the gender identity of those in court. 'The guidance, which features in the Equal Treatment Bench Book produced by the Judicial College, says: "It should be possible to respect a person's gender identity and their present name for nearly all court and tribunal purposes, regardless of whether they have obtained legal recognition of their gender by way of a Gender Recognition Certificate"'. This caused an outcry by Harry Potter author J K Rowling [81], even though Blake is to be sent to a male prison (for life). Rowling, whose blog rightly states that a trans-woman is a man, has been accused of a hate crime under the new Hate Crime and Public Order (Scotland) Act. This saga has yet to be played out (it was in 2015: for now see chapter 7). Were she to reside in Michigan, USA, it would be worse. In 2023, its House of Representatives passed a hate speech bill by which you are criminalised for using an inappropriate pronoun in regard to someone else. This can land you in prison for up to five years and result in a $10,000 fine [82]. But at least one trans-woman, as mentioned earlier, accepts Rowling's expression of reality.

Judges and barristers continue to refer in court to indicted criminals by the gender they decided to adopt *after* the time during which the offence occurred. Alexander Secker, now Lexi Secker, was sentenced to six years in prison at Swindon Crown Court for rape committed a year earlier, when his gender was male. Only subsequently did Secker decide to transition. Throughout the proceedings, Secker was referred to as 'she' [83]. I appreciate that to say 'now she' after reference to 'him' is clumsy, but surely accuracy is expected in court, especially as by law only a man can commit rape of a woman.

Kathleen Stock is not the only one who was hounded out of her university on account of her sensible views regarding the trans issue. More academics find themselves in this position year on year. A good example is Jo Phoenix, professor of criminology at the Open University (OU). Her views are clear. 'People can be who they want when they go to the cinema or park, but it's not so straightforward in places like hospitals and prisons'. She has been researching the issue of gender self-identity for some years and has set up an international network to that effect. This resulted in death threats and an open letter signed by 368 of her colleagues at the OU, accusing the network of being transphobic. She received no support from the OU. Her situation worsened and she resigned in 2021, having filed an injunction against the university for harassment, discrimination and bullying. The Watford Employment Tribunal upheld 20 out of 22 of her claims and concluded that the OU had allowed a 'fear of the pro-gender-identity section' to dominate. A sensible decision for once. But this is only an advisory judgement and if the OU appeals, Prof Phoenix may yet lose the case. Other universities across the UK likewise fail to support their staff and instead describe their gender-critical views as 'transphobic' [84]. It should be noted that most of those accused of being transphobic ('TERFS') actually bear no malice against trans-women. They oppose *institutions* that promote the rights of trans-women over those of cis-women, not individual *persons*.

The Civil Service, supposedly neutral on political and other issues, is no better than the Open University. In regard to matters of gender, it appears to take advice from Stonewall, the controversial LGBT organisation that championed homosexuality in the 1990s and is now active in promoting transgender issues. So, when Eleanor Frances, working in the Department for Digital, Culture, Media and Sport (DCMS), complained that the organisation was no longer impartial in that it considered a person's gender identity to be more important than their sex, thus allowing men to access female single-sex facilities, she was 'marginalised'. She complained to the head of her department but received no response. Instead, she was stripped of her team and responsibilities. Reluctantly, she resigned, but is taking her department (and the Department for Science, Innovation and Technology to which she was subsequently transferred) to an employment tribunal [85]. Thus is our belief in the objectivity of our public institutions eroded.

How one refers to a person's gender (as opposed to their biological sex) should be flexible. Calling a trans-woman like Jan Morris, and others like her who have transitioned for genuine reasons of dysphoria, a woman poses no problems for most of us. Doing so in respect of criminals like Isla Bryson who have transgendered for personal convenience is hard. If you were asked to describe Vladimir Putin as a statesman, you would probably be inclined to do so only if the word statesman were between inverted commas. We should apply these to the likes of Isla Bryson and refer to 'her' as a 'woman'. In any case, alluding to someone in an unconventional way has long been accepted, especially if made in a jocular manner. Queen Victoria was called Mrs Brown, though there is no evidence that she had sexual relations with her adored Scottish manservant John Brown, and the 20th-century architect Gerald Wellesley (later Duke of Wellington) was referred to as the Iron Duchess on account of his effeminate manner.

The National Health Service (NHS)

Youngsters and their parents seeking advice about puberty blockers and surgery for those wishing to transition should be careful whom they consult. The World Professional Association for Transgender Health (WPATH), for example, 'is not an international body of highly qualified medics ... Three-quarters of its members are based in the States and many are activists who advocate that anyone who identifies as trans may demand access to gender-confirming treatment, which for kids means puberty blockers'. The advice of organisations like WPATH should therefore not be used by the NHS as a basis for their transgender policies [86]. But the NHS continues to follow the bad advice given by the WPATH. That organisation is telling the NHS, which has set up a Young People's Gender Service in Nottingham, to abolish a minimum age for transitioning and to lower the age threshold for puberty blockers and surgery – both in direct contravention of the Cass report. As Helen Joyce, director of advocacy at the human rights charity Sex Matters, points out 'Dr Cass warned that [WPATH guidance] promoted childhood social transition without evidence that this was safe or beneficial. ... The point of closing the disgraced Tavistock was to learn from its mistakes ... This is a deeply concerning sign that the Nottingham clinic risks becoming Tavistock v2' [87].

Another worrying interference by the NHS is a pilot scheme to use General Practice staff (GPs) and nurses to 'carry out specialist assessments of adults with concerns around "gender dysphoria". The roles will see GPs taking decisions about whether patients should be prescribed hormone therapy, voice coaching to "feminise" or "masculinise" their voices or referred for gender reassignment surgery. ... all staff will be given specialist training from a centre for transgender health care in Nottingham' [88]. All well and good, except that GPs are currently too busy to see their own patients most of the time, resorting merely to conversations over the telephone or zoom. And nurses are among the most overworked members of the NHS.

TransActual, a lobbying group within the NHS, is campaigning to end single-sex wards and to reverse the ban on puberty blockers. Its director Chay Brown, who has held a senior position at the LGBT charity Stonewall and can now claim £150 per day of taxpayers' money as a 'patient voice', has written to NHS staff inviting them to an event in connection with Pride month. 'We do love to see NHS trusts celebrating Pride, but it's important that your LGBTQ+ inclusive work goes beyond that. TransActual are here to support you to develop your whole-trust approach to trans inclusion'. Jane Faye, a co-director of TransActual, also supports the Consenting Adult Action Network which lobbies for children to medically transition and for women-only spaces to be abolished. In response to these developments, Helen Joyce, director of the charity Sex Matters and author of *Trans: When Ideology Meets Reality*, considers it 'outrageous that activist employees within NHS England continue to engage groups like Trans Actual for programmes ... NHS England bosses need to act firmly to remove all traces of gender identity ideology throughout the healthcare system' [89].

On the other hand, NHS England rightly refuses to prescribe cross-sex hormone treatment to anyone as young as sixteen. It is therefore surprising that the Care Quality Commission (CQC) has registered a private organisation called Gender Plus to do just that. Moreover, some of the staff at Gender Plus previously worked at the disgraced Tavistock Clinic. But the decision of the CQC to register Gender Plus is being challenged in the Courts by a former Tavistock whistle-blower. Watch this space [90].

Is the transgender debate finally coming to its senses? Columnist Suzanne Moore thinks so. 'The medicalisation and mutilation of children's bodies is not a sign of being fashionable, it is a sign that many are in denial about children being gay'. But 'The cult is crumbling in the UK. It will take longer in America while there still is so much money to be made in harming children. No child is in the wrong body, but the fact that their bodies are put in the hands of some very wrong doctors is a terrible violation' [91]. In December 2024, the UK government rightly announced a nationwide ban on the use of puberty blockers. This did not prevent some transgender promoters from continuing their misguided mission. Susie Green, former chief executive of the charity Mermaids and co-founder of Anne Trans Healthcare, confirmed that the latter organisation would continue to provide 'legal routes to gender-affirming healthcare'. Not to do so would be 'morally and ethically wrong' [92]. She clearly considers the scandalous treatment of young children to be consistent with the Hippocratic Oath.

Dodgy advice to teachers

A group of Church of England schools, part of the Bath and Wells Multi-Academy Trust, is giving advice to their teachers that contains an incorrect assumption: '... they would probably be breaking the law if they said a person cannot change their biological sex' [93]. As mentioned earlier, if biological sex is defined by the chromosomes – X and Y or X and X – that are present in the cells of a person's body from birth to death, then the statement that a person cannot change their biological sex is correct. Gender dysphoria, hormonal treatment or surgery of one kind or another does not affect the situation. I am not aware of a law that negates this fact of nature.

Transgendering at its best

Several of the trans-females I have mentioned were bad characters – arrogant at best – whereas a trans-male person, such as James Barry, in the 19th century, was entirely benevolent. One might be tempted to think that some innate empathy in birth females who transition leads to a more benign outcome than the other way round. But the result of any transition surely depends mainly on the character of the person involved. So, when two good people, one trans-male and the other trans-female, met in 2015, the outcome was inspirational. What follows is taken from an extract [94] of an extraordinary book [95].

Jake and Hannah prefer not to mention their birth forenames. Their birth surnames, Graf and Winterbourne, respectively, are acceptable. The latter had always fancied an army career and rose to the rank of Captain in the Royal Electrical and Mechanical Engineers (REME). From his late teens, Winterbourne had realised that he wanted to be female and decided to become transgender. He told his commanding officer, who was surprisingly sympathetic. 'The first day I went to work as Captain Hannah Winterbourne and a soldier saluted me with a 'Good morning, Ma'am', I nearly cried with joy.'

Graf grew up as more than a typical tomboy. According to her, she realised at the age of two that she was in the wrong body, though she continued living as a female for nearly thirty years. Following testosterone treatment and other transgender therapies, Jake now sports an elegant moustache and short beard. He is an international award-winning director, screenwriter and actor.

Jake and Hannah met in 2015, fell in love, became engaged and married three years later. They lead a happy and contented life together. But something was missing: both wanted children. Fortunately, Graf had harvested her eggs and, through IVF (in vitro fertilisation) with donor sperm, a number of healthy embryos were produced. One of these was successfully implanted into a surrogate mother. Jake and Hannah had met Laura a few years previously, and she was delighted to help. Laura delivered a healthy girl whom the Grafs called Millie. Laura told them that she would be happy to repeat the process. A few years later, another girl, subsequently called Teddie, was born.

According to Jake, 'It will never stop feeling like some kind of miracle that we found each other, against all the odds, and built a world for ourselves as a family filled with happiness and love.' So, two persons, each transgender, have bonded just as two (cis) persons of the opposite sex have done since the dawn of humanity.

Notes

1. De Visser, J A G M & Elena, S F: The evolution of sex *Nature Reviews Genetics* 8: 139–149, 2007.
2. Arnold, Arthur P *et al*.: *Nature* **629**: 37–40, 2024.
3. Patrick Sawer and Hayley Dixon: 'AstraZeneca under fire over "sex is not binary" guidance' *Daily Telegraph* 2 March 2024.
4. Robin Aitken and Liam Kelly: *Daily Telegraph* 19 March 2024.
5. Zhou, J-N *et al.*: *Nature* 378: 68–70 (1995).
6. Kennis, Mathilde *et al.*: *Nature* **629**: 998–1000 (2024).
7. Joyce, p 79.
8. https://www.mayoclinic.org/diseases-conditions/gender-dysphoria/in-depth/pubertal-blockers/art-20459075.
9. Joyce, p 83.
10. Michael Searles: 'Trans men "becoming postmenopausal" in their 20s': *Daily Telegraph* 26 May 2024.
11. Margaret M McCarthy: Hormones reconfigure the immune cells of trans men. *Nature* **633**: 38–40, 2024.
12. Kathleen Stock: *Daily Telegraph* 6 March 2024.
13. Michael Searles: 'Labour looks to ban puberty blockers' *Daily Telegraph* 13 July 2024.
14. Suzanne Moore: 'Wes Streeting will suffer unhinged abuse simply for protecting children' *Daily Telegraph* 16 July 2024.
15. Michael Searles: 'Streeting to allow puberty blocker trial for children' *Sunday Telegraph* 9 March 2025.
16. Camilla Turner: *Sunday Telegraph* 7 April 2024.
17. E Cumming: '"We can now wake up from this nightmare": Has the turning point in the trans debate finally come?' *Daily Telegraph* 10 April 2024.
18. Charles Moore: 'The Cass Review shows it's a disaster for professionals to confuse opinion with expertise' *Daily Telegraph* 13 April 2014.
19. *Daily Telegraph* 13 April 2024.
20. Daniel Sanderson and Daniel Martin: 'Scottish primary schools will have pupils as LGBT champions' *Daily Telegraph* 18 April 2024.
21. Steve Bird: *Daily Telegraph* 16 April 2024.
22. Lucy Burton: 'Stonewall faces a corporate reckoning following the Cass report' *Daily Telegraph* 29 April 2024.

23. Joyce, p 71.
24. https://cass.independent-review.uk/home/publications/final-report/.
25. Michael B Young, p 3.
26. *ibid*, p 38.
27. Eg Ruse, p 134.
28. Maurice Lee Jr: *Great Britain's Solomon: James VI and I in His Three Kingdoms* (Urbana, Il, 1990), p 32.
29. Michael B Young, p 41.
30. Both Michael B Young, p 49.
31. Lamorna Ash: *Sunday Telegraph* Arts & Books section 23 February 2025.
32. Glendinning, p 40.
33. *ibid*, p 57.
34. *ibid*, p 105.
35. *ibid*, p 165.
36. *ibid*, p 155.
37. Harold Acton, W H Auden, Max Beerbohm, Gertrude Bell, Arnold Bennett, Bernard Berenson, Elizabeth Bowen, Winston Churchill, Ivy Compton-Burnett, Cyril Connolly, Albert Einstein, Robert Frost, David Garnett, Sinclair Lewis, Rose Macaulay, Somerset Maugham, Luigi Pirandello, William Plomer, Siegfried Sassoon, George Bernard Shaw, Edith Sitwell, Stephen Spender, Freya Stark, Hugh Walpole, Evelyn Waugh, Rebecca West, Virginia Woolf and W B Yeats.
38. Ruse, pp 22–26.
39. Scruton, R: *Sexual Desire* (London: Weidenfeld, 1986) p 208.
40. Medawar, P B: Review of *The Victim is Always the Same* by I. S. Cooper (*New York Review of Books*, 21, 1975) p 17.
41. Ruse, p 43.
42. *ibid* p 4.
43. Robert Plomin: *Blueprint. How DNA makes us who we are* (Allen Lane, imprint of Penguin Books, 2018).
44. Hu, S H *et al.*: 'Discovery of new genetic loci for male sexual orientation in Han population' *Cell Discovery* 7: 103, 2021.
45. Frans de Waal: 'Bonobo sex and society. The behavior of a close relative challenges assumptions about male supremacy in human evolution' *Scientific American* **272**: 82–88, 1995.
46. https://en.wikipedia.org/wiki/Homosexual_behavior_in_animals.

47. Zoe Strimpel: 'Woke studies have hit a new low – and your taxes are paying for it' *Sunday Telegraph* Sunday section 14 April 2024.
48. Goldsworthy, Adrian: *How Rome Fell: Death of a Superpower* (New Haven, CT: Yale University Press, 2009), p 81.
49. Michael du Preez and Jeremy Dronfield: *Dr James Barry: A Woman Ahead of Her Time* (London: Oneworld Publications, 2017).
50. Craig Simpson: 'Anglo-Saxon warriors were transgender, says academic'. *Sunday Telegraph* 4 January 2024.
51. Craig Simpson: *Sunday Telegraph* 12 October 2024.
52. Jan Morris: *Conundrum* (London: Faber and Faber, 1974).
53. Daniel Sanderson: *Daily Telegraph* 18 October 2023.
54. *Sunday Telegraph* 26 February 2023.
55. Max Stephens: *Daily Telegraph* 10 May 2023.
56. Hayley Dixon and Charles Hymas: *Daily Telegraph* 7 October 2023.
57. Sean Rayment: 'Majority of transgender prisoners are in jail for violent crime or sex offences' *Sunday Telegraph* 25 February 2024.
58. Will Bolton: *Daily Telegraph* 13 February 2025.
59. Tom McArdle: 'Trans child sex offender jailed after police sting' *Daily Telegraph* 15 February 2025.
60. Daniel Sanderson, *Daily Telegraph*, 23 March 2023.
61. Louisa Clarence-Smith: *Daily Telegraph* 27 February 2023.
62. Louisa Clarence-Smith: *Daily Telegraph* 30 March 2023.
63. Sanchez Manning: 'CBeebies hails drag queens as "inspirational mums" on site' *Sunday Telegraph* 23 February 2025.
64. Ewan Somerville: *Sunday Telegraph* 18 June 2023.
65. Louisa Clarence-Smith: *Daily Telegraph* 11 May 2023.
66. Celia Walden: 'Sexuality is so delicate and easily damaged – especially when people are still developing. Why are schools gambling with it?' *Daily Telegraph* 25 July 2023.
67. Alex Barton: *Daily Telegraph* 21 August 2023.
68. Gordon Rayner, *Sunday Telegraph* 29 October 2023.
69. Craig Simpson: *Sunday Telegraph* 6 August 2023.
70. Jeremy Wilson: 'Lia Thomas' transgender case thrown out after swimmer ruled ineligible' *Daily Telegraph* 13 June 2024.
71. Harry de Quetteville: The week the tide turned in the gender war: *Daily Telegraph*, 25 March 2023.

72. Sanchez Manning: 'Trans ice hockey players "are danger to girls"' *Sunday Telegraph* 2 June 2024.
73. Oliver Brown: *Daily Telegraph* 1 August 2024.
74. Lottie Moore, *Daily Telegraph* 29 December 2023.
75. Flora Bowen: 'Trans anglers given hook from women's events with global ban'; *Sunday Telegraph* 1 October 2023.
76. Gordon Rayner: *Daily Telegraph* Magazine 16 March 2024.
77. Helen Brown: 'Meet the bold "transsexual apostate" who's enraging every camp in the gender wars' *Daily Telegraph* 31 January 2024.
78. Debbie Hayton: *Transsexual Apostate: My journey back to reality* (Forum Press, 2024).
79. Peter Stanford: 'Chloe Cole: "I was told transitioning would save me. It destroyed my life"' *Sunday Telegraph* 27 August 2023.
80. Sanchez Manning: Features section in *Daily Telegraph* 14 August 2024.
81. Ewan Somerville and Gabriella Swerling: *Daily Telegraph* 27 February 2024.
82. Furedi, p 164.
83. *Daily Telegraph* 28 September 2024.
84. Gwyneth Rees, *Sunday Telegraph* 28 January 2024.
85. Camilla Turner: 'Civil Service "forced whistleblower out" over gender beliefs' *Sunday Telegraph* 19 May 2024.
86. Suzanne Moore: 'The NHS used controversial guidance from US organisation World Professional Association for Transgender Health to help shape trans policies' *Daily Telegraph* 12 March 2024.
87. Michael Searles: *Daily Telegraph* 19 October 2024.
88. Laura Donnelly: 'GPs taken out of day jobs to deal with gender services' *Sunday Telegraph* 24 March 2024.
89. Michael Searles: 'Trans "have infiltrated the NHS"' *Sunday Telegraph* 23 June 2024.
90. Hayley Dixon: 'Court review over clinic ex-Tavistock staff set up' *Sunday Telegraph* 10 November 2024.
91. Suzanne Moore: 'Tavistock whistleblowers and the Cass Review reshaped care for transgender children in the UK. In the States, the veil is slowly lifting' *Daily Telegraph* 10 December 2024.
92. Tim Sigsworth: 'Ex-Mermaids chief vows to defy puberty blocker ban' *Daily Telegraph* 21 December 2024.

93. Hayley Dixon: 'Denying pupils can change sex may be breaking the law, teachers warned' *Daily Telegraph* 5 April 2024.
94. Jake Graf and Hannah Graf: *Daily Telegraph* 16 June 2023.
95. Jake and Hannah Graf: *Becoming Us: A Story of Transgender Love, Joy and Family* (London: Coronet Books, 2023).

Political Correctness

Geoffrey Hughes, historian of the English language, considers that 'political correctness of one sort or another has been a feature of English society for centuries, certainly since the English Reformation' [1]. The words had their literal meaning during the mid-1930s [2] when Mao Zedong was leading the Chinese Communist Party (CCP) in its campaign against the ruling Kuomintang Party of Chiang Kai-shek. It behoved one to act according to the dogma of the CCP, as it does to this day, While the phrase may not have been widely used by the leaders of the Communist Party of the Soviet Union (from which the CCP was derived), the consequence of failing to act in a politically correct manner was clear. The same was true in Germany under Hitler in the late 1930s and remains so in the autocracies of China, Russia and North Korea.

In the free world, the words political correctness (PC) have come to imply social rather than political compliance. Journalist Anthony Browne defines PC as 'an ideology that classifies certain groups of people as victims in need of protection from criticism, and which makes believers feel that no dissent should be tolerated' [3]. According to Browne, the benefits of PC are matched by its drawbacks, and the more it 'strengthens its grip on the minds of policymakers and opinion formers, the more drawbacks it has. At the start of the 21st century, most of the benefits of PC have already been banked – the basic promotion of equality for women, homosexuals, disabled and ethnic minorities. With diminishing returns to the benefits, PC is now causing far more harm than good' [4]. Author Frederick Forsyth agrees. 'PC has changed. From its original plea for tolerance … it soon began to adopt a conviction of rigid self-righteousness. Long since, it has developed into a new and intolerant bigotry, the very thing it was supposed to oppose' [5].

The USA leads the world in PC doctrine (with the UK not far behind). As a result of increasing acceptance of transitioning, by which those who were male at birth refer to themselves as females and *vice versa*, another word should now be used to designate the original sex of a person. 'Those with XY' as opposed to 'those with XX chromosomes' is one suggestion. 'Sperm-producing' as opposed to 'egg-producing' or 'those who menstruate' is another. These appellations have been assembled by the EEB (Ecology and Evolutionary Biology) Language Project [6] founded by a group of academics in the US who claim that some terminology is not inclusive, and could be harmful [7]. Defining people in this way is problematic. First, sex chromosome abnormalities that include hermaphroditism occur naturally in some 0.2% of births, Second, deficiencies in the production of sperm or eggs are even more common. So, none of these wordy appellations is entirely specific, which makes their introduction into common usage pointless.

Language

Words like 'manmade', 'double-blind' (referring to the assessment of a novel drug or clinical procedure where neither the patient nor the physician is aware of whether they are given merely a placebo treatment or the real thing) or 'cripple' – deemed offensive to women, sightless or disabled persons, respectively – must be phased out. Similarly, of course, words like 'blackmail', 'blackguard', 'blackball', 'blacklist' or 'black day'. Even 'mum' and 'dad' are out – to be replaced by 'birthing parent' according to the Inclusive Language Guide published by the Local Government Association (LGA) of England. But 'Does the cripple rise from his wheelchair, or feel better about being stuck in it, because someone ... decided that, for official purposes, he was "physically challenged"'? [8]. Would you consider the word 'field' to be politically incorrect? Academics at the University of Southern California do, because phrases such as 'going into the field' or 'field work' may have connotations for descendants of slavery and immigrant workers that are not benign.

Some of the world's greatest poets and writers of fiction, history and law have written in English for a thousand years. When quality newspapers, the BBC and institutions of learning and culture such as the London Library (despite being called 'a symbol of civilisation' and 'a reminder of sanity and a promise of sanity to come' by Forster [9] refer to a person as 'they', the language is in trouble. I appreciate that we sometimes use 'they' in the singular, as in 'someone was spotted pushing a person off *their* bike, but then *they* ran away', but that is a colloquial expression. (In Russian, this is not a problem as there are three singular pronouns: masculine *oh* (on), feminine *oha* (ona) and neuter *oho* (ono).) Discarding the personal pronoun from any language because it may offend a percentage of humanity is unreasonable.

Yet children as young as eight are being encouraged by their local Scout group to use such non-binary language. In a game called Pronoun Pairs, children are dealt cards. When turned over, they reveal characters like Sam the dog or Leslie the ladybird. The participants then form sentences about the characters, using 'they' rather than 'he' or 'she'. The organisers discuss their choices with the aim of encouraging the participants to start using gender-neutral language for 'everyday communication'. Maya Forstater of Sex Matters considers that 'This game unquestioningly promotes the language of gender ideology. ... Many parents will rightly be shocked by Scouts when they learn the extent of what their children have been made to do in the name of "inclusivity"' [10].

In a free society, you can call someone anything you like, provided it is within the law. So, in the previous chapter, I suggested that a trans-woman (i.e. a male who has transgendered into a female) might well be referred to as *she* if the reason for the change is due to genuine dysphoria, but if the reason is simply the desire to be incarcerated in a female prison or to participate in sport as a member of a women's team, it is more appropriate to use inverted commas as in *'she'*. Best, of course, is to use a person's surname if that has not been changed. Presumably, *it* can still be applied to animals of either sex, though one has to be careful not to offend a 'sentient' [11] creature: cows and corgis, goats and gerbils also have rights, at least in the UK. As yet, it is largely the Anglo-Saxon language of the UK and the USA that has been corrupted. The languages of continental Europe have so far avoided much of this nonsense. Fortunately, most sensitivity readers are ignorant of the classical languages. So scholars are still able to enjoy the works of Thucydides and Euripides, Cicero and Caesar, in the way the authors intended.

The trend to make language 'inclusive' has now been extended to the sign language used by those unfortunate enough to be deaf-mutes. As former diplomat and journalist James Hansen has pointed out [12], a new gesture combining the raising of the right little finger (that indicates the letter B) and wiggling it together with a wink, refers to a transsexual, not previously part of the American Sign Language.

Accusations of Eurocentrism

Forty years ago, the wife of an English scientific colleague in the USA, who was teaching at a liberal arts college in Northern Ohio, was accused of being 'Eurocentric' (her subject was French history). Today, school teachers in Britain (including Alex Smith, head teacher of English at the independent Alleyn's school in London) [13] bemoan the fact that English literature taught to children is focused on 'white cis-male' authors, without regard for African writers. What do they expect? The printing press was invented in Europe during the 15th century. By the 17th century, it was producing novels by writers such as Miguel de Cervantes (*Don Quixote*) in Spain and John Bunyan (*Pilgrim's Progress*) in England. During the 18th century, popular novels like *Candide* by Voltaire appeared in France and *Robinson Crusoe* by Daniel Defoe, as well as *Evelina* by Frances (Fanny) Burney, in England. By the 19th century, female authors 'were accepted well enough for a literary magazine to suggest that the young Anthony Trollope might change his surname so as to avoid comparison with his famous literary mother' [14]. And what may be the world's first novel – *The Tale of Genji* – was written by a woman (Murasaki Shikibu, c 978–c 1016). The charge of 'cis-male' authors is unsustainable.

What about the accusation of 'white'? The printing press did not arrive in Sub-Saharan Africa until the 19th century, brought by Protestant missionaries [15]. It obviously took time for a literate (in English) writing class to emerge. The idea that Africans toiling in slavery in the Southern American colonies would be able to write any kind of book is absurd. Yet an African girl, brought to America at the age of seven, found herself in servitude to a Boston family who encouraged her to learn and subsequently to write in English. Her name was Phyllis Wheatley, and by the age of twenty, she had written a book of poems (*Poems on Various Subjects, Religious and Moral*). It was published in London in 1773 to great acclaim that included praise from George Washington himself [16]. Teachers of school and college students might also consider the works of Booker T Washington and W E B Du Bois in the 19th century and those of Maya Angelou and Nobel Laureate Toni Morrison in the 20th. Heineman's African Writers series, begun in 1962 in the UK, has published the books of authors like Chinua Achebe, Ngũgĩ wa Thiong'o, Steve Biko, Ama Ata Aidoo (Nadine Gordimer), Buchi Emecheta and Okot p'Bitek. The accusation of 'white' is spurious.

Today PC is determined not by parliament but by the ideologues who have penetrated schools and universities, the civil service and the National Health Service, the Church and the media, the police and the armed forces, businesses and banks, museums and libraries, public transport and trade unions. Some examples of their influence follow.

Civil Service

The UK Civil Service, which has implemented government policy for over a hundred years, was once considered a model of political and cultural neutrality with the highest standards. No more. Over several decades, civil servants have been hindering rather than carrying out their minister's programmes. They have also become work-shy. Many were still working from home a year after the COVID-19 pandemic, and there are plans for a four-day week. The output from many departments has fallen well below expectations. In 2006, Home Secretary John Reid considered the Home Office to be 'not fit for purpose', and it has not improved since then [17].

A Home Office functionary, writing anonymously, comments that 'I have worked for some time as a civil servant on immigration policy, and – in my experience – no priority is further from the Home Office in 2023 than stopping the boats or cutting net migration. ... Home Office officials have a moral and legal duty to do everything in their power to deliver the Government's priorities on immigration. Political impartiality is a central tenet of the civil service code, but this has morphed into a culture of "stewardship", as our permanent secretary Matthew Rycroft openly admitted in 2021 (when he was recorded telling colleagues there is no need to "slavishly" follow government policy on diversity). What this means in practice is accepting the bien pensant view that immigration cannot and should not be controlled, overruling the instructions of ministers and thereby their democratic mandates, with many of my colleagues viewing their role as being part of the resistance to what they see as a radical Right-wing Government determined to ignore the rules to punish innocent migrants. This culture of defiance is so widespread that any suggestion of border controls is sneered at or ignored' [18]. In addition to this, civil servants are simply incompetent. In 2023, the Department for Education miscalculated the budget for schools to such an extent that the average state school would lose £50,000 in the following year [19]. When those in the Office for National Statistics (ONS), who had been working from home since the COVID-19 pandemic, were asked to show up in the office two days a week, their response was to call for a strike [20]. Most people in jobs where working from home is not an option would consider a mere 2 days in the office very generous indeed. Another example comes from the HMRC (His Majesty's Revenue and Customs). 'If members of the public could actually get through when they call them, and receive correct advice, and if people's complaints were properly dealt with, then it would be fine for offices to sit empty. But that is not happening'. Why? Because only a third of staff are actually in the office (on a typical April day in 2024, a number that fell to a quarter in regard to the top mandarins) [21]. I appreciate that much of this section documents a general decline in work standards. This is related to PC in that members of the service consider being anyone's 'servant' to be politically incorrect.

So bureaucrats have turned from strict impartiality to promoting politically correct policies with open arms. The various departments, such as the Home Office, Ministry of Justice, Foreign Office, Department for Business and Trade, and Health Service, have initiated training courses for their staff on diversity, equality and inclusion. These have resulted in a million civil service days a year 'wasted on equality and diversity training' which cost the tax payer an estimated £150 m a year [22]. Such courses instruct, for example, that belief in two genders is 'a product and tool of colonialism and white supremacy' [23]. In order to run these courses, 90,000 extra civil servants have been recruited – despite the government's intention to reduce, not increase, numbers in the civil service. Not only that, senior civil servants are now eligible for a bonus if they can 'demonstrate that they have made a significant contribution ... for example involving leadership of functional initiative on capability building or diversity and inclusion' [24]. Thank goodness this mania of Equality, Diversity and Inclusion appears to be coming to an end – at least within the civil service [25].

By April of 2023, a group of civil servants that included senior managers and lawyers as well as policy advisors had had enough. 42 of them signed a letter (some anonymously for fear of reprisals) to the head of the Civil Service, Sir Simon Case. 'We are concerned that the widespread incorporation of the concept of "gender identity" into the language and internal policies of the Civil Service constitutes a significant breach of impartiality', they wrote. Typical of their views is that 'Freedom of speech does not exist for anyone whose personal or religious beliefs clash with the version of reality. ... Instead, those who exercise their legally protected right to gender-critical views, the belief that you cannot change your biological sex are: accused of bigotry and hate; compared to racists; and harassed or actively silenced'. Five months on, they were still waiting for a reply [26].

Kate Harris, a civil servant from the Department for Work and Pensions (DWP), was recently censured for pointing out – during a discussion on transgender issues – that 'it's useful to hear both sides of a subject'. She argued that 'One of the things I struggle to understand as a lesbian myself is, how can transwomen (i.e. biological males) be lesbian as lesbian is same sex attracted, not gender?' But a DWP official accused her of making 'inappropriate remarks in the wrong context' and she received an official reprimand [27]. In contrast, Saorsa-Amatheia Tweedale, who is the DWP's National Diversity Ambassador on Trans issues avows that 'the belief that sex is binary is not "the modern scientific view"'(Really?). Tweedale tells children who want to transition by taking puberty suppressing hormones that they should disregard the advice of the NHS and the concern of their parents [28]. The fact that Tweedale dresses in 'fetish gear' to come to the office [29] is of less concern.

The former Secretary of the Department for Business and Trade, Kemi Badenoch, thinks that one of the reasons why civil servants quite often 'bring in a Left-wing view of what fairness is' results from the fact that 'many Home Office staff ... have come from refugee campaigning charities ... They think that they are on the side of the righteous – and that they are correct. They think that we ministers shouldn't be political', which is of course the opposite of actuality: civil servants are supposed to be apolitical in order to serve a minister who is by definition a member of a political party [30]. Despite civil servants' inadequate performance, their remuneration continues to rise. Notwithstanding austerity elsewhere, senior civil servants are about to be given an above-inflation pay rise of 5.5%. So, the number receiving a six-figure salary has been rising steadily over the past decade. In 2024, 2,625 mandarins earned between £100,000 and £150,000. The previous year, the number was 1,850 [31]. Are these virtue-signalling bureaucrats worth it?

As mentioned earlier, some members of the civil service continue to believe in the myth that sex is a flexible characteristic. One such is suing two colleagues for their 'discriminatory' view that transgender people cannot change their sex [32]. To illustrate the fact that free speech itself is now under threat within the civil service, the defendants may lose their jobs [33]. However, the Department of Culture, Media and Sport and that of Science, Innovation and Technology have 'promised to review "gender assignment" policies [34]'.

But the number of civil servants who actually make it into the office is continuing to fall. This has been more marked since Labour came to office in July 2024. Those in private employment, such as banks (except the Bank of England), Boots or Amazon, have been told to be in the office five days a week. (The time when everyone – including those in schools and universities – worked Saturday mornings is but a distant memory). Government offices are barely 60% occupied, with the Department of Work and Pensions particularly devoid of human beings [35]. And it's getting worse by the month. Work-shy bureaucrats in the Public and Commercial Union are set to strike in 2025 after being told to go to the office for just 3 days a week [36]. Yet working from home is said to be 18 percent less productive than being in the office [37] and this now includes the BBC, NHS England, police and local government as well. Some of the latter are working not just from home but from holiday beaches too. Croydon is but one of six councils that have been granted emergency powers to increase council tax by up to 15% despite reducing their services, with some employees working from Botswana and Switzerland (for an entire year) [38]. As Baroness Bottomley, former Health Secretary under John Major, has pointed out 'We are social people, we need to go to work. ... The sooner we move away from thinking working from home is a very wonderful thing, I shall be delighted' [39].

It's not just council workers. Between them, thirteen government departments last year approved 2,348 out of 2,642 applications from civil servants not to work from the office. The Business Department, for example, allowed some 10% of its employees to put in their hours from Argentina, Australia and Brazil. Other destinations chosen by our devoted civil servants included Italy, Spain, Greece and France, as well as Jamaica, Barbados, Mauritius and Thailand [40].

HS2

Readers may be aware of the UK's decision in 2010 to build a high-speed rail link (HS2) between London and Birmingham, continuing to Manchester, Crewe and Leeds to the north. The project was doomed from the start, having received support from Lord (Andrew) Adonis, former Transport Secretary under Gordon Brown (when Parliamentary

Under-Secretary for Schools and Learners Adonis proposed teaching evolution alongside 'intelligent design'. A man who equates a billion-year-old fact of nature with a pseudoscientific form of creationism can hardly be said to possess a sharp mind). The cost of HS2 was estimated at £33 billion with a completion date of 2016. Currently, the cost is anticipated to be around £180 billion, with the first trains not arriving at their destination before 2034. Why is this? Much of the blame falls on the incompetence of those managing the tax payer-funded company High Speed Two Ltd that is building the line. But there is another reason: an obsession with Equality, Diversity and Inclusion goals. These include racially profiling staff to ensure that they exceed the 18% of non-white residents in England and Wales; guaranteeing that 4% of staff are lesbian, gay, bisexual, trans or 'questioning'; subsidising staff to participate in events such as Transgender Day of Visibility, International Asexuality Day, International Drag Day and Trans Awareness Week; establishing a Community Environment Fund that enables charities such as the Bengali Workers Association in London to hold 'activity sessions for the over 50s; and creating a gender-neutral menopause policy and relocating a 'drop-in centre' in Manchester that currently provides 'sexual health services' and a needle exchange for prostitutes. All undoubtedly worthy activities but of dubious relevance to building a railway line. As investigative journalist Guy Adams points out, the people in charge of HS2 'have all too frequently seemed to be more interested in social engineering than civil engineering' [41].

BBC

The BBC, an institution supposedly free of bias, censored broadcaster John Humphrys for pointing out – in a 2013 BBC2 documentary on the welfare state – that when he was growing up in Cardiff 'hardly anyone was on benefits. Now, vast numbers are. Why?' He was accused of 'supporting Tory policy, then found guilty of breaching guidelines on impartiality and accuracy.' *Spectator* editor Fraser Nelson points out that 'The BBC's own team of truth-deciders, modestly called "Reality Check", are rather selective in the realities they check' and gives several examples of this [42].

The following year, the Corporation told staff 'not to hire candidates who are "dismissive" of diversity and inclusion'. Applicants should be asked to 'explain what diversity and inclusion means to you and, should you be successful, what opportunities do you see for you to promote, celebrate or encourage diversity and inclusion in your role?' [43].

You might think that EDI is already in the very lifeblood of the BBC. But clearly not enough. It is now advertising for a £125,000-a-year Head of Diversity, Inclusion and 'Belonging' in order to create an 'inclusive workplace culture where everyone feels they can belong' – an aim that surely encompasses every organisation on the globe. The goal, surprise, surprise, is to 'embed inclusive practices into recruitment, retention, development and engagement'. As one MP has pointed out, 'Once again, British licence fee payers are being fleeced – more overpaid management roles means more rubbish on the telly' [44].

Armed Forces

Now, the armed forces, including the bureaucrats in the Ministry of Defence, have joined in. Britain's latest aircraft carriers HMS Queen Elizabeth and HMS Prince of Wales, costing £3.5 billion each, may be devoid of aeroplanes on their decks and the army bereft of fighting soldiers, but time and resources – at an all-time low – are being spent on ridiculous Diversity, Equity and Inclusion courses. 'The setting of seemingly arbitrary DEI targets should never be at the heart of recruitment activities for the British Army and the RAF – rather, the focus should be drafting in motivated individuals who are courageous, value routine, and are deeply protective of their country. Britain is at risk of pushing equality of opportunity to the sidelines in favour of an equalisation of outcomes which threatens to weaken the performance-related standards of some of its most treasured institutions' [45]. Recently, Britain was spending more than £50 billion a year on defence – more than any other European country – but not getting a proper return due to 'waste, incompetence, mismanagement, stupidity and reckless squandering of our money by those at the Ministry of Defence ...' [46].

Then, there is politically incorrect terminology. 14 Squadron of the Royal Air Force (RAF), one of its most senior squadrons, has for more than a hundred years been known as 'Crusaders' on account of its service in Palestine during World War 1. One of 14 Squadron's crew members has now petitioned for the nickname to be suspended because 'It is offensive to Muslims'. The complaint has been accepted [47]. Perhaps it's just as well that the army regiments collectively known as the Green Jackets (King's Royal Rifle Corps and Rifle Brigade, joined by the Oxfordshire and Buckinghamshire Light Infantry in 1966) were amalgamated with other regiments to become The Rifles in 2007. For today, the name would presumably be problematic for the Irish nation as well as for members of the All England Lawn Tennis and Croquet Club. The 11th Hussars (amalgamated with the 10th Hussars in 1969), nicknamed the Cherry Pickers, would have been disrespectful for agricultural workers, and the Black and Tans (as the constables of the Royal Irish Constabulary were known) ... but such musings are best left alone.

NHS

Columnist (Lord) Charles Moore mentions a friend and front-line hospital doctor who writes to him in regard to the NHS's preoccupation with politically correct matters such as net zero. 'Having come through Covid and now battling with the effects of strikes, he gets short-tempered with "being bombarded endlessly by email by diversity, LGBTQ+ network/month identity spam"; but this is nothing beside the mountain of material about decarbonisation which flows from hospital trusts, royal colleges and NHS leaders. He goes on, "There are endless Microsoft Teams meetings announced on this stuff and of course I have never had time to attend and don't imagine anyone who is actually involved in treating patients does attend them." A good way of cutting waste "would be to sack all those who do have time for it and then stop any further such events/news from slowing down the health service". The doctor also senses hypocrisy, since he believes the NHS to be the biggest greenhouse gas producer in the UK. And while it is true that air pollution "does have a measurable impact on people's respiratory health in large urban centres, all other claims of morbidity and mortality are absurdly indirect, speculative and falsifiable'" [48].

Instead of engaging in 'politically correct' EDI training schemes, such as the 18-page trans diversity and inclusion document drawn up for its staff by the Lewisham and Greenwich NHS Trust [49], the NHS should concentrate on deficiencies in clinically important diseases such as cancer. The survival rate for most cancers in the UK is the worst in the G7 group of countries. This is due largely to an inadequate General Practitioner (GP) service. Cancers are diagnosed too late, by virtual rather than by face-to-face contact, which jeopardises effective treatment. Cancer specialist Meirion Thomas considers GPs to be the most entitled 'workers' in Britain [50]. This does not stop them from industrial action, orchestrated by the British Medical Association (BMA), in order to achieve an 11% pay rise (which they are likely to get [51]) for their efforts in seeing as few patients as possible face-to-face.

The situation appears to be getting even worse for patients. Encouraged by the BMA, GPs have been told that instead of referring patients directly to hospitals, they can revert to the earlier system of writing a referral letter. This means even longer delays, with some patients never reaching the hospital at all, as clerks there cope with voluminous paperwork. For cases of suspected cancer, the situation is disastrous, as cancer specialist Prof Sikora has pointed out, 'creating a massive workload for clerks creates a needless obstacle. The consequence can only be delay – and delay is lethal for cancer' [52].

The NHS wastes money on ridiculous forms, which it then expects its patients to complete. One such form, designed by the Royal Brompton Hospital, which is part of the Guy's and St Thomas' NHS Trust, asks patients to select their identity from one of the following options: Agender, Another gender not listed here, Choose not to disclose, Demiboy, Demigirl, Female, Gender fluid, Male, Non-binary, Other, Questioning, Transgender male and Transgender female [53]. I trust that members of the NHS staff are able to draw clinically relevant conclusions from the replies in order to justify the time spent on this exercise.

Senior executives at Lewisham and Greenwich NHS Trust defied the then Health Secretary Victoria Atkins and drew up an 18-page trans diversity and inclusion policy document for their staff [54]. Derbyshire NHS Foundation Trust is advertising for a Head of Equality, Diversity and Inclusion. The job description is to 'champion new ways of thinking and hearing the voices of our people and local population to improve equitable, diverse and inclusive experiences for all. ... The role is fundamental to creating innovative approaches to diversity and inclusion which will support our work at Derbyshire Healthcare NHS Foundation Trust.' Of 'patient' or 'waiting time', there is no mention, but the successful candidate will enjoy an £80,000 salary. MP Robert Lowe has called this 'an insult to taxpayers' [55].

Universities

In the Introduction, I mentioned the role of the University of Sussex, a member of the elite Russell Group, in the hounding out of Professor Kathleen Stock for her factually (but not politically) correct views concerning trans-women. Three years on and another Russell Group university is singing the same song. The University of Essex is asking its staff to sign six pledges, approved by the LGBT charity Stonewall, to show that they are 'the kind of person that LGBTQ+ can confide in and feel safe around'. These include a promise that they are 'against transphobia, bi-erasure, acephobia (discrimination against asexual people) and intersexism (prejudice against people with variations in their sex characteristics)'. Staff are encouraged to educate themselves in regard to LGBTQ+ topics and to bring these into their teaching material. Those who sign will be identified on their staff profile (meaning that those who don't will be recognised by students and others) [56].

The University of Liverpool considers that being white and heterosexual is a problem, though it doesn't give advice on how to eradicate these deficiencies in the billions of people afflicted by them. Instead, it is asking its history lecturers to 'think creatively' and asks whether a module that teaches race relations could do more to 'problematise and de-centre whiteness' [57]. Another study concerned about whiteness is launched by the University of Sheffield. The project will 'take an unflinching look at the white-centricity of folk music repertory, performers and audience by conducting fieldwork to shed light on long-standing vernacular singing practices of ethnic minority cultures in England'. The aim is to 'increase accessibility to the folk club scene and take the first step in a process of decolonisation within the folk music canon'. UK Research Innovation is funding this project to the tune of £1.5 million [58]. And Leicester University is dropping Chaucer 'in favour of modules on race and sexuality' [59].

Meanwhile, a researcher at the University of Edinburgh has received a grant from the Economic Research Council in order to study 'home educating communities of colour', because it is 'crucial to understand how home educating families of colour are impacted by race, class, gender and coloniality'. Lucy Marsh of the Family Education Trust comments that 'Accusations that academia is out of touch are justified when tax-payers money is being wasted on pointless research like this' [60]. Is pole dancing a subject fit for a doctorate? The Arts and Humanities Research Council seems to think so. It has just awarded a two-year grant to a research student at the University of Lancaster to complete her thesis on 'Pole dancers' digital media practices through an international feminist framework that centres lived experience' [61].

King's College London (KCL) is hosting Dr Annabel Sowemimo, a sexual and reproductive health registrar in the NHS and founder of the Reproductive Justice Initiative (RJI), to carry out a PhD. The RJI believes in the 'redistribution of wealth' and aims to dismantle structures that perpetuate 'state-driven violence'. It is committed to 'decolonisation by illuminating the impact of colonialism' and supports the call for 'reparations'. It has received over £85,000 from government grants, which will presumably finance Dr Sowemimo's PhD. The title for this is 'Reproductive (In)Justice: Understanding the experiences of Black women in Britain with fertility control methods (contraception and abortion) in the United Kingdom' [62]. Let's hope that future NHS patients will benefit from such research. KCL continues to use NHS funds for its PhD programmes. A course on 'addressing whiteness' for those studying for a PhD in clinical psychology is one example. Resulting from its obsession with identity politics, it initially sought to segregate white and non-white students (thus seeding racial divisions even further and a sense of victimhood on behalf of ethnic minorities). But KCL appears to have changed its mind on such a retrograde policy. The course itself is said to promote the notion that white students bear a responsibility for the colonial policies initiated by their ancestors. It has received criticism not only from the chairman of the Common Sense Group of parliamentarians but also from one of its participants who considers that its approach 'was damaging relationships between those of different races' [63].

The University of Nottingham, in its move to 'decolonise the curriculum', is following the decision in 1983 of the International Society of Anglo-Saxonists to change its name to the International Society for the Study of Early Medieval England. This resulted from Canadian academic Mary Rambaran-Olm's resignation from the society because the term Anglo-Saxon evokes 'an imagined medieval past that justifies beliefs in white, Western superiority' [64]. So, a teaching module at Nottingham called 'Research Methods in Viking and Anglo-Saxon Studies' has had the latter words replaced by 'Early Mediaeval English Studies' (removing 'Saxon' may strike some readers as an abrogation of historical fact). But that's not all. The word 'Viking' is also considered problematic because of concerns over connections to 'race, empire, Nazism' [65]. Will the word 'Roman' be next to go?

Taxpayers' money continues to be spent on absurd schemes. The University of Derby has been awarded over £80,000 by the Arts and Humanities Research Council for a research project entitled 'Dracula returns to Derby'. In fact, it isn't even a proper research project at all. The aim is to 'contribute to the national conversation on equality, diversity and inclusion in horror' by organising events in order to establish Derby as a 'gothic tourism destination and a place of historical significance in literature' [66].

Over 50 leading professors claim that the Quality Assurance Agency is trying to make students 'pay for their own indoctrination'. Academics at top UK universities have signed an open letter criticising guidance on academic standards that states that values of Equality, Diversity and Inclusion 'should permeate the curriculum and every aspect of the learning experience' [67].

Britain's leading universities have succumbed to the idea that students from poorer or minority backgrounds perform less well in traditional examinations than their peers. This was not one of the findings of the Commission for Race and Ethnic Disparities (see Chapter 2), nor would one expect it to be the case. Intellectual ability is not a quality determined by social status or ethnic background. It is therefore unlikely that 'more "inclusive assessments" such as open-book tests or take-home papers instead of in-person, unseen exams' are likely to make much difference. Two members of parliament have criticised the proposals on further grounds. Richard Holden points out that 'This knee-jerk and patronising approach to dumbing down university education serves no one', while former Education Minister Sir John Hayes considers that the proposals are 'deeply insulting to students from minority backgrounds ... and would undermine the integrity of the assessment process' [68].

More on EDI

The UK government spends vast amounts on projects related to Equality, Diversity and Inclusiveness. By 2021, it was spending £557 million a year on jobs related to EDI, with a further £212 million on training days and contracts. 'That's before we get to the £7 billion on quangos which, as it were, incidentally promote identity politics' [69]. The value of such expenditure is beginning to be questioned. The last Conservative UK Government set up an Inclusion at Work Panel to assess the value of its Equity, Diversity and Inclusion measures. Its conclusions were that such initiatives are a waste of money. Kemi Badenogh, the former Equalities Minister who commissioned the investigation, wrote that '... many practices have not only been proven to be ineffective, they have also been counterproductive. ... No group should ever be worse off because of companies' diversity policies – whether they be black women, or white men ... Performative gestures such as compulsory pronouns and rainbow lanyards are often a sign that organisations are struggling to demonstrate how they are being inclusive' [70]. Businesses too are beginning to row back on EDI projects. Simon Fanshawe, one of the founders of the LGBT charity Stonewall, now admits that 'It seemed self-evidently right [in the past] but now they're saying, "Actually I'm not convinced that a high-street retailer should take a position on anti-conversion therapy, because what's that got to do with the price of beans?"' [71]. But other 'nonsense' research projects continue. Under the new Labour government, £6 billion will be spent on 'literary decolonisation' of Africa, as well as on LGBT rights in China and the marketing of vegan meat products [72].

Political scientist and former academic Matthew Goodwin has criticised the proponents of EDI by asserting that 'if you look at our national conversation you can only talk about Britain if you're equating Britishness with diversity. It's almost like saying we don't have an identity of our own.' Victoria Treadell, Australia's High Commissioner, agrees and has criticised Australia's Foreign Minister Penny Wong for asserting that Britain must confront its history of empire and stop 'sheltering in narrower versions' of its past. Politician Nick Timothy concedes that diversity may be one of Britain's strengths, but 'Britain is proving that it can succeed as a multiracial democracy precisely because of the legacy of the many generations who built this country over centuries. Diversity matters, as does the inclusion of all our citizens in our national identity. But what matters most is the common thread: the shared story that binds us all together' [73].

Columnist Zoe Strimpel considers that EDI (DEI in her article) is dying faster in the USA (whence it arrived) than in Britain. A recent essay in the *New York Times* points to the University of Michigan as a particularly strong supporter of DEI. In January 2024, it had awarded its Martin Luther King Jr Spirit Award to a pro-Palestine student group (since rescinded). Over a decade, Michigan 'spent a quarter of a billion dollars on instilling DEI in every corner, every individual, every word, every thought and response'. That is now being reversed. According to the *New York Times*, 'everyday campus complaints and academic disagreements were now cast as crises of and harm, each demanding some further administrative intervention'. But according to Strimpel, it is too late. 'A generation has been destroyed, rewarded for insisting that wrong is right' [74].

One cannot but agree. US-based Walmart – the world's largest company based on revenue – is abandoning EDI. 'While diversity and inclusion are certainly worthwhile values to strive for in any company, they lost practically all their meaning along the way. The pursuit of diversity pushed out diversity of thought. Inclusion meant ugly box-ticking exercises. Rather than uniting workforces, they alienated employees from each other'. Walmart is not alone. As Mark Zuckerberg has pointed out, 'it feels like we're in a new era now' [75]. The omens for the UK don't look so good. The British Business Bank, owned by the Department for Business and Trade, is spending £64,500 on 'embracing diversity', despite the fact that the opposition has warned the government that its proposed diversity drive is likely to cost the City of London up to £1 billion [76].

In fact, the USA is not entirely out of the picture. While not blaming any one person for the air crash between an American Airlines plane and an army helicopter over Ronald Reagan National Airport in Washington DC on 30 January 2025, it is possible that the diversity policy of the Federal Aviation Administration (FAA), that oversees the air traffic control at major airports, may have contributed by not choosing the best-qualified candidates. Andrew Brigida, an applicant for a job with the FAA, achieved top marks in the air traffic control selection and training examination but failed the biographical questionnaire because he 'didn't fit the preferred ethnic profile' [77].

In the UK, a report by the National Fire Chiefs Council finds insufficient diversity in the fire service because the proportion of women (9.3%) and those from ethnic minorities (5.4%) is considerably less than in the population as a whole. This is hardly surprising. Fighting a blaze in a house or a high-rise building like the Grenfell Tower in 2017 is not an occupation typical of the majority – like teaching or working in a shop. As Paul Embery, former executive council member of the Fire Brigades Union, points out, 'fire chiefs should focus on putting out fires rather than "manipulating the workforce demographic"' [78].

EDI measures within certain NHS Trusts are wasting effort and money, according to UK Health Secretary Wes Streeting. He has pointed to some health workers celebrating their 'anti-whiteness' instead of focusing on important issues like cancer diagnosis and treatment. Some 35 EDI positions, at a cost of £750,000 in salaries alone, have been advertised since his own government took power in July 2024 [79]. However, Ashford and St Peter's Hospitals Foundation Trust, Buckinghamshire Healthcare NHS Trust, Hillingdon Hospitals NHS Foundation Trust and Whittington Hospital NHS Trust (among others no doubt) continue to use ridiculous words like 'birthing people' and 'pregnant people' [80] instead of the simple term 'mother' that has worked well for at least ten centuries.

Companies wishing to bid for government contracts have been told to focus on net-zero and diversity goals. Former Business Secretary Sir Jacob Rees-Mogg considers that 'When the public finances are under such strain trying to use (the Procurement Act 2023) for woke virtue signalling is especially foolish and potentially unlawful' [81].

Lawyers

An example of how lawyers are following deluded ethnic principles is illustrated by the Sentencing Council's new guidelines. A Pre-Sentence Report (PSR) – that can make the difference between being sent to prison or not – will now be required only if the defendant is from an ethnic minority, a cultural or faith minority, transgender or pregnant. In other words, 'if you are a white working-class man who has faced hardship, tough luck – you will not get the same consideration as someone from a different background'. The much-cited principle of equality appears to operate only in favour of non-whites [82].

Publishers

Publishers like Penguin Random House and others consider themselves to be arbiters of Equality, Diversity and Inclusion. So, they feel obliged to add a trigger warning when reissuing works of some of the 20th century's greatest authors (which they realise are their bread and butter), from P G Wodehouse, Virginia Woolf, Ernest Hemingway, Evelyn Waugh and Nancy

Mitford to Roald Dahl. Hemingway's *The Sun Also Rises*, for example, is accompanied by a warning that 'this book was published in 1926 and reflects the attitudes of its time', while potential readers of Mitford's 1945 novel *The Pursuit of Love* are told that it contains 'prejudices that were common in British society that were wrong' (and for good measure, 'are wrong today') [83]. Yet anyone able to read a book is surely aware that all these authors – long dead – couldn't possibly have been aware of today's deluded attitudes.

Sensitivity readers scan books for any mention of a disability that might offend a person suffering from an impairment. So, in Roald Dahl's children's story *Charlie and the Chocolate Factory*, the description of the gluttonous boy Augustus Gloop has been changed from 'enormously fat' to just 'enormous'. Referring to someone as 'fat' is seen to be discourteous to fat children. Yet, surely, if an overweight boy were to say to his mother, 'Mummy, I don't want to be fat any more', that would be admirable, as he could then be encouraged to go on a diet so as to avoid complications like type-2 diabetes in later life. Every obese person (BMI over 25) costs the British Health Service (i.e. taxpayer) more than £700 per year. Dahl does not use words like 'cripple' or 'blind' about a child, for that would not be considered funny. Amusement may cause a smile or outright laughter. And the latter is, according to philosopher Roger Scruton, 'one of the raw materials from which culture is built. ... All rational beings laugh – and maybe only rational beings laugh. And all rational beings benefit from laughing. ... Laughter helps us to overcome our isolation and fortifies us against despair' [84]. The best-selling author Alexander McCall Smith has taken virtue-signalling sensitivity readers to task in their quest to 'sanitise' disturbing passages in children's books. As most parents are aware, it is precisely the 'nasty' bits in books by authors like Roald Dahl that children enjoy most.

Publishers take the issue of 'insensitivity' seriously. As journalist Melanie McDonagh points out [85], 'Some of the censorship is down squarely to cowardly publishers who cancel books lest they offend one' [86]. So, Puffin publishes rewritten versions of Roald Dahl as though they were the original, and Bloomsbury cancels a book by historian Nigel Biggar about the British Empire. In the future, such books may not even reach a publisher. Ash Literary agency, for example, states that 'We are not interested in stories about white, able-bodied WW2 evacuees but would welcome that story from a disabled, LGBTQ+ or BIPOC (black, indigenous, and other people of colour) perspective' [87]. Some publishers are holding their own. Pan Macmillan, publisher of Hilaire Belloc's *Cautionary Tales for Children* (1907), has refused to rewrite any of the verses, arguing that '... changing the text to reflect today's world would undermine the authenticity of the original'. It has, however, printed a trigger warning in its latest edition, stating that 'Readers should be aware that there may be hurtful or indeed harmful phrases and terminology that were prevalent at the time this book was written in the context of the historical setting of this book' [88]. Let us hope that a future generation of better-taught children won't need such self-evident warnings.

Editor Madeline Fry Schultz quotes Ian McEwan's criticism of sensitivity readers: '... saying we can't read Nabokov or Conrad or whatever, seems beyond contempt'. But she goes on to point out that 'The sensitivity reader isn't the only specter plaguing the publishing industry as authors, editors, and stories have become more obsessed with race, class, and sexuality than prose and narrative' [89]. Her point about race is well taken, though the problem is the opposite as far as authors are concerned, because Israeli publishing houses are 'facing public boycotts by prominent writers', according to a leading article in the *Sunday Telegraph* [90].

Libraries

Publishers are not the only ones to have been seduced by the new ideology. Public libraries appear to take a similar stance. When 49 local council libraries were surveyed by the Free Speech Union (FSU), they were found to contain 720 books on transgender topics between them. Of these, 60% extolled the right of people to decide their own gender, with only 40% expressing the view that male and female are distinct biological entities. Toby Young, founder and general secretary of the FSU, comments that 'There are still a lot of sensible librarians out there who believe that public libraries shouldn't take sides on contentious ... issues. But too many libraries have been captured by woke activists behaving like bespectacled zealots in the culture war' [91]. The Calderdale council-run public library goes further. Works such as those by Kathleen Stock (*Material Girls. Why Reality Matters for Feminism*) and Helen Joyce (*Trans: When Ideology Meets Reality*) have been concealed from view and are now prevented from being promoted in displays 'in order to protect the public from offence'. The only other book to have been treated like this is Adolf Hitler's *Mein Kampf*. [92].

York St John University in the UK has placed some 3,000 books donated by a former librarian into its restricted-access collection because 'Within the 150 years of children's writing which is represented in the collection, there is a widespread occurrence of colonialist narratives which centre white supremacy, and racist and orientalist methods of both fictional and historical storytelling'. Hardly surprising. What are these books that are likely to 'include language and visual imagery which is racist, and (that) many people may find their contents upsetting and offensive'? Internationally acclaimed children's stories (beloved as well by adults across the world) such as JM Barrie's *Peter Pan*, Lewis Carroll's *Alice in Wonderland* and Jules Verne's *Around the world in eighty days* [93]. In 2022, the Welsh (Labour) government initiated an 'Anti-Racist Welsh Action Plan' created by the Chartered Institute of Library and Information Professionals (CILIP) in order to secure £130,000 of public funding for a project of 'critical whiteness studies' in order to manage the 'dominant paradigm of whiteness'. Some 93 buildings, which include schools, community centres and pubs as well as libraries, have been identified as sites 'associated with empire and the slave trade'. Needless to say, this includes Gladstone's Library (note the vilification of Gladstone mentioned in Chapters 1 and 3). But author Rakib Ehsan considers that a 'more worthwhile use of time, energy and resources' would be to 'improve educational, economic, and health outcomes ... especially (in) former coal mining parts' [94].

As far as school libraries are concerned, a fight back against today's ideologues by concerned parents and some teachers has begun. A survey conducted by the Index on Censorship finds that 28 out of 53 British school librarians have been asked to remove books such as those dealing with controversial LGBTQ+ issues. But is this really a desired outcome? Journalist Ben Lawrence is right in that 'Curious minds will always seek out good writing ... Book banning may be a global industry – but the freedom to read will always prevail' [95].

Museums and Galleries

Punch and Judy marionettes have been entertaining children (and adults) since the 17th century. The sight of nasty Mr Punch hitting his wife Judy does not upset viewers because they realise that these puppets are not real people. Nevertheless, the Tate Modern, which is showing a film called *Cabaret Crusades: The Horror Show Files* that is enacted by traditional 200-year-old Italian marionettes, finds it necessary to warn the audience that the film 'depicts acts of violence and dead bodies' [96].

You might consider that the purpose of a museum is to display objects of interest to the public. Think again. New guidance published in 2023 states that museums should 'stimulate positive explorations of gender' for children. A 44-page guide produced by the University of Leicester's Research Centre for Museums and Galleries aims to address the 'growing uncertainty and anxiety surrounding trans-inclusive practice'. It claims that 'outspoken objections to trans content frequently intersect with homophobia, misogyny and racism' [97]. Not surprising, then, that the following year the Bronte Parsonage Museum in Haworth produced LGBT-themed resources as part of its series 'Pride at the Parsonage: The Brontes and Gender Identity'. Columnist Madeline Grant considers that '... trying to shoehorn 21st century concepts of the "queer" into the lives and works of three vicar's daughters from the mid-19th century isn't just deranged but faintly insulting' [98]. It's difficult to disagree with her.

The Natural History Museum in South Kensington has decided not to accept support from the previously generous oil companies and others 'now stigmatised as environmental villains, or worse'. Instead, it will use £550 million (£400 million from the taxpayer) in a major redevelopment.

According to its director Doug Gurr, 'our revitalised museum will be the heart of a global mission to create 100 million advocates for the planet, powered by our scientists' work to find solutions to the planetary emergency' [99]. Meanwhile, the Pitt Rivers Museum in Oxford has organised a project, 'Beyond the Binary', to demonstrate its solidarity with LGBT+ communities. The project and its accompanying exhibition state that the Pitt Rivers Museum 'is rooted in colonialism ... We hope that this exhibition is a positive step in tackling oppression, which LGBTIAQ+ communities often feel in spaces such as this one' [100].

The titles of artwork displayed by the council-run Aberdeen Archives, Gallery & Museums are to be renamed in order to erase language that might be 'racist, offensive and discriminatory'. Unsurprisingly one picture entitled 'A Negress' becomes 'Imogen' and one depicting metal workers called 'African Group' is changed to 'A copper foundry, Katanga' [101]. But to change the title of another portrait also called 'A Negress' to 'A Woman' is surely a retrograde step. I thought the word 'woman' had been outlawed by the ideologues of political correctness.

The Tate Gallery in London is replacing some of its best-loved pictures to make room for works on colonialism and other topics that provide a more 'inclusive view of art history'. Its Victorian rooms now warn visitors that artists of the 19th century 'often overlook, caricature or romanticise the experiences of women, people of colour, workers or those living in poverty'. Visitors to a room of Georgian works are reminded that 'English furniture in the 18th century was often made from mahogany produced by enslaved people in the Caribbean' [102]. The following year, it launched an exhibition entitled 'The 80s: Photographing Britain'. Viewers are informed that photography has a 'sexist and racist past' and 'was a valuable tool for colonial powers ... that legitimised the mission of empires'. So, choosing the Thatcher years to build on this was an obvious approach for a gallery espousing today's anti-colonial vogue. Pictures relating to the miners' strike of 1984–1985 are naturally included, implying culpability by the prime minister herself. But illustrations of the AIDS crisis can hardly be laid at her door [103].

Deluded New World: Current Controversies and Why the Free World is on Edge

Statues and Eponymous Buildings

Elsewhere, I have referred to the removal of W E Gladstone's name from the university of Liverpool's halls of residence (Chapter 1) and his bust from the front of a church in Seaforth near Liverpool (Chapter 3) on account of his father's links to slavery (he himself was a fervent abolitionist). Now, the Albert Memorial, opposite the Royal Albert Hall in Southwest London that was sought by his grieving widow Queen Victoria and paid for by public subscription, is considered 'offensive' because it reflects a 'Victorian view of the world' (hardly surprising) 'that differs from mainstream views held today' (quite: the fact that a sense of duty and economy, of taking personal responsibility for one's actions and subscribing to a strong work ethic, are no longer considered desirable characteristics is indeed regrettable). The offending feature of the monument is not the seated figure of the prince but the politically incorrect figures at the base depicting the people and animals of four continents [104].

The emeritus professor of sociology at the University of Kent, Frank Furedi, notes that 'The British Parliament has launched a probe to make its art collection "more representative of diversity". One of the first high-profile casualties of this inquisition has been the 18th century conservative philosopher and Member of Parliament Edmund Burke. Even though Burke opposed the practice of slavery and was a fierce critic of the excesses of the British Empire in India, his statues and portraits in the Palace of Westminster have been targeted by members of the review board because, according to Parliamentary documents, his younger brother made money from Caribbean plantations' [105]. So an enlightened critic of slavery can be retrospectively taken down because of his relative's sins (like Gladstone).

Cemeteries

Cemeteries have not escaped stricture either. Highgate is using a £100,000 National Lottery Heritage Fund grant to ensure that the diversity of those buried in there 'is reflected in the stories which are told about it'. The grave of menagerie owner George Wombwell, for example, would have depended on 'European colonial connections in Africa and South America', raising 'questions around colonialism and links to empire' [106].

Religion

Religion is supposed to be colour-blind. Not so the Anglican Church. Having been accused of favouring white people over past ages, it has turned 180 degrees and now discriminates against the white majority [107]. It is not alone. Academic, commercial and other institutions have been following this approach for a number of years. Perhaps we shouldn't worry too much about it in as far as the Church of England is concerned, since it is anyway in a period of sharp decline [108]. In fact, some Anglicans themselves have decided that the very word 'church' is no longer relevant. The Rev Dr Will Foulger, vicar of St Nicholas's in Durham, considers that the word is not comprehensive enough to describe what some new dioceses are doing, and suggests that the phrase 'new things' may be more appropriate. Needless to say, others disagree with such language of 'culture change' [109].

In Chapter 1, I pointed to the fact that some Anglicans – including the Archbishops Justin Welby (since resigned) and Stephen Cottrell – take the view that God should no longer be considered male. Now, one diocese has declared that 'God is not a white man', a surprising statement in view of the fact that Genesis 1:27 tells us that 'God created man in his own image', not the other way round. The assertion concerning God's colour has been passed to the Church's racial justice unit in order for it to determine how dioceses should meet the 'diversity and inclusion targets' set by the archbishops' anti-racism taskforce in 2021. Naturally, the ethnicity of Jesus (depicted in various colours throughout the Christian world over time – including black in a stained-glass window of 1877 in a Rhode Island church – is part of the survey [110] (though one might be forgiven for assuming that Jesus of Nazareth – like other Judeans in Palestine – might be depicted as off-white). What is clear is that PC now trumps any theological doctrine.

Religion was certainly involved in the Charlie Hebdo affair when Muslims rightly complained about the caricatures of the Prophet

Mohammad that had appeared in the Danish newspaper *Jyllands-Posten* and were subsequently reprinted in the satirical French magazine *Charlie Hebdo*. To accept that the cartoon (as a French court subsequently did) has less to do with freedom of speech and more with a lack of respect for someone else's religion seems obvious. But the ensuing arson of the editorial office and murder of 17 people involved in the magazine by an Islamist terror group in January 2015 was a needless and barbaric criminal act. If the magazine's editor (who subsequently became one of the victims) had apologised for an inappropriate jest, all this might have been avoided.

Spiritual succour has given way to ideological guidance. The Church of England is advertising for a 'head of racial justice priority' within the Diocese of London. The role of the successful candidate, who will receive a salary in excess of £66,600 – double that of the average vicar – will be to 'foster a culture ... built on love, fairness, equity, justice, collaboration and integrity' in order to facilitate 'learning' on 'the injustice and impact of racism' [111].

Christmas may be a religious feast, but faith is disappearing from the carols sung by the Anglican community. Clergy have been told to alter 'problematic phrases' – such as Jesus as the 'true Messiah'. No wonder churches are empty [112].

Banks

Coutts Bank closed politician Nigel Farage's account in June 2023 because his stance on Brexit, his friendship with Donald Trump, and his other views were 'not aligned' with the bank's 'values or purpose'. Dame Alison Rose, the person responsible for this action, has since resigned and the word 'debanking' has entered the HarperCollins' English Dictionary [113]. Yet Nigel Farage's speeches during Brexit were no more inflammatory than those of Enoch Powell, whose 'rivers of blood' speech in 1968 caused Leader of the Opposition Edward Heath to sack him as Shadow Secretary of State for Defence. Fiery speeches, provided they do not contravene laws relating to incitement to violence, are surely what politics in a democratic society is about. Now, it appears that they may lead to a loss of your freedom of action brought about by someone who is simply an official at a bank.

The US online payment facility (not an actual bank) terminated the account of one of its clients in 2022 (only recently admitted) because her views did not coincide with theirs. Molly Kingsley, founder with Liz Cole of the campaign group UsForThem, fought against the government's policy of closing schools during the COVID-19 epidemic. In their book *The Children's Inquiry*, they write, 'Some may maintain that restrictions applied to children were a necessary evil. We say that a public health paradigm which strives to protect adults without weighing up the costs to children is the very antithesis of "public health"'. The Covid enquiry has now admitted that Cole and Kingsley – as well as others at the time [114] – were right [115].

The Co-operative Bank is more tolerant. It considered debanking Rose West, a serial killer responsible for the torture and murder of at least nine young women between 1973 and 1987, but subsequently decided to allow her to retain her bank account. Others, whose actions seem considerably less heinous, are not so lucky. The bank declined to offer its services to a feminist group on account of their views that oppose transgender issues [116].

Yorkshire Building Society, actually a bank, sends monthly newsletters to its clients inviting them to respond with their views ('How are we doing? We want to hear from you!'). When Richard Fothergill received a newsletter promoting an upcoming LGBTQIA+ Pride month, he decided to reply. As a clergyman, he expressed concern over the impact of transgender ideology on children. He also wondered whether promoting Pride was really a good use of the bank's time. Eventually, he received a reply. Far from thanking him for taking time off his duties, the letter stated that 'Your comments will not stand ... we must protect our workforce from prejudice' [117].

It's going on everywhere. Staff at the Bank of England have been told to use 'gender neutral' language when speaking at meetings or to customers. It has initiated 'trans inclusion' sessions and is promoting a 'trans day of visibility', a 'trans day of remembrance' and a 'trans awareness week' [118]. Is all this really relevant to its role? Many would consider that getting its forecasts right for once is of greater value.

Failing to follow a bank's policy in regard to its views on matters such as diversity might not only lose you your account but you could lose your job. Carl Borg-Neil has been an employee of Lloyd's Bank for 30 years. During an online training session, Neil asked what one should do if someone from an ethnic minority used a word that was deemed unacceptable by others. When asked to explain to what he was referring to, he inadvertently used the N word in full (being dyslexic, he sometimes blurts things out before losing his train of thought). He was called a racist, told not to contact his colleagues and was sacked (though he was subsequently awarded handsome damages when he appealed to a court for wrongful dismissal) [119].

National Trust

The National Trust's recent report entitled 'Connections between Colonialism and Properties Now in the Care of the National Trust, including Links with Slavery' aims to 'make us question our assumptions about the past'. It has little to do with the actual history and upkeep of its properties. Its intention appears to ensure that the elderly, the disabled, families and others who pay for the NT are no longer allowed to enjoy the beautiful gardens, countryside or coastal walks without feelings of guilt [120].

Excessive Zeal

On the evening of 22 May 2017, as the concert goers who had been enjoying a performance by American pop star Ariana Grande were leaving the Manchester Arena, they were met by a hail of shrapnel: Islamic terrorist Salman Abedi had just detonated his homemade bomb containing triacetone triperoxide and a selection of lethal nuts and bolts. Twenty-two people aged between eight and fifty-one were killed outright (including Abedi). Over a thousand were seriously injured. It was subsequently revealed that Abedi, wearing a backpack, had been spotted by several transport police security guards as he was making his way from Victoria railway station to the arena's foyer. None had stopped him. As journalist Allison Pearson subsequently wrote, 'Political correctness is a gift for terrorists. ... Twenty-two people are dead in part because someone who was supposed to be protecting them feared an allegation of Islamophobia more than a mass slaughter of innocents ... ... Suella Braverman, the then Home Secretary, said she would "wholeheartedly" adopt the 34 recommendations in the [William] Shawcross report, promising "major reform" to Prevent which, in future, must "focus on security not political correctness"' [121].

Music

If literature is to be 'corrected', surely there's a case for evaluating 'difficulties' in music? Shouldn't the Chorus of the Jewish Slaves in Verdi's *Nabucco* be rewritten as, say, the Chorus of Gypsies, in the way that Agatha Christie's *Ten Little N.....s* was for several years titled *Ten Little Indians* on the (probably false) assumption that Indians were less likely to be offended? The implication of Wagner's *Götterdämmerung* and the other works that comprise the *Ring der Nibelungen* is clearly racist, and not just the text but the strident music also. Then, there's the mocked hunchback of Verdi's *Rigoletto*, the betrayed gypsy *Carmen* in Bizet's opera of that name, the abandoned geisha of Puccini's *Butterfly*. And what about Odette in Tchaikovsky's *Swan Lake*? Animals have rights too.

There is work to do here. Perhaps by a team of writers and musicians in a (government-funded) institute devoted to removing politically incorrect themes from an evening's entertainment. But to suggest that someone of a sensitive nature should not go to an opera without first checking the programme, should not purchase a book without prior knowledge of when it was written, should not enter a library that has not been cleared of questionable material would probably be considered an affront and a lack of regard for one's human rights.

Re-Naming Species

The rewording of plants and animals named according to the taxonomic system devised by Carl Linnaeus during the eighteenth century is on its way. The genus of many flowers has been named after people for centuries:

Bougainvillea (Louis-Antoine de Bougainville, French naval officer and explorer), *Forsythia* (William Forsyth, 18th c Scottish botanist), *Fuchsia* (Leonhart Fuchs, 16th c German physician and botanist), *Hydrangea* or *Hortensia* (Hortense Lepaute, 18th-century astronomer, who also had an asteroid and a lunar crater named after her). They arouse no antagonism. Nor could anyone object to *Blakea attenboroughi* (a tree flower native to Ecuador), *Nepenthes attenboroughii* (the pitcher plant found on a single mountain in the Philippines that is large enough to digest rats and shrews) or *Zaglossus attenboroughi* (a long-beaked spiny anteater) and other species named after the iconic naturalist. But the yellow *Hibbertia* flowers, honouring the 18th-century George Hibbert, should be renamed. Hibbert may have been a 'patron of botany', but he was also a wealthy owner of slaves and a supporter of the practice [122].

The names of animal species, too, are under threat. *Uta stansburiana* (the common small-blotched lizard), named after Howard Stansbury in 1852, is one. Stansbury was a naturalist who collected many types of lizards in what is now Utah. But he had also been involved in the massacre of more than a hundred innocent Timpanogos at Battle Creek in 1849. Then, there is the Confederate soldier John P McCown, who served in many campaigns against Native Americans during the 1840s. He was then stationed on frontier duty along the Rio Grande, during which time he began to collect specimens of local birds. The thick-billed longspur *Rhynchophanes mccownii* was named after him. That honour might well be revoked as a result of McCown's subsequent leadership in the maintenance of slavery.

Surprisingly, the blind cave beetle named *Anolphthamus hitleri* in the 1930s has escaped rewording by the ICZN (International Code of Zoological Nomenclature), but the future of *Melidectes whitemanensis*, a honeyeater bird native to Melanesia, must be in doubt. In contrast, if there is to be a renaming of species, perhaps the recently described South American four-eyed opossum might be called *Metachirus aritanai*, as a tribute to the Indigenous leader Aritana Yawalapiti, who died of COVID-19 in 2020 [123]. Then, there's the Gypsy Moth (*Lymantria dispar*). The Entomological Society of America has decided to remove this insect from its list of approved names [124], presumably because of possible offence to the Romany population (though these do not appear to have crossed the Atlantic).

The rewording of species as a result of 'grievance archaeology' [125] will soon be funded by the taxpayer. The University of Cambridge is advertising for a PhD student (with a generous stipend) to 'root out imperial connections' in its collection of plants and animals. Thus does cultural doctrine trump scientific enquiry these days [126].

The attitude of white Europeans towards black Africans and their treatment of them a hundred and more years ago are of major concern to the ideologues of political correctness. Memorials to prominent persons only remotely connected to slavery or colonialism must be removed. Children need to be taught about the errors of such people's ways. University research projects on this issue, which are of little intrinsic value, should be funded by the taxpayer. But were Africans themselves any better? In the empires of Sub-Saharan Africa in the west, such as ancient Ghana (not to be confused with the modern country of that name 500 miles to the southeast on the coast of the Bay of Guinea) and Mali (that supplanted ancient Ghana during the 13th century), slavery as a form of employment was the norm: on the land and in the home. Slaves were exported as goods for profit (alongside gold and salt) to willing buyers along the Mediterranean coast and beyond [127].

In this Chapter, I have given as many examples as possible of absurd PC across a wide range of activities during the second decade of the 21st century. The good news is that some, like EDI, are slowly on their way out, as illustrated in Chapter 7.

Notes

1. Hughes, p 7.
2. *ibid*, p 17.
3. Browne, p 4.

4. *ibid*, p 41.
5. *ibid*, p 30.
6. https://www.eeblanguageproject.com/.
7. Sarah Knapton: *Daily Telegraph*, 14 February 2023.
8. Robert Hughes, quoted by Geoffrey Hughes, p 33.
9. London Library Magazine October 2024, p 12.
10. Craig Simpson: 'Scouts teach eight-year-olds non-binary pronoun game' *Sunday Telegraph* 3 November 2024.
11. Animal Welfare (Sentience) Act 2022: https://www.legislation.gov.uk/ukpga/2022/22.
12. in one of his Italian language *Nota Diplomatica* (23 July 2023) by reference to an article in the *Washington Post*.
13. Ruth Comerford, *Sunday Telegraph* 6 August 2023.
14. Victoria Glendinning: *Trollope* (London: Pimlico Press, 1993), p 166.
15. see Julia Cagé and Valeria Rueda: The Long-term Effects of the Printing Press in sub-Saharan Africa; *American Economic Journal: Applied Economics* 8: 65-99, 2016.
16. see Henry Louis Gates, Jr: *Trials of Phyllis Wheatley: America's First Black Poet and Her Encounters with the Founding Fathers* (Basic Civitas Books, 2010).
17. Steven Edgington: How 'death by paperwork' is killing Home Office, *Sunday Telegraph* 14 January 2024.
18. Anonymous comment *Daily Telegraph* 15 November 2012.
19. Louisa Clarence-Smith: *Daily Telegraph* 7 October 2023.
20. Lucy Burton: 'Civil servants to strike over office work rule' *Daily Telegraph* 6 April 2024.
21. Guy Adams: *Daily Mail* 25 May 2024.
22. Camilla Turner, *Sunday Telegraph* 11 December 2022.
23. Steven Edginton and Gordon Rayner: 'Whitehall "taken over" by woke zealots': *Daily Telegraph* 23 September 2023.
24. Edward Malnick: Top civil servants get bonus to push diversity; *Sunday Telegraph* 11 December 2023.
25. Esther McVey: 'Wasteful Whitehall diversity and inclusion spending will end' *Sunday Telegraph* 12 May 2024.
26. Stephen Edgington and Gordon Rayner: *Daily Telegraph* 22 September 2023.

27. Steven Edgington: 'Civil servant taken to task after saying trans debate has "two sides"' *Sunday Telegraph* 7 January 2024.
28. Steven Edginton: 'Civil servant says children can ignore parents on puberty blockers' *Sunday Telegraph* 14 January 2024.
29. Dominic Penna: 'Transgender civil servant wearing "fetish gear" sparks Whitehall row' *Daily Telegraph* 5 August 2024.
30. Liam Halligan: The Saturday Interview with Kemi Badenoch, *Daily Telegraph* 3 August 2024.
31. Dominic Penna: 'Civil servants on over £100k rises by 40pc in a year' *Daily Telegraph* 10 August 2024.
32. Alex Barton: 'Civil servants sued by colleague over claims transgender people can't change sex' *Daily Telegraph* 22 October 2024.
33. Ella Whelan: 'The civil service is becoming a cesspit of intolerance and censorship' *Daily Telegraph* 24 October 2024.
34. Ethan Croft: 'Civil Service ends "climate of fear" trans policy' *Sunday Telegraph* 12 January 2025.
35. Nick Gutteridge, Eric Williams and Ruby Cline: 'Number of civil servants at their desks has fallen since Labour came to power, leaving the private sector to pick up the slack.' *Daily Telegraph*, 3 December 2024.
36. *Daily Telegraph* 28 December 2024.
37. Camilla Tominey: *Daily Telegraph* 7 December 2024.
38. Dieter Snepvangers: 'Thousands of council staff allowed to "work from beach"' *Daily Telegraph* 30 December 2024.
39. Amy Gibbons: 'Working from home is bad for grumpy old colleagues' *Daily Telegraph* 7 December 2014.
40. Nick Gutteridge: 'Civil servants allowed to "work from the beach"' *Sunday Telegraph* 16 February 2025.
41. How wokery has derailed HS2, *Daily Mail* 30 September 2023.
42. Fraser Nelson: 'There's a chilling new punishment for those who question certain "facts". It's 'political correction': the narrowing of debate by fact-checking bodies that purport to defend truth' *Daily Telegraph* 11 May 2023.
43. Steven Edginton: 'Critics believe guidelines act as mechanism to maintain "groupthink" and promote controversial ideas', *Daily Telegraph*, 29 January 2024.

44. Andrew Levy: 'BBC hires "head of belonging" on £125,000 salary' *Daily Mail* 8 March 2025.
45. Rakib Ehsan: The obsession with 'diversity' is putting Britain in danger, *Daily Telegraph* 13 February 2024.
46. Andrew Neil: 'Incompetence. Stupidity. And reckless squandering', *Daily Mail*, 10 February, 2024.
47. Connor Stringer: 'RAF squadron drops "Crusaders" nickname after complaint it is offensive to Muslims' *Daily Telegraph* 29 July 2024.
48. Charles Moore: 'Net Zero is the NHS's latest excuse to skip work' *Daily Telegraph* 7 Oct 2023.
49. [Gareth Corfield: 'NHS staff ordered to apologise for using "wrong" pronouns under trust trans policy': *Daily Telegraph* 27 May 2024.
50. J Meirion Thomas: *Daily Telegraph* 24 July 2024.
51. Laura Donnelly: *Daily Telegraph* 16 August 2024.
52. Laura Donnelly: *Sunday Telegraph* 4 August 2024.
53. Charlotte Gill: *Sunday Telegraph* 3 December 2023.
54. Gareth Corfield: 'NHS staff ordered to apologise for using "wrong" pronouns under trust trans policy': *Daily Telegraph* 27 May 2024.
55. Max Stephens: *Sunday Telegraph* 1 September 2024.
56. Sanchez Manning: 'University staff "feel coerced" to sign anti-transphobic pledge' *Sunday Telegraph* 9 June 2024.
57. Sanchez Manning: 'Discuss how whiteness is a problem, dons told' *Sunday Telegraph* 16 June 2024.
58. Charlotte Gill: 'Taxpayer foots £1.5m bill to 'decolonise' folk music' *Sunday Telegraph* 23 June 2024.
59. Furedi, p 142.
60. Charlotte Gill: '"Coloniality" study in early years' *Sunday Telegraph* 16 June 2024.
61. Charlotte Gill: 'Poledancing study paid for by taxpayers' *Sunday Telegraph* 30 June 2024.
62. Charlotte Gill: 'Charity's "decolonise" contraception plan' *Sunday Telegraph* 30 June 2024.
63. Laura Donnelly: 'Psychology students in "segregated" race classes' *Sunday Telegraph* 19 January 2025.
64. Furedi, pp 138 and 139.
65. Craig Simpson: *Sunday Telegraph* 1 September 2024.

66. Connor Stringer: 'University Dracula project sucks up taxpayers' money' *Sunday Telegraph* 2 June 2024.
67. Louisa Clarence-Smith: 'Top mathematicians warn curriculum being "politicised" with diversity guidance' *Daily Telegraph* 23 May 2023.
68. Neil Johnston: 'Oxbridge moves away from exams to boost results of minorities' *Sunday Telegraph* 26 January 2025.
69. Daniel Hannan, *Sunday Telegraph* 3 September 2023.
70. Daniel Martin: 'Britain's diversity drive has back-fired' *Daily Telegraph* 20 March 2024.
71. Lucy Burton: 'Inside the plot to take back control from diversity zealots' *Daily Telegraph* 6 May 2024.
72. Nick Gutteridge: 'Whitehall bill for "nonsense" hits £6 billion' *Sunday Telegraph* 15 December 2024.
73. Nick Timothy: 'The UK's success as a multiracial democracy is not in spite of our history, but directly because of it' *Sunday Telegraph* 19 March 2023.
74. Zoe Strimpel: *Sunday Telegraph* Features 20 October 2024.
75. Kate Andrews: 'The US has dropped diversity targets – will Britain cling on?' *Daily Telegraph* 11 January 2025.
76. Natasha Leake: '£65,000 bill for diversity drive at trade body's bank' *Daily Telegraph* 11 January 2025.
77. Connor Stringer: 'Diversity schemes "cost promising recruit a job in air traffic control"' *Daily Telegraph* 1 February 2025.
78. Tim Sigsworth: 'Firemen are too male and too white, say chiefs' *Daily Telegraph* 22 February 2025.
79. Laura Donnelly: 'Health Secretary says staff boasted of "anti-whiteness" as part of "daft" equality and inclusion agenda' *Daily Telegraph* 4 February 2025.
80. Tim Sigsworth: 'Mothers still "birthing people" as NHS defies Streeting crackdown' *Sunday Telegraph* 2 March 2025.
81. Ethan Croft and Sam Ashworth-Hayes: 'Go green and embrace diversity to win public contracts, firms told' *Sunday Telegraph* 23 February 2025.
82. Suella Braverman: 'Equality before the law is now well and truly over' *Daily Telegraph* 6 March 2025.
83. see Furedi, pp 165–166.
84. Scruton, p 6 *et seq.*
85. Simon Johnson: 'Children prefer Dahl and Blyton unsanitised, says McCall Smith' *Daily Telegraph* 27 August 2024.

86. *Evening Standard* 6 September 2023.
87. Charlotte Gill: We don't want able-bodied, white stories, say agents; *Sunday Times* 10 September 2023.
88. Craig Simpson: 'Belloc's comic verse given warning for "hurtful" rhymes *Sunday Telegraph* 7 April 2024.
89. Madeline Fry Schultz: 'Woke books and sensitivity readers have destroyed publishing' *Daily Telegraph* 19 December 2023.
90. 8 December 2024.
91. Ewan Somerville: Public libraries prioritising 'trans books'; *Sunday Telegraph* 29 October 2023.
92. Craig Simpson: Gender-critical works 'treated like Hitler's Mein Kampf'; *Sunday Telegraph* 29 October 2023.
93. Craig Simpson: *Daily Telegraph* 27 March 2024.
94. Rakib Ehsan: 'Even library buildings aren't safe from the woke witch-hunt' *Daily Telegraph* 20 August 2024.
95. Ben Lawrence: 'Books are being banned across Britain. We are not as tolerant as we pretend' *Daily Telegraph* 21 August 2024.
96. Blathnaid Corless: 'Tate puts trigger warning on puppet show' *Daily Telegraph* 6 January 2024.
97. Craig Simpson: 'Help children to explore their gender identity, museums told' *Daily Telegraph* 12 September 2023.
98. Madeline Grant: 'Our culture is in the hands of people who hate it' *Daily Telegraph* 22 June 2024.
99. Michael Mosbacher: 'Museums should be custodians of history, not climate evangelists' *Daily Telegraph* 13 September 2024.
100. Furedi, p 149.
101. Craig Simpson: 'Aberdeen gallery renames art said to have "unacceptable" titles' *Sunday Telegraph* 10 November 2024.
102. Anita Singh: 'Gallery takes classic works down for more contemporary ones and also updates labels to emphasise roles of slavery, colonialism, and racism' *Daily Telegraph* 23 May 2023.
103. Craig Simpson: 'Photography has sexist and colonial past, claims Tate Gallery' *Daily Telegraph* 23 November 2024.
104. Craig Simpson: 'Albert Memorial is "offensive" for its Victorian views, says Royal Parks' *Sunday Telegraph* 21 July 2024.
105. Furedi, p 77.

106. Craig Simpson; 'Highgate to dig into "empire links" of graves' *Sunday Telegraph* 21 January 2024.
107. Michael Deacon: 'Why is the Church of England so horrified by "whiteness"?' *Daily Telegraph* 26 March 2024.
108. Peter Stanford; 'The Anglican "doom spiral"' *Sunday Telegraph* (Sunday section) 31 March 2024.
109. Janet Eastham: 'We're more of community and less of a church, say Anglicans' *Daily Telegraph* 17 August 2024.
110. Craig Simpson: 'God is not a white man, declare Church of England clergy in Jesus diversity drive' *Daily Telegraph* 9 November 2024.
111. Tom Sigsworth: 'Church to pay racial justice worker double salary of its vicars' *Sunday Telegraph* 22 September 2024.
112. Celia Walden: 'Woke carols are the latest sign of a church that's lost faith in its convictions' *Daily Telegraph* 24 December 2024.
113. Craig Simpson: *Daily Telegraph* 1 November 2023.
114. Charles Pasternak, ed: *Evaluating a Pandemic* (World Scientific Publishing 2024, p xiv).
115. Camilla Turner: 'How Covid vaccine sceptics were "debanked" because of their views' *Sunday Telegraph* 19 January 2025.
116. Katie Morley: *Daily Telegraph* 24 August 2023.
117. Richard Fothergill: 'Not even Reverends like me are safe from the banks' woke purge' *Daily Telegraph* 25 July 2023.
118. Camilla Turner: '"Woke" Bank of England tells staff to share their pronouns' *Sunday Telegraph* 1 September 2024.
119. Robert Mendick: 'Bank worker "sacked for not being diverse enough"' *Daily Telegraph* 6 January 2024.
120. Furedi, pp 133 and 134.
121. Alison Pearson: *Daily Telegraph*, 9 Feb 2023.
122. Scientific names need to reflect the values of today: *Nature* **640**: 857, 2025.
123. Guilherme S T Garbino: *Nature* **616**: 433, 2023.
124. Furedi, p 76.
125. *ibid*, p 75.
126. Craig Simpson: 'Cambridge to "decolonise the dodo" in taxpayer-backed project' *Daily Telegraph* 31 March 2024.
127. see Levtzion.

Chapter 6

Free Speech

'Freedom is the open window through which pours the sunlight of the human spirit and human dignity'.

Words spoken by Herbert Hoover, 31st President of the United States, on his 90th birthday in 1964.

In his idiosyncratic opus, *There's No Such Thing as Free Speech and it's a Good Thing, Too*, American literary theorist Stanley Fish considers that '... "Free Speech" is just the name we give to verbal behaviour that serves the substantive agendas we wish to advance; and we give our preferred verbal behaviours *that* name when we can, when we have the power to do so ... the label "free speech" is the one you want your favourites to wear. Free speech, in short, is not an independent value but a political prize ...' [1]. Fish is right in so far as the ability to express one's opinions freely depends on their nature and on the mood of the authorities at the time.

In the Greece of the 5th century BCE, for example, Euripides and Aristophanes could ridicule all and sundry. Outside the amphitheatre, one had to be more circumspect. Although a man could argue about any topic in the spirit of Athenian democracy, it behoved him to bear in mind the fate of Socrates: condemned to death in 399 BCE for impiety and corrupting the young. Two millennia on, by which time the Church of Rome had become all-powerful, any views inconsistent with its dogma were off limits. Giordano Bruno, originally a Dominican friar, subsequently a Calvinist, was inspired by the ideas of Copernicus and more. He considered the stars to be distant suns, each encircled by its own planets, a suggestion said to have been hinted at by the 5th-century BCE Greek philosopher Anaxagoras. (It was only in 1925 that Cecilia Payne [2], a research student who moved from Cambridge in England to Radcliffe College of Harvard University, showed in her PhD thesis that stars had the same consistency as the Sun. Her work was subsequently described by astronomer Otto Struve as 'the most brilliant PhD thesis ever written in astronomy' [3].)

Bruno antagonised the Inquisition in other ways. His remark that 'Perhaps your fear of passing judgement on me is greater than my fear in receiving it' [4] fell on deaf ears, and he was burned alive at the stake together with his books in Rome in 1600. If you supported the heliocentric view of Galileo Galilei – whose work became 'a keystone of modern science' [5] – in any Italian university during the 17th century, you were in trouble. Yet elsewhere, universities continued to live by standards such as those enshrined in the 14th-century Jagiellonian University of Krakow: *Plus ratio quam vis* (Let reason prevail over force). We are returning to former times by silencing the views of academics and students who oppose the current dogma.

One of the first actions of the National Constituent Assembly that was inaugurated at the start of the French Revolution was to guarantee freedom of speech and thought. Within a few years, that noble objective had already been forgotten, and the books of Voltaire, originally a hero of the Revolution, were being burned once again. As recently as the mid 19th century, the writer and cleric Sir Leslie Stephen (father of Virginia Woolf) argued for the destruction of 'poisonous' works, even though it 'would be equivalent to the suppression, not of this or that theory, but of thought [itself]' [6].

For several years, the ideas of Karl Marx were debating points. But in Russia, after 1917, they became the central dogma of the state. Communism, of course, is not the utopia Marx envisioned. As we know, it proved to be – not just in Russia but in adherents like China, North Korea, Cuba, Angola and Mozambique (the latter two between 1975 and 1992) – a totally repressive form of government that denies its people freedom to express themselves by speech or script.

From curtailing free speech in the Free World, it is but a short step to curtailing freedom of action. In previous chapters, I have shown how museums and art galleries, libraries and publishing houses, churches and civic authorities (in regard to the display of statues and memorials) have fallen victim to the warped dogma of 'sensitivity, diversity and inclusion'. Artistic expression in the form of dance is not immune, as choreographer Rosie Kay has found. 'A culture of self-censorship and groupthink has become normalised, which fundamentally damages the arts. The demand for ideological compliance and the avoidance of controversy is impoverishing our institutions which were once spaces for free thought and open debate. This intolerant activism is now an existential threat to the arts'. To tackle this, she has set up a project entitled Freedom in the Arts [7]. Good luck to her.

Language

The 17th-century philosopher John Locke considered speech to be 'the great bond that holds society together' and through language, 'knowledge is conveyed from man to man and down the generations' [8]. A century later, Samuel Taylor Coleridge made the same point. 'The care of the national language I consider as at all times a sacred trust and a most important privilege of the higher orders of society. ... A nation which allows her language to go to ruin is parting with the last of her intellectual independence, and testifies her willingness to cease to exist' [9]. Frank Furedi warns that 'The Culture Wars today are so intertwined with conflicts over words because language reflects the norms and beliefs that underpin culture' [10]. Trans ideologists and others now challenge those norms.

For example, the word 'female', in use since the 14th century meaning 'woman' or 'girl' according to *The Oxford English Dictionary*, should now be applied to trans-women whereas trans-men are now 'male'; cis-women may still be called 'female'. Then, there's the *Inclusive Language Guide*, published by the Local Government Association (LGA) of England, which considers the words 'mum' and 'dad' to be 'unacceptable' [11]. The suggested alternative of 'birthing parent' lacks the ring of informality and does not enhance the English language.

The World Intellectual Property Organisation (WIPO), a United Nations agency based in Geneva which protects patents and trademarks globally, has ruled that using 'masculine-specific' terms risks giving the impression that 'women are not represented in certain groups'. 'Brotherhood of man' and 'Forefathers' are clearly out. 'Cave dwellers' (for 'Cavemen'), 'Wood chopper' ('Lumberjack') and 'Ordinary citizen' ('Man in the street') are fairly obvious replacements. But 'Faithful dog' for 'Man's best friend'? They're still struggling with 'Sportsmanlike' [12]. Perhaps 'Sportspersonlike' is after all too clumsy for the scholarly members of the WIPO. Hunting alternatives for 'problematic patriarchal connotations' may be good fun and provide a new parlour game, but is this really the best use of the UN's limited resources when we could be on the cusp of World War 3?

Hate Speech

Censorship – the opposite of free speech – has been around since ancient times. In today's deluded world, it is being pursued by the ideologues of political correctness. An opinion such as 'there are only two sexes', that many would consider an obvious fact, is considered by others to constitute 'hate speech' [13] and hence to be condemned.

A good example of hate speech in the UK were the fascist exhortations of Sir Oswald Mosley during the 1920s and 1930s. Today, voicing a fact of nature such as the one just mentioned, or 'trans-women are biologically male', is considered hate speech. The trans lobby among students at universities (as mentioned in relation to Kathleen Stock in Chapter 1) is particularly vociferous in this regard. Anyone expressing such views in public should be cancelled. So, it is not surprising that when Helen Joyce, whose sensible views concerning gender change were mentioned in Chapter 4, was invited to speak at Gonville and Caius College in Cambridge on the subject of sex and gender, its students tried to cancel her appearance. Worse, the Master and Senior Tutor attempted to disrupt the meeting by accusing Joyce of views 'offensive, insulting and hateful to members of our community' [14].

Anthony Stevens, a local councillor from Wellingborough, Northamptonshire, was arrested at his home because of a 'hate crime'. What was the nature of the crime? He had shared a video showing the arrest of a Christian street preacher, Oluwole Ilisanmi, in 2019. The preacher's bible had been snatched by the police, who accused him of Islamophobia. He was taken miles away before being de-arrested and left with no means to get home (Ilisanmi was later awarded £2,500 for wrongful arrest). As Stevens pointed out, 'The accusation of racial hatred is ridiculous and insulting. My only crime has been supporting the only black local councillor in Northamptonshire'. Toby Young, director of the Free Speech Union, agrees. 'Northamptonshire police have made a serious mistake in this case. Defending free speech isn't a crime and Cllr Stevens should never have been arrested, let alone held in custody for 9 hours' [15].

Hate speech is a problem only outside the USA. Here, there is no such thing because free speech is enshrined in the First Amendment. This 'prevents the government from making laws that: regulate an establishment of religion; prohibit the free exercise of religion; abridge the freedom of speech, the freedom of the press, the freedom of assembly, or the right to petition the government for redress of grievances'. But according to feminist scholar Catharine MacKinnon, the efficacy of the First Amendment has changed. 'Legally what was ... a shield for radicals, artists and activists, socialists and pacifists, the excluded and the dispossessed, has now become a sword for authoritarians, racists and misogynists, Nazis and Klansmen, pornographers and corporations buying elections' [16]. Nevertheless, philosopher Sam Harris opines that 'if I could wave a magic wand and give everyone the First Amendment, I would' [17].

However, even in the USA, speech – or rather instruction – on topics that might offend someone is restricted. So, for example, the principal of Tallahassee Classical School in Florida was fired from her post because of complaints from parents that their children had been shown Botticelli's 'Birth of Venus' and Michaelangelo's 'David' and 'Creation of Adam' (all, of course, in the nude). The topic of the class? Renaissance Art [18].

Restricting Free Speech

Ai Weiwei, the charismatic Chinese artist and critic of the regime who fled his country in 2015, has warned of the decline of free speech in the free world. 'Freedom of the press and expression is integral to freedom of speech ... when these freedoms are curtailed or eliminated, society stagnates, akin to stagnant water emitting a foul odour and incapable of sustaining life'. He challenges the lack of freedom of expression today. When individuals 'cannot express their opinions freely, questioning serves as a catalyst for critical thinking'. He warns against the power of artificial intelligence (AI) to limit critical thinking. Instead, it provides answers to everything, based on knowledge without feeling, experience or inspiration. 'The advancement of AI technology had transformed into a powerful tool, capable of monopolising and controlling existing knowledge and information. Its rapid processing and authoritative knowledge dissemination pose a threat to individual thinking abilities, representing a danger to humanity's development' [19].

The concept of freedom to think, to speak and to act as we like, provided it is within the law of the land, is gradually being eroded throughout the world. An international non-governmental organisation based in London called Article 19, founded in 1987, 'works for a world where all people everywhere can freely express themselves and actively engage in public life without fear of discrimination. We do this by working on ... the Freedom to Speak and the Freedom to Know'. That freedom is in sharp decline. In 2023, Article 19 reported that 6.3 billion people living in 81 countries have less freedom than they had a decade earlier. Most of them live in countries that are rated as 'restricted', 'highly restricted' or 'in crisis'. Only 13% of the world's population now lives in countries rated as 'free' [20]. These include the USA and Canada, Australia and New Zealand, Japan and South Korea, a few in South America and most European countries (of which the UK ranks near the bottom).

The situation has deteriorated since then. In Brazil, the largest democracy in Latin America, a judge has banned X (formerly Twitter) because some of its content was critical of the government. Asked to remove this, the owner of X – Elon Musk – refused. Hence the ban. This means that anyone wishing to express their view, for which X has been an appropriate platform used by 22 million subscribers, will no longer be able to do so. A clear abrogation of free speech. Columnist Andrew Neill notes that 'We have come a long way since the days we thought progress was best served by allowing all manner of opinions to be expressed, to be tested by time, events, argument and scrutiny, with the best emerging triumphant to guide us forward. Now we have a ruling elite, increasingly dominant in public life, which is hostile to free speech if it means the expression of opinions of which it disapproves. ... Of course we're still a free society compared to the dictatorships. But bit by bit our freedoms are being eroded, above all when it comes to free speech' [21].

Non-Crime Hate Incident

Anyone can now be investigated (though not necessarily charged) for a non-crime hate incident (NCHI). Journalist Allison Pearson was just getting up on Remembrance Sunday in 2024 when two young police officers arrived at her house. She was accused of a non-crime hate incident regarding something she had posted on X a year ago and was 'invited to attend a voluntary interview on the matter'. The police officers would not tell her what the offending article was about, or who had reported it. The Free Speech Union's Toby Young commented that 'it's little wonder that 93% of car-related crimes went unsolved in Essex last year. The local officers are too busy policing journalists' tweets to police their streets' [22].

Columnist Daniel Hannan takes up the issue of Allison Pearson's subjection to police inquiry. 'This really has become a country where freedom of speech has become subordinated to the presumed sensibilities of minorities, and where saying the wrong thing, even if you have plainly not incited anyone or risked public disorder, can bring the cops to your door. ... Perhaps there was never a golden age of free speech, only an interregnum between the old religious ascendancy and the new trinity of Diversity, Equality, Inclusion ...' Hannan is clear in his view concerning the role of Police Crime Commissioners. 'If the duty of a PCC ... is to hold the police to account, the role of the press is to uphold free expression' [23].

Hate speech can include voicing a scientifically correct opinion. In 2024, Murdo Fraser, a Member of the Scottish Parliament (MSP), was reported to the police for saying that 'choosing to identify as "non-binary" is as valid as choosing to identify as a cat'. Police Scotland judged that the post was not a crime but still logged it as an NCHI, without telling Mr Fraser. His lawyers have stressed that additional safeguards were needed to protect freedom of speech [24]. Reporter Janet Eastham comments that the press watchdog's ruling in favour of a trans writer amounts to a negation of free speech. It concerns a complaint by author June Dawson that the Independent Press Standards Organisation (IPSO) ruling – regarding the description of a trans author as 'a man who claims to be a woman – breached the (Spectator) Editor's Code of Practice. [25]. On the other hand, we must accept that trans-women, such as Jan Morris, who have taken on a completely feminine role, deserve to be referred to as 'she' and hence as a 'woman' (see Chapter 4).

The police have been Investigating non-crime hate incidents for some time. Currently, more than 50 NCHIs are reported to the police in England and Wales *every day*. In 2019, the author Julie Bindel was visited at her home and told that they were investigating a hate incident attributed to her. The nature of the event or who had reported it were not revealed but she was invited to attend a police station. She refused to do so and the case was eventually dropped, but as she points out, 'A criminal record is a serious issue and can have a terrible effect on a person's livelihood, reputation and self-esteem. Police coming after those of us that do nothing more than speak the truth about gender madness and refuse to bend the knee to the crazy cultists, are doing a massive public disservice' [26].

Others agree. The chief leader writer for the *Observer*, Sonia Sodha, considers that 'The police have an appalling record when it comes to policing speech. Any liberal who cares about our fundamental democratic rights should be worried about it'. Donna Jones, a former chief police and crime commissioner, admits that 'police officers should not go to people's homes over offensive online posts. If the police determine it's not a crime, it's not a hate crime, then they should not be going and knocking on someone's door and encouraging them to come in for a voluntary interview' [27].

A former head of MI6, Sir Richard Dearlove, considers that 'officers shouldn't be wasting their time on these sorts of issues. ... I think those of us who have grown up in an era of free speech just can't understand the way things have developed. It's extraordinary. There are other ways of tracking extremism and I don't think doing stuff which prejudices people's freedom of speech is a sensible starting point'. Lord Stevens, a former Met commissioner concurs. 'If it's the activities of the Iranian Revolutionary Guard Corps in the UK or serious stuff to do with Hamas, that's what they should be looking at. ... We need officers on the streets for prioritising things like knife crime and violence' [28].

One cannot help being reminded of a possible future as imagined by George Orwell in his novel *1984*, published in 1948. 'A day never passed when spies and saboteurs ... were not unmasked by the Thought Police ... Winston's hatred was ... turned against ... the Thought Police; and at such moments his heart went out to the lonely, derided heretic ..., sole guardian of truth and sanity in a world of lies. ... The Thought Police would get him ... He had committed ... the essential crime that contained all others in itself. Thoughtcrime, they called it. Thoughtcrime was not a thing that could be concealed for ever. You might dodge it successfully for a while, even for years, but sooner or later they were bound to get you. ... You were abolished, annihilated: *vapourized* was the usual word' [29].

Fifteen years before Orwell wrote his story, Aldous Huxley in *Brave New World* (1932) had speculated on life – in this case, 600 years into the future – under an autocracy of a different kind. This is eugenics brought to its most extreme form. People are no longer born in a mother's womb, but raised artificially. Though sexual relations between male and female are the norm, extreme contraceptive methods are mandated to prevent a natural birth. Instead, fertilisation is achieved by mixing millions of donor ova and sperm in a dish. Words like 'mother' and 'father' do not apply and are actually proscribed. Huxley, of course, had no idea that IVF (in vitro fertilisation) would be achieved in the late 1970s (as the first stage for treating infertility). In *Brave New World*, the fertilised embryos are cultivated in bottles all the way to babies. Although this has not yet been achieved, a recent experiment with sheep [30] shows that a premature human baby might in the future be brought to term outside the womb. In Huxley's story, the growing embryos are selected for, and indeed treated with chemicals to achieve, persons of differing IQ: from elite *alphas* and *betas* – at the top of society – to lowly *gammas*, *deltas* and *epsilons* at the bottom. People are no longer free to act as they will but are circumscribed by *alpha* men (such as the 'Resident World Controller for Western Europe').

For example, '"A New Theory of Biology" was the title of the paper which Mustapha Mond', Director of Hatcheries and Conditioning, 'had just finished reading. He ... wrote across the title page, "The author's mathematical treatment of the conception of purpose is novel and highly ingenious, but heretical and, so far as the present social order is concerned, dangerous and potentially subversive. *Not to be published.* ... The author will be kept under supervision. ... ." A pity, he thought, as he signed his name. It was a masterly piece of work.

But once you began explanations in terms of purpose – well, you didn't know what the result might be. It was the sort of idea that might easily de-condition the more unsettled minds among the higher castes – make them lose their faith in happiness as the Sovereign Good and take to believing, instead, that the goal was somewhere outside the present human sphere; that the purpose of life was not the maintenance of well-being, but some intensification and refining of consciousness, some enlargement of knowledge' [31]. So, Huxley foresaw today's 'sensitivity readers' by almost a century.

An early warning sign already exists with the Hate Crime and Public Disorder (Scotland) Act that was promoted by Scotland's First Minister Humza Yousaf. It took effect from 1 April 2024 (All Fools Day). But it's no joke. Anyone who feels that they have been affronted in any way will be able to report you – anonymously if they wish – to one of more than 400 centres (that include a Glasgow sex shop). Your word will be proof enough. In other words, 'if I think what you said is a hate crime, it's a hate crime' [32].

Universities

Matters are particularly acute in universities, despite the fact that one of their main functions is surely the free debate of novel ideas. As the then Education Secretary Gavin Williamson pointed out in 2023, 'It is a basic human right to be able to express ourselves freely and take part in rigorous debate ... Our legal system allows us to articulate views which others may disagree with... this must be defended, nowhere more so than within our world renowned universities'. Journalist Inaya Folarin Iman agrees. 'The fear to speak freely still haunts university campuses ... brighter, more curious students feel bullied into obedience by a culture that cannot countenance diversity. And that diversity of *thought* must be constantly defended, particularly if liberal philosophy is to be freely discussed among younger generations. ... This is not to speak of the cultural implications. Our literature, arts and music will become increasingly monotonous, with only those artists who share the dictated world view receiving attention. ...' [33].

But the UK and USA are slipping fast. 'Free speech will return to our great universities' says philosopher Arif Ahmed [34]. Let us hope so, but there is little evidence of this at present. The freest universities according to the Global Academic Freedom Index prepared by Friedrich Alexander University in Erlangen, Germany (https://academic-freedom-index.net/),

Free Speech

are in Czechia, Estonia, Belgium, Italy and Germany. The UK is ranked 59th and the USA 74th (figures for 2022).

Not surprising then that no less a university than Harvard has been criticised for the 'Ivory Tower's march towards a monoculture of like-minded, intolerant liberal views'. Or that Florida Governor Ron de Santis has introduced legislation in his state aimed at stopping 'the tactics of liberal elites who suppress free thought in the name of identity politics and indoctrination' [35]. In the UK, the top universities (Russell Group) consider statements like 'everyone can succeed if they work hard enough' or 'the most-qualified person should get the job' to be 'microaggressions.' (Then there's author Maisie Hill's recommendation, when advertising for an assistant, that TERFS, i.e. those who believe in two sexes and might be the best-qualified, are advised not to apply.) Who is being aggressed is not spelt out, but as Dr Edward Skidelsky, director of the Committee for Academic Freedom, has pointed out 'the effect is to undermine a culture of free inquiry' [36].

When the government introduced its Higher Education (Freedom of Speech) Bill 2 years ago, it seemed that Westminster had finally acknowledged the seriousness of the threat to open debate on university campuses. But Bridget Phillipson, the Labour government's Education Secretary, halted the act days before it was due to come into force [37]. Opposition to her action has not been slow in coming. More than 150 academics have signed a letter to the Education Secretary urging her to reconsider her decision. The Free Speech Union is considering taking the government to court if the act is now dropped. Its founder Toby Young has accused the Education Secretary of having 'at a stroke made it virtually impossible for students and academics to challenge radical progressive ideology on campus' [38].

Toby Young was born in 1963, a son of Labour peer Lord Young of Dartington. He studied, sequentially, at the universities of Oxford, Harvard and Cambridge. In 1991, he co-founded the *Modern Review*, publishing popular and cultural articles as its Editor until it ran out of funds 4 years later [39]. He moved to New York where he joined *Vanity Fair* [40]. He also met Caroline Bondy, his future wife with whom he has fathered four children. His time in New York is described with his inimitable combination of humour, ridicule and self-deprecation in a page-turning memoir [41]. He then wrote for the *Sun on Sunday*, *Daily Mail*, *Daily Telegraph* and *Spectator* (of which he subsequently became Associate Editor). He also served as a judge on the television show *Top Chef* and wrote a food column in the *Evening Standard* for 5 years. If these early incursions into journalism and other ventures make him seem a peripatetic amateur, the reader should be aware that Young is also possessed of a singularly sharp mind – witness his gaining first class honours in Philosophy, Politics and Economics at Brasenose College, Oxford in 1986 (to be followed in the same college with exactly the same result by former Prime Minister Lord (David) Cameron a couple of years later).

When I asked Toby what has been his greatest achievement to date, he hesitated before replying 'Probably helping to set up the West London Free School, the first free school to sign a funding agreement with the Department for Education. That was probably the hardest thing I've ever done. Took 2 years of hard labour – 80 hours a week, unpaid'. The school, which caters for 11- to 18-year-old girls and boys, is situated in King Street, Hammersmith. It offers its pupils a classical liberal education, with more than half taking up a musical instrument of one sort or another. All children up to 14 years old study Latin. It was rated 'good' by OFSTED in 2013 and 2017. Despite some criticism regarding turnover of its teaching staff, it is one of the most oversubscribed taxpayer-funded schools in the land. In 2024, the *Sunday Times* named it London Comprehensive of the Year.

In 2020, Young co-founded the Free Speech Union (FSU), of which he is Director. 'The Free Speech Union is a non-partisan, not-for-profit membership organisation that stands up for people whose right to freedom of expression has been violated. Not only do we pressure institutions to uphold their own free speech policies through direct challenges and media scrutiny, but we also litigate when we believe they've acted unlawfully. This work is particularly urgent in the present climate, with people being cancelled every day for daring to challenge the latest ideological dogma, either in the workplace or public square' [42].

One of its first actions was to condemn the Hate Crime and Public Disorder (Scotland) Bill mentioned earlier, though the Act did not come into effect until 2024. The FSU has filed several lawsuits and lobbied the government on behalf of academics. One example of this concerns a law lecturer at the UK's Open University. Dr Almut Gadow voiced concerns over plans by the department of Equality, Diversity and Inclusion to 'incorporate its political ideologies' in order to 'liberate the curriculum' (which illustrates the anomaly to which the purpose of a university has now sunk). As part of her teaching criminal law, she rightly pointed out that 'no offender should be allowed to dictate the language of his case in a way which masks relevant facts'. But her opinions were not sufficiently 'inclusive' or 'trans-friendly' and she lost her job at the university [43]. With the Free Speech Union's support, she eventually won a six-figure settlement from the OU.

Toby Young is clear about his vision for the future of the FSU. 'I want the FSU to become the world's leading human rights group – like Amnesty International, but bigger.

There are now sister organisations in Australia, New Zealand, South Africa and Switzerland and there's soon to be one in Canada' he told me. A noble vision that no one would wish to deprecate. Given Young's recent appointment to the House of Lords and the entrepreneurial qualities that enabled him to set up FSU in the first place, there's every reason to assume that he will be successful.

At least one institution has decided to reaffirm the importance of free speech in a university. More than 650 academics at Oxford have signed an open letter to the Education Secretary outlining their concern: 'free speech duties on universities have long been neglected, despite being enshrined in law'. As a result, the university's vice-chancellor, Professor Irene Tracey, proposes to initiate termly debates on a variety of subjects of which democracy will be the first. 'It is clear we need to reaffirm the importance of free and inclusive speech, diversity of thought and vibrant exchange of ideas. The spirit of these events will be one of examination and exploration, of curiosity and challenge' [44].

The situation in US universities regarding free speech is similar, if not worse, to that in Britain. A recent poll by the American not-for profit Knight Foundation finds that college students consider that the security of free speech rights on campus has declined. Some 6 in 10 students feel that the climate on campus 'prevents some people from saying things they believe, because others might find it offensive', while 7 out of 10 believe that some speech 'can be as damaging as physical violence' [45].

The influence of politicians on freedom of action in universities – a problem almost as old as universities themselves – can be a double-edged sword. In the USA, Florida Governor Ron DeSantis aims to stop 'the tactics of liberal elites who suppress free thought in the name of identity politics and indoctrination'. Good. But the legislation, interpreted broadly, could also 'rule out any activities or even research efforts that seek to mitigate climate change, make birth control more accessible or increase vaccination rates.' Not so good (as far as some are concerned). Irene Mulvey, president of the American Association of University Professors, points out that 'The language is ... deliberately vague, so that people will overcompensate and self-censor, so they won't get into trouble' [46].

Students need to be careful of what they say even in the privacy of their room. Robert Ivinson, a first-year University of Exeter philosophy student, mentioned to a friend on the telephone that he considered veganism to be wrong and gender fluidity stupid. His remarks were overheard by his neighbour who considered them 'offensive' and 'transphobic' and reported Ivinson to the authorities. What did they do? Instead of chastising the neighbour for eavesdropping, Ivinson was placed on a 'behavioural contract' for the remainder of his studies. He received a formal warning and was told that he would be expelled if he broke any other of the university's rules. Edward Skidelsky, director of the Committee for Academic Freedom, considers it 'extraordinary that in 21st-century Britain eavesdroppers can be rewarded, and a student punished for remarks made to a friend in the privacy of his room'. Robert Ivinson put it more bluntly: 'It was like the Stasi had come to my door' [47].

Teachers themselves continue to be under threat (recall the hounding out of Professor Kathleen Stock from the University of Sussex). King's College, a constituent institution within London University, has ruled that staff will not be promoted unless they support its 'pro-trans diversity policy'. They 'should provide evidence of what they have done to promote inclusion, such as participating in activity run by Stonewall, the charity which has come under fire for its support of puberty blockers' [48]. What has this to do with the purpose of a university? The role of its staff is surely to engage in meaningful research and to instruct the students. Box-ticking unrelated topics does not lead to academic excellence.

Several universities in the USA such as Stanford, University of North Caroline at Chapel Hill, Georgetown University in Washington, DC and the University of Florida at Gainesville have been accused of failing to maintain free speech on campus. To counter this trend an organisation called the Foundation for Individual Rights in Education (FIRE) was established in 1999 in order to sponsor legal challenges against colleges and universities that it considers a violation of the First Amendment. Its remit was extended to American society at large in 2022, renaming it the Foundation for Individual Rights and Expression, thus retaining the acronym FIRE. It therefore now competes with the American Civil Liberties Union (ACLU) for funds to support its aims. Some of FIRE's right-wing supporters – as possible members of The Scheme [49] – may have been behind the US Supreme Court's decision on 30 June 2023 to uphold a person's religious belief when it conflicted with LGBTQ policy on same-sex marriage.

The indulgence of some faculty members in the USA towards vociferous students promoting LGBTQ and similar issues has led other academics to create a private, non-profit university devoted to academic freedom in Austin, Texas (UATX) – not to be confused with the 120-year-old state University of Texas at Austin (UTA). UATX, whose sponsors include former President of Harvard Larry Summers, is committed to the 'fearless pursuit of truth' [50].

In the UK, more than 100 academics have formed the London Universities' Council for Academic Freedom. The non-partisan group, which includes Imperial College, King's College London (KCL), the London School of Economics (LSE) and University College London (UCL), 'aims to defend the principles of free enquiry, intellectual diversity and civil discourse, following a spate of free speech rows in recent years and escalating campus rows over the Hamas-Israel war'. The organisation states that '"academic freedom safeguards the pursuit of knowledge and truth, which is central to the mission of higher education" and underpins the knowledge universities can produce in a democracy' [51].

Schools

We should however applaud Education Secretary Bridget Phillipson's proposal to revamp the school curriculum in the light of the riots that occurred across some British cities in early August of 2024. 'Schools will use lessons such as English, ICT (Information and Communication Technology) and maths to "arm" pupils against "putrid conspiracy theories" ... pupils as young as five would be given the critical thinking skills to identify misinformation online under the new plans' [52]. All sounds fine, but should five-year-olds really be given access to online material? In any case, it seems that the teaching unions, that wish to end the rote learning of 'times tables', are going to be the arbiters on the curriculum, in which case future generations will be unable to multiply 8 x 12 without a calculator or to appreciate the difference between 'its' and 'it's'. Equally worrying is the fact that the Department for Education has decided to stop teaching Latin in state schools. Yet as Oxford lecturer Lola Salem has pointed out, 'To study Latin is to grapple with the roots of our own language, to see how ideas and values have been transmitted across centuries. It fosters intellectual curiosity and analytical thinking. These are not esoteric skills for an elite; they are the bedrock of a well-rounded education' [53]. Because so many English words are based in part on Latin (and Greek) prepositions, a knowledge of Latin helps youngsters speak their own language correctly.

Bridget Phillipson's proposed Children's Wellbeing and Schools Bill is in two halves. The first half is a sensible proposal to close illegal schools and to improve the protection of vulnerable children. The second half prevents failing schools from becoming academies, placing them instead under local council control. Yet it is academies – initiated by Tony Blair during the last Labour government – as well as Free Schools (see earlier) that have achieved the best results and are the most oversubscribed schools in the country. Why? Because they are school-led and not subject to the ideological constraints of the Education Union and local government that seek to 'dumb down the curriculum and undermine the three Rs (reading, writing and arithmetic)' [54]. Columnist Charles Moore takes a similar stance. Academies provide a 'a system in which the best talent seeks to answer the greatest need. That is a virtuous circle. It is a mystery of politics that Labour now wants to create a vicious circle of mediocrity instead' [55].

False Speech

Here, I introduce the concept of False Speech – maintaining Fake News or similar falsehoods. For example, if someone were to assert that 'Britain was not invaded by the Normans in 1066' that would be considered as False Speech, since all historical research confirms the statement to be correct. But to contend that 'The Princes in the Tower were murdered by Richard III in the 15th century' would not be False Speech as there is some doubt over the fate of Edward V and his brother Richard, Duke of York.

The contention that 'The Holocaust (the murder of six million Jews and others by the Nazis in World War 2) did not happen' is False Speech. Moving on to today's deluded world, the statement that 'Israel deliberately targets Palestinian civilians in their attempt to eliminate members of Hamas' is considered likewise to be False Speech. This conclusion is supported by the views of the High-Level Military Group (HLMG), an independent body of former chiefs of staff, senior military officers and cabinet ministers from NATO countries. They write that 'We gained insight into the IDF (Israeli Defence Force) military justice and accountability mechanisms and found them consistent with the highest standards of our own armed forces' [56]. Moreover, the unavoidable deaths of civilians in order to bring a major conflict to its end appear to be justified by international criteria. During World War 2, between 300,000 and 600,000 German civilians were killed by allied bombs from 1940 onwards, plus some 20,000 French civilians during the invasion of Normandy in 1944. The victorious allies were not prosecuted for such unavoidable loss of life. Nor were they indicted for the bombing of Hiroshima and Nagasaki.

Free Thought

Physiologists have shown that the nervous system consists of two arms. One that originates in the brain (autonomic) and sends impulses to the rest of the body – causing movement of limbs, beating of the heart and so forth – and one that receives external impulses through sound and sight, taste and touch (sensory). Thinking is somewhat similar. Some thoughts arise in the brain – such as the 18th century philosopher René Descartes's *cogito ergo sum* (I think therefore I am), though psychologist Simon McCarthy-Jones considers this wrong in so far it is not 'I' who thinks but our brain [57]. To what extent Descartes considered this distinction significant is debatable.

Other thoughts are triggered by what we hear and see. Reading a book or enjoying a view of the countryside brings new thoughts into our mind. Reading, of course, as McCarthy-Jones reminds us [58], is a reflection about what we read rather than the act of reading itself. Stimulating thoughts brought into our mind by nature is most effective when it is accompanied by movement [59]. I can think of no better example than that of Charles Darwin walking along the Sandwalk at his home Down House in Kent, when he formulated the theory of evolution by natural selection.

Such thoughts are essentially 'free' in that they result from activities carried out at our behest. In autocratic regimes, they are not. External triggers to thinking are deliberately forced into our consciousness by the government's propaganda machine. Chairman Mao's China and Stalin's Soviet Union of half a century ago are good examples of regimes in which freedom of thought (and expression) was restricted. This endures under Presidents Xi Jinping and Vladimir Putin, despite the fact that Freedom of Thought was enshrined in Article 18 of the 1948 UN Universal Declaration of Human Rights. Even in the free world, we are sometimes unaware of how external impulses affect our thought and consequential actions. In *The Hidden Persuaders* (1957), Vance Packard showed how corporations use subliminal stimuli to advertise their goods and services.

McCarthy-Jones asserts that freedom of thought 'is necessary for us to have an autonomous mind that is sovereign over itself ... By releasing us from the yoke of fallible authority, freedom of thought gives individuals and society the best chance of finding truth' [60]. But the development of artificial intelligence (AI), which is becoming cheaper by the day [61] threatens this. AI may well prove effective in identifying the origin of metastatic cancer cells [62], predicting the weather [63] or discovering new drugs – particularly by Africans for Africans in Africa [64] – but its influence on our minds [65], especially in the hands of a malign autocracy, is unpredictable.

'The idea that machines should think for us may be the last thought we ever have. *Homo sapiens sapiens* will have been a brief candle flittering in the darkness between ape and AI' [66]. On the other hand, futurist Ray Kurzwell envisages the possibility of hybrids of humans and AI [67] (See also [68] and [69]).

How to avoid such outcomes? 'We need to develop a culture of free thought ... which occurs most effectively in groups, when we think aloud together ... It means seeing people as networked creatures imbedded in communities of thinking' which would 'benefit from shifting away from competitive enquiry, in which one person is attempting to persuade another, and towards collaborative enquiry, in which multiple people are seeking the truth together. ... We need to re-establish a civil society with institutions that promote free thought ... Only by protecting free thought will we walk, not fall, into the future' [70]. Wise words indeed.

This chapter began with a definition of freedom. The freedom to write and speak your mind, whether in university or any organisation that subscribes to the real (as opposed to the deluded) principles of Equality, Diversity and Inclusion, is a hallmark of democracy. The leaders of the Free World must ensure that this remains the case.

Notes

1. Fish, p 102.
2. Moore, Donovan: *What Stars Are Made Of: The Life of Cecilia Payne-Gaposchkin* (Cambridge, MA: Harvard University Press, 2020).
3. https://www.amnh.org/learn-teach/curriculum-collections/cosmic-horizons-book/cecilia-payne-profile#:~:text=Horizons%20Curriculum%20Collection-,Cecilia%20Payne%20and%20the%20Composition%20of%20the%20Stars,and%20explained%20in%20her%20Ph.
4. Berkovitz, p 75.
5. Rovelli, p 35.
6. Berkowitz, p 155.
7. Rosie Kay: 'I saw cancel culture in the arts up close and had to act' *Evening Standard* 1 February 2024.
8. quoted by Furedi, p 156.
9. Coleridge, S T: *The Collected Works of Samuel Taylor Coleridge*, Vol. 10: *On the Constitution of Church and State* (ed J Colmer). (Princeton: Princeton University Press, 1976 [1829]) pp 69, 43.
10. Furedi, p 158.
11. *ibid*, p 156.

12. Celia Walden: 'It's tempting to keep on laughing at this kind of idiocy, but it's dogmatism of the most dangerous kind and we must treat it as such' *Daily Telegraph* 9 September 2024.
13. Defined by the Cambridge Dictionary as 'public speech that expresses hate or encourages violence towards a person or group based on something such as race, religion, sex, or sexual orientation'.
14. Robert Tombs: 'Labour's war against freedom of speech is built on a lie' *Daily Telegraph* 24 August 2024.
15. Louisa Clarence-Smith: 'Tory councillor arrested for "hate crime" after sharing video criticising police' *Sunday Telegraph* 27 August 2023.
16. Berkowitz, p 294.
17. *Evening Standard* 30 November 2023.
18. David Aaronovitch: 'Censorship to avoid causing offence is still just censorship'; *Evening Standard* 22 August 2023.
19. Martin Robinson: 'Exile, censorship and art: Ai Weiwei lets rip' *Evening Standard* 9 February 2024.
20. https://www.article19.org/resources/the-global-expression-report-2023/.
21. Adrew Neill: *Daily Mail* 7 September 2024.
22. Charles Hymas: 'Telegraph writer in "Kafkaesque" hate crime inquiry' *Daily Telegraph* 13 November 2024.
23. Daniel Hannan: 'Britain's liberal reputation has been trampled by the bleak reality of our DEI police state' *Sunday Telegraph* 24 November 2024.
24. Simon Johnson: *Daily Telegraph* 13 November 2024.
25. Janet Eastham: 'Press watchdog accused of chilling effect on free speech over trans writer ruling' *Daily Telegraph* 10 December 2024.
26. Julie Bindell: *Sunday Telegraph* 17 November 2024.
27. Ethan Croft: 'It may be us after Pearson, journalists warn' *Sunday Telegraph* 17 November 2024.
28. Nick Gutteridge and Henry Bodkin: *Sunday Telegraph* 17 November 2024.
29. Orwell, pp 12–17.
30. Max Kozlov: Human trials of artificial wombs could start soon. *Nature* **621**: 458–460, 2023
31. Huxley, 1932: chap XII, p 208.
32. Andrew Neil: *Daily Mail* 30 March 2024.
33. *Sunday Telegraph*, 30 April 2023.
34. *Daily Telegraph* 27 March 2024.

35. https://www.flgov.com/eog/news/press/2023/governor-desantis-elevates-civil-discourse-and-intellectual-freedom.
36. Louisa Clarence-Smith: 'Saying "hire the most-qualified person" is a microaggression' *Daily Telegraph* 24 February 2024.
37. Poppy Wood and Nick Gutteridge: 'Free speech "in peril" after law tackling cancel culture is shelved' *Daily Telegraph* 27 July 2024.
38. Poppy Wood: 'Scrapping of law to protect free speech on campus faces legal challenge' *Daily Telegraph* 3 August 2024.
39. Young, pp 22 and 26.
40. *ibid*, pp 17, 28 and 29.
41. Young, 2001.
42. https://freespeechunion.org/.
43. Louisa Clarence-Smith, *Daily Telegraph*, 19 August 2023.
44. Poppy Wood: 'The new Sheldonian debates will celebrate "curiosity and challenge", says vice-chancellor' *Daily Telegraph* 8 October 2024.
45. Emma Camp, writing in the magazine *Reason* that is published by the Reason Foundation, on 31 July 2024.
46. Emma Marris: How culture wars are affecting US universities. Scientists and other academics worry that political pressure on universities is growing and could limit research and teaching. *Nature* **626**: 474–476, 2024.
47. Max Stephens: *Sunday Telegraph* 21 April 2024.
48. Daniel Martin: 'University's trans policy "may be unlawful" *Daily Telegraph* 20 April 2024.
49. Whitehouse, 2022.
50. Niall Ferguson, *Daily Mail* 28 October 2023.
51. Ewan Somerville, *Sunday Telegraph* 5 November 2023.
52. Nick Gutteridge: 'Schools to wage war on "putrid" fake news' *Sunday Telegraph* 11 August 2024.
53. Lola Salem: 'Scrapping Latin in state schools will impoverish us all' *Daily Telegraph* 21 December 2024.
54. Julie Henry: 'How Labour plans to torch 30 years of school *Daily Telegraph* 18 January 2025.
55. Charles Moore: 'Labour is creating a vicious cycle of mediocrity – and kowtowing to China' *Daily Telegraph* 21 January 2025.
56. Letters to the Editor: 'Israeli conduct in Gaza' *Daily Telegraph* 17 August 2024.

57. McCarthy-Jones, p 66.
58. *ibid*, p 78 *et seq.*
59. *ibid*, p 55 *et seq.*
60. *ibid*, p 8.
61. see Gemma Conroy and Smriti Mallapaty: How China created AI model Deepseek and shocked the world *Nature* **638**: 300–301, 2025.
62. Smriti Mallapaty: AI traces mysterious metastatic cancers to their source. *Nature* **628**: 699–700, 2014.
63. Carissa Wong: How AI is improving climate forecasts. *Nature* **628**: 710–712, 2014.
64. Gemma Turon *et al.*: AI can help to tailor drugs for Africa – but Africans should lead the way. *Nature* **628**: 265–267, 2024.
65. Helen Pearson: Are the internet and AI affecting our memory? *Nature* **638**: 26–28, 2025.
66. McCarthy-Jones, p 296.
67. Alex Gomez-Marin: A pseudo-religion dressed up as technoscience promises human transcendence at the cost of extinction. *Nature* **632**: 497–498, 2024.
68. Helena Kudiabor: The super-charged virtual lab powered by 'AI scientists'. Could human-AI collaborations be the future of interdisciplinary studies? *Nature* **636**: 532–533 (2024).
69. Mariana Lenharo: What happens if AI becomes conscious? It's time to plan. *Nature* **636**: 533–534 (2024).
70. McCarthy-Jones, pp 310–312.

Chapter 7

Conclusion

The concept of a 'free world' as opposed to an 'unfree' one goes back to the last century. Slavery had been eliminated (more or less) during the 19th century and colonialism a hundred years later. India, for example, gained its freedom in 1947 and is by far the largest independent country today. Following the end of the Second World War, it became clear that those living in Eastern and Central Europe were not 'free', but subject to the authority of the Soviet Union (despite Stalin's earlier reassurance to Churchill that there would be free elections). These countries would continue under its authority until the fall of the Soviet Union at the end of 1991. Its own citizens, of course, had been living under a dictatorship since 1922. After Putin's rise to power, Russia is once again a dictatorship in all but name.

The opening years of the 21st century saw no remarkable changes in the lives of most people in the free world. Cancer and heart disease remain the major causes of death. Science continues to improve medical treatments but we're still waiting for a new and effective antibiotic. The commercialisation of nuclear fusion is, as it has been for the past half century, less than a decade away. Governments change democratically every few years within the European Union, the United Kingdom, the United States (just) and elsewhere. Arguments about how to deal with anthropogenic warming of the Earth persist. Homosexual couples are leading happy lives. The death penalty continues to await murderers in much of the USA.

Deluded Dogma

Sporadic national elections may be proof of the democratic principle (see the following), but there is nothing democratic about denying women a space of their own in changing rooms or on the sports field.

Slavery and colonialism may have fizzled out, but the ideologues of political correctness assert that anyone even remotely associated with those episodes must be reprimanded. So, statues and other memorials to the 19th-century four times prime minister, W E Gladstone, who argued vehemently for the abolition of slavery, need to be removed because the politician's father owned plantations in British Guyana and Jamaica. On the other hand, the freedom to write and speak your mind, especially in universities, is in jeopardy. Trans activists, abetted by doctors who have forgotten their Hippocratic Oath, endanger the lives of children unsure of their sexual orientation.

Literature and art have to surrender spontaneity in favour of blandness driven by dogma. Authors have been writing books for the pleasure of others since the 17th century. Themes that amused readers at the time, now considered by 'sensitivity readers' to be potentially offensive to certain people, need to be rewritten. Such 'bowdlerisation' [1] is surely unnecessary. Teachers of literature who follow the trend need to reconsider their position. Anyone of a sensitive nature can presumably avoid opening a book that was published before their time. Denying scholars and those wishing to enjoy the wit of a previous generation is retrograde.

In any case, sensitivity readers are wrong to protect the young against reading unsettling literature. First, because many actually enjoy the acerbic parts of P G Wodehouse, Evelyn Waugh, Nancy Mitford or Roald Dahl. Second, because mollycoddling today's youth will lead to a generation of timid individuals. These will not be ones to confront the despots of the autocratic world who threaten our freedom. Resilience, not timidity, has been a feature of humanity since *Homo* diverged from *Pan*. We have been able to exercise our innate curiosity [2], which has led fearless humans to set forth across the oceans without any idea of what lay ahead and explore

Conclusion

every inch of the globe. Aristotle recognised that 'All humans naturally desire knowledge'. We should not allow deluded ideologues to push humanity backwards.

Today, those who conspire to silence one's views are no longer institutions like the Roman Catholic Church and its Inquisition. They now include individuals in universities, the very places that once championed unfettered debate on any topic of interest. Radical students, forever a feature on university campuses and now abetted by deluded faculty, are able to impose their views on the rest. The ousting of Professor Kathleen Stock (Chapter 1) is a good example. In previous chapters, I have also shown how museums and places of worship, schools and medical centres, newspapers and broadcasters, corporations and banks have succumbed to a minority of self-righteous ideologues determined to inflict their opinions on the majority. Lack of 'inclusivity' is often cited by these proselytisers of dubious concepts, by which they mean excluding those who disagree with them.

Historians are no longer able to record past events as they happened but as they should have happened by today's standards. That is the way history was rewritten in autocracies such as the Soviet Union and continues in Russia and China to this day. It is not the way of the free world.

Two thousand years ago, Cicero pointed out that *historia magistra vitae*: 'history is life's teacher'. We ignore these words at our peril. But as the historian Gertrude Himmelfarb reminds us, 'having been spared the revolution that Marx predicted, we have succumbed to the cultural revolution' [3]. The free world needs to protect itself against purveyors of dubious concepts. Historian Robert Tombs finds that such 'nihilistic attacks on national history and culture (are) now visible in practically every school, museum and university in the land' [4]. The following year, he warned that 'We are threatened by external and internal dangers. We see and feel them. Politicians, generals and diplomats sound the alarm. Our defences are weak. Our enemies are emboldened. Our streets are disorderly. What follows the stark warnings? Not much. Words do not announce action but cover inaction' [5].

Writer Paul Kingsnorth likewise considers that 'The West's ongoing decline has caused its elites to lose faith in their cultural inheritance, and this loss of faith has now reached pathological proportions. As a result, the leading lights in Western society – the cultural elites, and sometimes the political and economic elites too – are dedicated not to upholding the cultural forms they inherited, but to turning them on their heads, or erasing them entirely' [6]. The current leader of the opposition in the UK, Kemi Badenoch, considers that 'We are giving away our freedoms by stealth. Because we don't know the value of what we have, and we are failing to adapt as the world is changing and new threats emerge, and we don't recognise when opposing ideologies are taking over. Ideologies and beliefs that demand our tolerance even as they seek to undermine the very culture and institutions that create that tolerance' [7].

Some Clarity

On 16 April 2025, the Supreme Court of the UK ruled that the word 'woman' refers only to a biologically born female: trans-women are therefore now excluded from this definition. Referring colloquially to a trans-woman as 'she' (see Chapter 4) should obviously remain acceptable in the future. Gender transitioning itself is not affected by the Supreme Court ruling and should remain as much part of a free society as homosexuality. Jake and Hannah Graf, like Jan Morris and James Barry before them (see Chapter 4), threaten no one. But just as aspects of homosexuality – like paedophilia – are indefensible, so are actions by trans-women that deny women their rights.

The expense of the Supreme Court action could have been avoided if the government had ensured that its citizens were aware of a simple biological fact: that every cell in one's body contains two chromosomes, XX (female) or XY (male), which are faithfully reproduced at every cell division from birth to death, irrespective of any hormonal or other treatment a person may undergo. (The fact that some people – less than 1 in a hundred – are born with certain chromosomal abnormalities does not affect this conclusion.)

Origins

In the Introduction, I mentioned that this book is not about politics. Yet the new ideologies have been associated with left-wing views, even if these are not the main reason for their emergence. According to philosopher Susan Neiman, the *Left is Not Woke* [8]. Nor can the deluded tendencies of the 21st century be ascribed to a lack of democratic principles. Since the end of World War II, Americans have oscillated nine times between electing a Democrat (largely left-wing) and a Republican (largely right-wing) president [9]. In the UK, there have been six Labour and eleven Conservative prime ministers during that time. In the rest of Europe as well as in Asia and South America, the people have likewise elected leaders of successively different hues from time to time. Such changes are the very essence of democracy. The one occasion when the losing candidate in the USA refused to accept the will of the people, in 2020, left a stain not on the electoral process but on the reputation of the contender. The German election of 1933 was democratically conducted. It was a deluded majority that voted for the Nazi party. Outside the free world, it is not the most popular or able person but the most powerful who becomes leader. But even within a democracy, a minority view may yet exert considerable influence.

In her book *Ten Years to Save the West*, former UK Prime Minister Liz Truss considers that our currently deluded world is very much the product of left-wing dominance and therefore can only be fought by those on the right. 'The madness of identity politics and wokery is doing huge damage to our society and our public services, and it needs to be taken on. Conservatives need to dismantle the architecture that has enabled these fringe ideas to flourish and instead restore the primacy of individual liberty, the family and parental authority. I am not prepared to leave the field until the battle is won' [10]. Let's hope she succeeds in her quest.

Those with left-leaning views may well bear responsibility for our present dilemma, but they are not politicians. Tony Blair, prime minister of New Labour from 1997 to 2007, introduced no provocative social changes (apart from banning hunting with dogs, which he subsequently admitted had been a mistake). His championing of free academies, on the other hand, proved to be precisely what the educational system needed (see previous chapter). Left-of-centre politicians may support deluded dogma but they did not introduce it in the first place.

Sympathy for the downtrodden, which is in the blood stream of most people, forced political leaders during the 19th and 20th centuries like Robert Owen to bring about the changes that improved the condition of the working classes. By the beginning of the 21st century, they were no longer being exploited and mass unemployment had not returned since the 1930s. Whose plight then, apart from ethnic minorities, could the liberal classes espouse? Reforming idealists began to campaign instead on behalf of an assumed victimhood: children who might be upset by certain texts or pictures that refer to the values of a bygone age; students whose radical views are not necessarily accepted by the faculty (or anyone else); transgender persons who believe themselves to be entitled to behave as they wish; any who consider themselves threatened or offended by certain types of normal speech.

A Word of Caution

In 1969, the philosopher Isiah Berlin wrote that 'We cannot remain absolutely free, and must give up some of our liberty to preserve the rest. ...' [11]. Of course, like others before him, he was right. Democracy is dependent on the rule of law. Expression of one's views, in writing or speech, is acceptable only if it does not incite violence or the overthrow of established institutions. Currently, free speech is under threat (see previous chapter).

Another warning comes from the 19th century. 'Eternal vigilance is the price of liberty'. This remark has been attributed, probably incorrectly, to Thomas Jefferson. It is more likely to have been coined by the American abolitionist Wendell Phillips, 'the only white American wholly color-blind and free from racial prejudice'. The best example of a failure of vigilance is that of Germany's Weimar Republic, established after World War 1. Vigilance is now required to prevent Kemi Badenoch's fears [7] from becoming reality.

The purveyors of political correctness must not be allowed to abrogate our freedom of action and speech. The danger of succumbing to our deluded acceptance of false ideology, cancel culture and virtue signalling is clear. For 'should the negative and destructive narrative of the past consolidate its growing authority, it will succeed in undermining people's confidence in themselves, their communities, and their capacity to confront the challenges posed in the future. Once the past is cast in an entirely negative light, there is little possibility of cultivating a sense of hope for the future. In such circumstances, the past ceases to provide any guidance. The continuous serving up of the horrors of the past has the effect of lowering human ambition' [12].

Can Today's Ideologies Endure or will they Fizzle out?

I do not believe that the present state of affairs will persist, for it serves no purpose for society. Has the avoidance of words like manmade, manhandle, manpower or manservant improved the life of a single woman? Deluded ideologues would be more effective if they tried to dissuade leaders in Muslim countries from denying women and girls a proper role in civic society. Has the encouragement of young children unsure of their gender to undergo life-changing procedures been of benefit to them? In many cases, they have come to regret the outcome and wish they had never listened to such advice in the first place. Has the removal of statues commemorating past philanthropists been of benefit to anyone? Has the ability of criminals to declare themselves of changed gender made the world a better place? Is 'inclusivity' a better criterion for employing someone than ability or experience? Does a (factually correct) remark made by one person and reported to the police by another, such as 'a trans woman is biologically a man' constitute a 'non crime hate crime'? If so, what is the point, apart from causing the first person distress and the police to waste time, of following this up?

If today's ideologies are unlikely to endure, when will they begin to decline? In the USA, its irrepressible president vows to prevent transwomen from competing in the ladies' section of any elite sporting event, while companies like Walmart are abandoning EDI on their own initiative [13]. There are signs that in some cases this has started to happen in the UK too. In an article about the recruitment of firemen that I referred to briefly in Chapter 5, reporter Tim Sigsworth has included a graph showing the number of advertised DEI jobs in Britain. I appreciate that DEI (EDI) is but one of the several deluded ideologies documented in previous chapters, but for what it's worth the graph (Fig. 1) shows that DEI started to increase towards the end of 2020, reaching a peak in 2022. Thereafter, there was a sharp drop that has continued at a more leisurely pace since 2023. Because the generality of Fig. 1 is not known, my warning about our *Deluded New World* should not be discarded just yet. (Moreover, DEI has been interpreted and applied in different ways – for beneficial as well as for mistaken aims. In universities in the USA, for example, DEI is used to *improve* 'investment in workforce development, economic mobility and institutional excellence' [14].) I also note that, according to columnist Zoe Strimpel, we should not expect the next generation to return to common sense on their own. Most of those in their 20s and 30s are the present

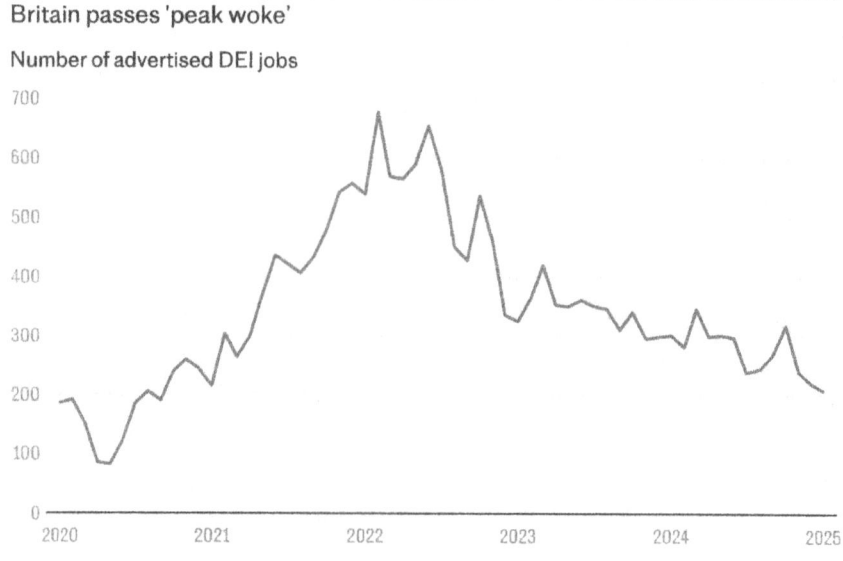

Figure 1. Number of advertised DEI jobs.
Source: Adapted from Tim Sigsworth: *Daily Telegraph* 22 February 2025.

ideologues' 'greatest cheerleaders, demanding access to safe spaces, trigger warnings and grievance airings wherever they go' [15].

I have avoided using the word 'woke' throughout this book. I use it now in the hope that it and its deluded implications are indeed beginning to disappear. But a greater danger lurks outside the free world in the autocracies of Russia, China, North Korea and Iran. I alluded earlier to the need for vigilance. Failure to act by the leaders of the free world when action was required resulted in the rise of Hitler, Nazism and World War 2. A lack of response to provocative acts by Russia a decade ago has led to the first major war on European soil since 1939. These events, as well as a rare glimpse into wartime Germany, are presented in the Epilogue that follows.

Notes

1. Thomas Bowdler (1754–1825) produced expurgated editions of Shakespeare's plays that removed disagreeable language.
2. Charles Pasternak: *Curiosity and Quest* in *What makes us human?* (ed. Charles Pasternak, Oxford: Oneworld Publications, 2007.
3. Himmelfarb, G: *One Nation, Two Cultures: A Searching Examination of American Society in the Aftermath of Our Cultural Revolution* (New York: Vintage, 2001) p 118.
4. Robert Tombs: *Daily Telegraph* 18 November 2023.
5. Rober Tombs: 'It may now be too late for the West, a corpse that cannot be galvanised. Elected governments no longer have the power or will to do what is needed to save our free societies' *Daily Telegraph* 11 March 2024.
6. Quoted by Furedi, p 11.
7. Daniel Martin: 'Badenoch: Western liberalism has been "hacked" by woke ideologies' *Daily Telegraph* 6 December 2024.
8. Wiley, 2023.
9. Truman, Dem; Eisenhower, Rep; Kennedy, Dem followed by Johnson, Dem; Nixon, Rep followed by Ford, Rep; Carter, Dem; Reagan, Rep; H W Bush, Rep; Clinton, Dem; G W Bush, Rep; Obama, Dem; Trump, Rep; Biden, Dem; Trump, Rep.
10. Truss, p 147.

11. Isaiah Berlin, "TWO CONCEPTS OF LIBERTY," Four Essays On Liberty, (Oxford, England: Oxford University Press, 1969), pp 118–172.
12. Furedi, p 16.
13. Kate Andrews: 'The US has dropped diversity targets – will Britain cling on?' *Daily Telegraph* 11 January 2025.
14. Rebecca Calisi Rodriguez: Universities must fight the anti-DEI crackdown *Nature* **639**: 277 (2025).
15. Zoe Strimpel: *Sunday Telegraph* Features 2 February 2025.

Chapter 8

Epilogue

Every society contains some people with noble aspirations and others with evil intent. Most fall into what has been described as a silent majority. The governments of free nations need to maintain vigilance so that the second do not prevail. As the 18th-century statesman and philosopher Edmund Burke observed, for evil to triumph, all that is required is 'for good men to do nothing' [1]. The best example of a failure of vigilance comes from the leaders of Germany's Weimar Republic and the flawed (due to the absence of the USA) League of Nations which was established after World War 1. Neither prevented the rise of Hitler and the consequent ravages of the Second World War.

Rise and Fall of Nazi Germany

By 1918, hyperinflation had led to 'starving billionaires' scavenging for food on the streets. In reviewing *Vertigo* by Harald Jähner [2], a study of the downfall of the Weimar Republic, Julian Evans observes that the author 'makes the point that many Germans didn't want to engage in a rational analysis of their situation because the national awakening that Hitler promised was vastly preferable to an acceptance of reality. But rational examination had always been the Weimar Republic's weakest suit' [3]. We must not allow a malevolent upstart to emerge and threaten the rest.

In 1919, the year he joined the Deutsche Arbeiterpartei or DAP (German Workers Party), Adolf Hitler was relatively unknown. He had served as a lance-corporal during the war and been awarded the Iron Cross

First Class in 1918 on the recommendation of Lieutenant Hugo Gutmann, the (Jewish) adjutant of his regiment. It was at this time that he developed an unwavering belief in his ability to become a leader. Comparison with Winston Churchill's view about himself at this period is apt. Both were persuasive orators: Hitler by ranting, Churchill by inspiring. The DAP became the Nationalsozialistische Deutsche Arbeiterpartei or NSDAP (National Socialist German Workers' Party), better known as the Nazi Party in 1920. By the following year, Hitler had become its leader. An attempted coup to seize power over the government in 1923 was unsuccessful, and he was sent to prison for five years. While there, he composed *Mein Kampf* (My Struggle). In it, Hitler attacked the Versailles Peace Treaty, espoused a greater German Reich and denounced communism and Judaism. He was released after just one year. Hitler continued to articulate his views in public, with intimidatory actions by the paramilitary wing of his party, the Sturm Abteilung or SA (Stormtroopers also known as Brownshirts) at every meeting and on the streets.

The Federal election of July 1932 saw the Nazi Party win 37% of the popular vote, beating the SDP (Social Democratic Party) with 22% and the KPD (Communist Party of Germany) with 14%. To form a government required a two-thirds majority. The other parties refused to join a coalition with the Nazis, leading to another election in November of 1932. The Nazi Party actually lost 34 seats, finishing with 33%, with significant gains by the Communists. Nevertheless, former Chancellor Franz von Papen, perhaps encouraged by the erstwhile Crown Prince Wilhelm Hohenzollern, persuaded President Paul von Hindenburg – against his better judgement – to appoint Hitler as Chancellor in January of 1933. The feeble Weimar Republic now became a one-party Nazi dictatorship under its charismatic Führer, described by historian Ian Kershaw as 'the embodiment of modern political evil'. Persistence and determination by one man had won, due to lack of vigilance by his countrymen and the feeble Versailles Treaty.

In 1933, Hitler had predicted a 'thousand-year Reich'. It lasted just 12. Its end came with Germany's unconditional surrender to the Allies on 6 May 1945. By this time, Berlin was a heap of rubble, and the Führer, unable

Epilogue

to face the world he had created, committed suicide. At the height of his power, Hitler, like Napoleon a century earlier, commanded most of Europe. After the collapse of their respective ventures, the boundaries of Germany and France were pretty much back to where they had been at the beginning. Napoleon had initiated decimalised quantities (the metre, the litre, the gram) and the principles of civil liberty, equality before the law and a secular state (the Code Napoléon), which have since been adopted by countries throughout the world and are still in use today. Hitler brought the German people the shame of the Holocaust (over 6 million Jews and others murdered), the destruction of their cities and an estimated 5 million civilian and military deaths.

On 12 March 1938, Hitler's troops had marched into Austria to the delight of its Nazis and foreboding on the part of its Jews. Six months later, he annexed the German-speaking Sudetenland within the borders of Czechoslovakia and on 1 September invaded Poland. British Prime Minister Neville Chamberlain's policy of appeasement had not brought 'Peace in our time' to Europe, though its rejection by Hitler finally woke a somnolent British government to begin rapid rearmament. Younger readers of this book will find accounts of the Second World War, such as the masterly 900-page account by Antony Beevor [4], written with hindsight 60 years after its end, instructive. In it, several attempts on Hitler's life during the last 2 years of the war are mentioned: all failed. Unsurprisingly, the White Rose is not in the index.

This is because the White Rose was not an attempt on Hitler's life. It was an endeavour by a group of medical and other students at the Ludwig Maximilian University of Munich to end the attrition on the Eastern Front. The German assault eastwards had been halted at Stalingrad in July of 1942. The battle to take the city was the bloodiest of the entire war. Half a million Germans were killed, with the 6th Army surrounded and annihilated. The Soviets lost twice as many of their fighters. By 1943, the Germans were in retreat. The origin of the words *Weisse Rose* is unclear, perhaps no more than the purity of a white flower compared to the pollution of Nazi ideology.

The instigators of the White Rose movement were five students and one professor: Hans and his sister Sophie Scholl, Alexander Schmorell, Christoph Probst (married, the father of a newborn child) and Willie Graf. Professor Kurt Huber soon joined them. (My mother, who was taught philosophy by Huber in the 1930s, considered him to be an inspired teacher and the kindest of men.) Between 27 June and 12 July, four flyers or pamphlets were composed, printed secretly at night on an old hand-operated photocopier in an upstairs room in Alexander Schmorell's family home, and sent to writers, academics, headteachers, booksellers, doctors, restaurant owners and others in the Munich area.

The first flyer was written in a somewhat intellectual tone with quotations from Friedrich Schiller and Goethe. It urges Germans to mount resistance to the regime. 'Is it not so that in the present day every honourable German is ashamed of their government? And who among us can foresee the extent of the infamy that will be on us, and on our children, when the veil is lifted from our eyes and the most horrific crimes, crimes beyond all measure, come to light? If, in their innermost being, the German people have been corrupted and degraded enough to betray the greatest quality humanity possesses ... – free will – without so much as lifting a finger ... then, yes, they truly deserve their own demise. ...' [5]. The second flyer quotes the ancient Chinese philosopher Laozi (Lao Tzu) and asks, 'Why do the German people behave so apathetically in the face of all these most atrocious, most inhumane crimes?' Germany must not only feel 'collective suffering, no much more: COLLECTIVE GUILT. ...Everyone wants to exonerate themselves from such a collective guilt, everyone does so and returns to sleeping soundly with the calmest, clearest conscience. But no one can exonerate themselves, everyone is GUILTY, GUILTY, GUILTY! ...' [6].

The third flyer gets to the point and urges Germans to show passive resistance, and more. 'SABOTAGE of arms factories and other strategic operations ... SABOTAGE of all academic and intellectual groups that actively support the continuation of the war ... SABOTAGE of all cultural events that might raise the fascists' "prestige" with the people. SABOTAGE of all branches of the arts that have the slightest connection to National Socialism or stand in its service. SABOTAGE of all publications, all newspapers that are in the pay of the "government", that propagate its ideas and spread the brown lie. ...' [7]. The fourth flyer takes on a religious tone. Hitler is attacked as a liar. He blasphemously speaks of God when he really means 'the power of the Evil One, of the fallen angel, of Satan'. It ends with what is the White Rose's central message: 'We will not be silent. We are your bad conscience. The White Rose will never leave you in peace' [8]. Like the previous three pamphlets, its final message is to ask the recipient to make as many copies as possible and to distribute them.

Following the dispatch of the fourth flyer in July 1942, Hans Scholl, Alexander Schmorell and Willie Graf were ordered to the Russian front for a three-month tour of duty as student soldiers in the Wehrmacht medical corps. Their journey through Warsaw, where they witnessed the clearing of the Jewish ghetto and the deportation of its starving men,

Epilogue

women and children to Auschwitz, Treblinka and other death camps, must have convinced them that the folly of what they and their colleagues had embarked on was justified, honourable (and probably fatal). In January 1943 (a month before the German army began its retreat from Stalingrad), a fifth flyer was written and distributed. Entitled 'An Appeal To All Germans!' It pointed out that 'Hitler Cannot Win the War; He Can Only Prolong It! ... Break away from everything associated with National Socialism Before It's Too Late!' [9]. During the first two weeks of February, Hans Scholl, Alexander Schmorell and Willie Graf began daubing buildings in Munich at night with slogans like 'Down with Hitler' and 'Freedom'. Miraculously, they were not observed. 3,000 copies of a sixth flyer – 'Students! The German people look to us! ... Berezina and Stalingrad have gone up in flames, the dead of Stalingrad beseech us' [10] – were printed.

On 18 February, Hans and Sophie Scholl went to Munich University with a large suitcase containing flyers. While lectures were in progress, they left some on window sills, outside doors and scattered the remainder from the balustrade on the upper floor. At this point, they were spotted by an ardent custodian who promptly took them to the rector's office. Having tried, unsuccessfully, to bluster their way out, they were handed over to the Gestapo. Hans and Sophie's luck had run out. Four days later, they were in the Palace of Justice, together with Christoph Probst, a letter from whom had been found on Hans's person. All three were accused of high treason. The sentence of death was predictable. The method of execution – by guillotine – was not. The same afternoon, all three had breathed their last.

Unaware of what had just been enacted, the campaign continued. More students joined the movement, with a separate group opening in Hamburg. Individuals would leave Munich with a suitcase full of leaflets for another town. From there, these were posted elsewhere in order to make tracking their origin more difficult. But it was extremely dangerous work as the Gestapo and military police were everywhere. Nevertheless, thousands of leaflets were disseminated throughout Southern Germany and as far north as Berlin and Hamburg [11]. In August 1943, leaflets were smuggled into Britain and dropped by Allied aircraft over Germany. By this time, the main participants had been identified and arrested. A thousand Reichsmark reward had been offered for Schmorell's capture – dead or alive – and he was betrayed while hiding in a cellar. On 19 April 1943, Graf, Huber and Schmorell were tried for high treason and sentenced to death by decapitation. Eleven of their compatriots were accused of lesser crimes and received prison sentences of varying lengths. Huber was stripped of his professorship and other positions. His wife Clara was now a widow and destitute at that. She also received a bill for 3,000 Reichsmark to pay for the execution and 'depreciation costs of the apparatus'.

Today, there is a bust of Sophie Scholl near a white marble carving of a rose in the atrium of Ludwig Maximilian University of Munich. Above are inscribed the names of those who gave their lives in opposition to the Nazi regime. In 1946, the plaza in front of the university was renamed Geschwister (Siblings)-Scholl-Platz, while that around the corner is now Professor Huber Platz. In 2005, a German TV station held a competition for 'The Greatest Germans'. Konrad Adenauer, the first chancellor of West Germany in 1949, headed the poll. He was followed by Martin Luther, then Karl Marx. In fourth place came Hans and Sophie Scholl. And in 2012, Alexander Schmorell was proclaimed a saint in the Russian Orthodox Church: Alexander of Munich.

The attempt to rein in Hitler was bound to fail. But the heroism of the White Rose participants gave Germans a sense of honour. Evidently, not all were in thrall to Hitler. A large number were not inherently Nazis anyway. Admiral Wilhelm Canaris, head of the Abwehr (Intelligence Organisation for the Army) itself, was a confirmed anti-Nazi. He may even have been a source of information for the allies [12]. In 1944, Hitler ordered his execution, though he was not one of the conspirators in the plot to kill the Führer. Erwin Rommel, 'one of the few eminent commanders who have gained distinction as military thinkers and writers' [13], never joined the Nazi Party and 'totally ignored an order that captured Jewish enemy soldiers were to be treated not as prisoners of war but as Jews'. When, after he took Tobruk in 1941, he was asked by the South African General Klopper to segregate black prisoners from the whites, he refused on the grounds that 'the blacks were South African soldiers, had fought alongside whites, worn the same uniform and were all captives together' [14]. The idea that Germans are a cruel, antisemitic people is nonsense. Antisemitism thrives in countries throughout the world. A Hitler could emerge anywhere, provided he is helped into power, as Hitler was by Franz von Papen in 1933. Germans are no more instinctively evil than the inhabitants of other nations. Romania produced Nicolae Ceaușescu as president in 1967, but few of its citizens shared his innate cruelty.

On 30 April 1945, following Adolf Hitler's suicide, Admiral Karl Dönitz was appointed Head of State. On 4 May, he ordered the troops facing the British and Canadian 21st Army Group in Northern Germany to surrender to their commander Field Marshall Montgomery at Lüneburg Heath. Three days later, Dönitz instructed Adolf Jodl, who had been Chief of Operations Staff of the Oberkommando der Wehrmacht (OKW) – German Armed Forces High Command – throughout the war, to sign the instruments of unconditional surrender to the allies (USA, UK and the Soviet Union) at the Supreme Headquarters of the Allied Expeditionary Force (SHAEF) in Reims. The Second World War in Europe was over, but hostilities in the Pacific continued. The detonation of an atomic bomb over Hiroshima on 6 August did not induce Japan to surrender to the allies, but one over Nagasaki three days later did. (The development of the bomb had been a controversy of huge dimensions. In August of 1939, Albert Einstein wrote to US President Franklin Roosevelt informing him that the Germans were working on an atomic bomb and urging him to proceed with the American version. The President agreed. In March of 1945, by which time it was clear that Germany was losing the war, Einstein wrote again, urging him to stop. This time the President disagreed, realising that an invasion of Japan would be extremely costly in terms of American lives.)

Post WW2

The end of hostilities brought no more than a short-lived peace to the world. Within 2 years, tension between the Soviet Union and the West evolved into the Cold War. Both sides had developed ever more powerful nuclear weapons, but hostilities never broke out because of pragmatism by the respective leaders: each side realised that a nuclear conflict was to no one's advantage. When the Soviet Union collapsed at the end of 1991, it seemed that amity between the major nations of the world had finally arrived. Francis Fukuyama called it 'the end of history'. Alas, it was not to be. The free world may be on edge for the reasons enumerated in the previous chapters of this book, but it is now threatened from outside by the belligerent regime of Vladimir Putin's Russia, abetted by China, North Korea and Iran, whose own citizens live under constant repression.

In China, for example, Xi Jinping rules with an iron fist. Any freedoms won in the past have been abrogated. 'Hong Kong was once a haven. But the freedoms promised to it after handover are first ground down and then crushed outright ... Teachers, lecturers, lawyers and judges are targeted by pro-Beijing media. There is far worse in Xinjiang, where perhaps a million "unreliable" residents, almost all Uighur or other Muslim minorities, have been herded into camps. They call them vocational training centres, for "transformation through education", but with their barbed wire and control towers they look like what they are: prisons for people held without charge or trial. Some of the detainees are sent to de facto orphanages. Women report forced sterilisations and sexual violence. Mosques and other cultural sites are razed' [15].

The Falun Gong, a recently founded spiritual organisation of admittedly somewhat outlandish beliefs, is brutally repressed – imprisoned and tortured – by the government. Its members constitute a major source for the internationally illegal practice of removing organs for transplantation into needy recipients for financial gain. 'In the long-term practice in the PRC (People's Republic of China) of forced organ harvesting it was indeed Falun Gong practitioners who were used as a source – probably the principal source – of organs for forced organ harvesting' [16]. One forced organ donor, Cheng Pei Ming, tells how he woke up three days after being dragged into a 'hospital' to find himself shackled to a bed. A large scar across his chest is testimony to the removal of parts of his lung and liver. Twenty years later, he still feels 'extreme pain' [17]. Political opponents of Xi Jinping's rule simply disappear. 'His goal is to restore China to its former glory, and to overcome a past century of humiliations ... We face ideological warfare, economic espionage and influence operations as the Chinese Communist Party tries to counter Western narratives with propaganda' [18].

Russian Invasion of Ukraine

During the writing of this book, two unprovoked attacks on democratic countries within the free world took place. The first was on Ukraine, at the eastern edge of Europe, by its Russian neighbour. A year later, one of Iran's sponsored terrorist groups launched an attack on Israel. I will describe each in detail shortly.

Russia had been meddling in Ukraine's Donbas region since 2014. That year, Vladimir Putin sent Russian soldiers into the Crimea and announced its annexation to Russia. The leaders of the free world met, passed resolutions and refrained from further action. The brutality of

Epilogue

Putin's invasion of Ukraine on 24 February 2022 would have given Attila cause for jealousy, though the Kremlin refers to its invasion as no more than 'military operations' against 'Nazi elements' in the country. Sergei Lavrov, Russian Foreign Minister, caused ripples of laughter to break out when he informed the UN Security Council that the invasion was the result of 'western provocation'. The fact that Russian tanks rolled into their neighbour's land without provocation of any kind, that Russian shells have targeted schools and hospitals, that prisoners have been found dead with their hands tied behind their backs, that women have been raped, that over a million Ukrainian prisoners were taken to Siberia, that more than 7,000 children have been abducted and sent into Russia's interior for adoption, that some 9,000 civilians and 15,000–17,000 military personnel have died during the first 15 months of the war, is unexplained. Following investigations by the International Criminal Court, an arrest warrant for Russia's president on charges of war crimes, crimes against humanity and genocide was issued on 17 March 2023. Within Russia, opponents of the regime spend their lives in prison or flee the country. Some are poisoned by polonium or Novichok; if that fails to kill, they are murdered by other means. Anyone who as much as mentions the war is arrested, with outright criticism of it punishable by imprisonment for up to 25 years. Others merely fall off their balcony [19].

Opposition to Putin

On Saturday, 17 February 2024, I was walking westwards along High Street Kensington towards Palace Gate when I noticed that part of the street had been closed to traffic on account of a kind of tent that had been erected in the middle of the road. That week's march by the 'Free Palestine' movement (see in the following) was clearly going to end here, near the fenced-off Israeli Embassy in Palace Green. But I had not come to hear speeches by deluded anti-Israel protesters. I had come to lay a bunch of flowers outside the Russian Embassy at the other end of Palace Green as a mark of respect for Alexei Navalny, who had died the previous day in the freezing Polar Wolf penal colony in Kharp.

Deluded New World: Current Controversies and Why the Free World is on Edge

Alexei Navalny was an honest, kind and patriotic man, fighting against a lying, malevolent dictator. The only thing they had in common was resolve. In Navalny's case, it was to rid Russia of Vladimir Putin. In the latter's case, to prevent this coming to pass. There was never much doubt who would win. That is how, in an autocracy, martyrs are made. Recall my earlier comments about the members of the White Rose. Roman Borisovich, an insurance executive who met Navalny in 2011, considered him to have 'enormous charisma. He was the most charismatic Russian I ever met. ... The second thing that comes to mind was his necessity, his need to lead. ... He had this gift of leading people' [20]. What an inspirational president he would have made, given half a chance.

Alexei Anatolyevich Navalny was born on 4 June 1976 in Butyn, outside Moscow. His father was an officer in the Soviet army, and for the first 2 years of his life, Alexei was brought up by his paternal grandmother in Zalyssia, a village close to Chernobyl, then within the Ukrainian Soviet Socialist Republic. Alexei read law (as had Putin in Leningrad) at the prestigious People's Friendship University in Moscow, followed by a second degree in securities and exchanges at the Financial University, also in Moscow. In the meantime, he had met Yulia Abrosimova, whom he married in 2000 and with whom he would produce two children. In the autumn of 2010, he spent a term at Yale University, having been elected to its World Fellows Program for emerging leaders from around the world.

Navalny's first arrest came a year later, on account of his derogatory remarks concerning the elections to the Duma. He was sentenced to 15 days in prison. He had joined the Russian United Democratic Party Yabloko ('apple') in 2000, and in 2013 became one of thirteen candidates for Mayor of Moscow. This resulted in him being charged with embezzlement and sentenced to 5 years in a penal colony. He was freed on bail, but his conviction (on trumped-up charges) prevented him from running for office.

In 2015, the Anti-Corruption Foundation that Navalny had set up found that Lopatina, former wife of Deputy Prosecutor-General Gennady Lopatin, had close links to the wives of the Tsapok crime syndicate that had massacred twelve people in Kushcheveskaya 5 years earlier. The victims included three children and a newborn baby who was thrown in a fire 'while he was still alive' [21]. Such revelations, made by team Navalny in a YouTube film, did not endear him to the regime.

Three opposition candidates were likely to contest the presidential election to be held in 2018. Boris Nemtsov was eliminated in 2015 by being shot four times in the back as he walked across the Bolshoy Moskvoretsky bridge near the Kremlin. No one was ever arrested or charged with his murder. Mikhail Kasiamov, Putin's first prime minister but subsequently a severe critic, was exposed making love to his girlfriend in a film obtained secretly and then shown to the nation on NTV. Alexei Navalny was prevented from running on 'legal' grounds, namely that he was subject to a suspended prison sentence. Thus are presidential elections in today's Russia decided.

Epilogue

On 20 August 2020, Navalny was flying back to Moscow from Tomsk in Siberia when he fell desperately ill. The plane was diverted to Omsk, where he was rushed to the local hospital. In a coma and on a ventilator, staff treating him considered that he might have been poisoned, though the hospital's chief physician thought this was only one of several possibilities. (Of those actually treating him, one subsequently resigned, another 'suffered a fatal stroke' and a third died 'from heart failure'.) His wife Yulia was informed, and she rushed to Omsk and managed to get Angela Merkel to send a plane to take him to the Charité Hospital in Berlin. Here, he was diagnosed with poisoning by a modified version of Novichok, and his life was saved.

On his discharge from the hospital in Berlin, Navalny – like Caesar camped before the Rubicon – paused before returning home. He spent a few weeks in the Black Forest to regain his strength. On 17 January 2021, he boarded a plane for Moscow. It was the last freely made decision of his life. He was arrested as soon as the aircraft touched down, charged with violating parole while lying in hospital in Berlin and sentenced to over 2 years in prison. Whether he died a natural death after 3 years of being moved from one penal colony to another and finishing up in the Arctic Circle with temperatures down to -25 C, fed starvation diets, tortured, incarcerated in ever smaller solitary confinement, denied daylight and any medicines, or whether he received more poisons is beside the point. Alexei Navalny will be remembered as a hero, Vladimir Putin as his murderer.

The free world received another jolt, this time in the Near East, on 7 October 2023. To understand the conflict, I need to diverge somewhat from the narrative.

Hamas Attack on Israel

Many Jews – who are like Arabs of Semitic origin – began to leave their homeland of Palestine more than a thousand years ago because of continued oppression in order to settle elsewhere. By 1900, some 10 million were living outside Palestine. In Europe, they were treated as second-class citizens and have been subject to much abuse. In 1897, an Austro-Hungarian journalist named Theodor Herzl founded a political movement aimed at enabling Jews from across the world to return to their traditional homeland in Palestine. It was called Zionism.

On 2 November 1917, Arthur Balfour, the British Foreign Secretary, wrote to his friend Lord Rothschild, a leader of the Zionist Movement, that

177

his government had decided to establish a homeland for the Jewish people in Palestine, then part of the shortly-to-be defeated Ottoman Empire. This became known as the Balfour Declaration. It was followed up by a League of Nations conference at San Remo in April 1920 that agreed on a Mandate for Palestine, assigning administration of the area (the land enclosed by Lebanon, Syria, Jordan, Egypt and the Mediterranean) to Britain. The Mandate was signed by representatives of Britain, France, Italy and Japan. No member of the indigenous, largely Arab, community was consulted. During the 1940s, European Jews naturally sought refuge in Palestine, but numbers were restricted, and many entered illegally. Skirmishes between the British and incoming Jews, as well as between resident Arabs and Jews, ensued. Finally, on 14 May 1948, the Declaration of the Establishment of the State of Israel was proclaimed.

At no point between 1917 and 1948 – or indeed subsequently – have the Palestinian residents (who had accounted for 93% of the population in 1917) been granted their own government. Britain gave up its mandate in 1947, and this passed to the United Nations. That body voted for a two-state solution (with Jerusalem under international control). Yet at no time during the next 75 years, despite numerous summits and 'Accords' (that of 1993 leading to the Nobel Peace Prize shared between the Palestinian leader Yaser Arafat and Israeli politicians Shimon Peres and Yitzhak Rabin), has the two-state project come to fruition.

Hamas is an Iranian – and Qatari (until late 2024) – backed group elected by the people of Gaza in 2006 to administer their land. Instead of providing good governance, it has stolen humanitarian aid sent to Gaza and has used the local population as human shields. Rockets are discharged into Israel from densely populated areas, including hospitals and schools, in order to minimise Israel's response. Any return of fire that harms the local population and destroys their buildings is then attributed to murderous aggression by the State of Israel. Needless to say, Hamas has not put itself up for re-election since it gained control of Gaza. Worse still, when 26-year-old Ahmed-al-Masri was holding a banner saying 'Hamas does not represent us', he was subsequently abducted by Hamas gunmen and brutally tortured. 'In recent weeks, reports have multiplied of people being dragged out of aid lines, tortured in basements, or simply executed in broad daylight. One video, published gleefully by Hamas-affiliated social media accounts, showed masked figures using a long metal pole to smash a blindfolded man's kneecaps. His screams for mercy are too visceral to describe' [21a].

What happened on 7 October 2023 is that the Israeli Defence Force (IDF) momentarily took its eyes off the ball – yet another failure of vigilance [22] – enabling a large group of Hamas assassins to enter peaceful kibbutzim in Southern Israel. More than 1400 people were massacred, with women raped and their babies decapitated. A further 200 – including children and the elderly – were abducted. It was the worst slaughter of Jews since the Holocaust, eighty years before. The fact that the crimes against civilians committed by Hamas mirror in some ways those inflicted on Ukrainian citizens by Vladimir Putin has not prevented the Russian president from offering to mediate in the Middle East (and welcoming Hamas leaders to Moscow). No example can better illustrate the danger in which the democracies of the world now find themselves.

Israel's response to the 7 October massacre has been unambiguous: the annihilation of the entire terrorist group (thought to number around a thousand fighters, with its leaders living in style in Qatar). But this is fraught with difficulties, as Hamas has hidden itself and its weaponry within the Palestinian community. So, to achieve Israel's aim has resulted in the unavoidable deaths of peaceful Palestinians (see False Speech in Chapter 6). The outcome has been condemnation of Israel, with pro-Palestinian and anti-Jewish demonstrations and marches throughout the cities of the USA, Britain and other countries. The LGTB lobby has enthusiastically joined in with a placard displaying their rainbow flag and urging 'Queers for Palestine'. Whether from ignorance or stupidity, the absurdity of this exhortation (Arab countries are notoriously anti-homosexual) seems lost on them. Anti-Israel protests and sit-ins by university students, abetted by some faculty, erupted in some of the leading academic institutions and on the streets of America and Britain. It took a world war and 29 countries to defeat Hitler. Israel is having to destroy Hamas on its own.

And not only Hamas. Hezbollah, another Iranian-backed terrorist organisation that is ten times larger than Hamas, has infiltrated Lebanon to the point of its members holding seats in the Lebanese parliament and its military occupying land in the north and south of Lebanon (not to mention assassinating its prime minister, Rafic Hariri, in 2005). It threatens Israel with missiles and rockets on a daily basis. On 27 September 2024 Hassan Nasrallah, secretary-general of Hezbollah, was killed by an Israeli air strike. It was followed by an Israeli incursion into Southern Lebanon. Iran responded by firing rockets into Israel. To say that Hezbollah is a major reason for the dangerously escalating conflict in the Middle East and beyond is an understatement.

United Nations

The United Nations (UN) was founded after the Second World War in order to prevent bullies like Hitler from ever exercising power again. Its first engagement was in Korea. The peninsula had been occupied by Japan since 1910. In 1948, it was divided into North Korea, administered by China and the Soviet Union, and South Korea, under the control of the USA and its allies. When North Korean troops crossed the border in 1950, the UN assembled a force of 16 nations to support South Korea. After 3 years of bitter fighting between the two factions, a ceasefire was agreed upon and the border between the two nations at the 38th parallel was reinstated. But no peace treaty has ever been signed.

UN peace-keeping forces have been involved in more than 50 conflicts around the world, mostly to little effect. In Bosnia during the early 1990s, UN soldiers watched impotently as Radovan Karadzic's men, abetted by Serbian President Slobodan Milosevic, raped and murdered innocent civilians. Up to 100,000 died in this 'ethnic cleansing' of Muslims by Serbs. On a single day in July 1993, '3,777 artillery shells fell on Sarajevo, a UN-designated "safe area"'. On 11 July, 'the Muslim "safe" enclave of Srebrenica fell to the Serbs. UN Dutch troops stood by while between 38,000 and 42,000 Muslims were expelled from the area. A group of mainly women, children, and elderly men were taken in trucks, some of which were driven by UN personnel, to UN headquarters at Potocari, where upon arrival they were forcibly seized by armed Serbs. Beatings, abduction of women, and acts of physical violence often resulting in death then occurred; witnesses reported executions. There were many reports of shots and screams in the nearby cornfield during the night.' [23].

Such lack of teeth by the UN (as was the case with the League of Nations before it) is compounded by the fact that China (suppressor of democracy that it guaranteed to the people of Hong Kong in 1997) and Russia (headed by an indicted war criminal) are permanent members of the Security Council, able to veto any proposal with which they disagree. Iran, whose supreme leader sponsors terrorism abroad and the repression of women at home, has been chair of the Human Rights Council. Some members of the terrorist organisation Hamas were recruited to serve on UNRWA (United Nations Relief and Works Agency for Palestine Refugees in the Near East) in 2024. Later the same year, UN Secretary-General Antonio Guterres himself gave succour to Russia's murderous regime by attending a regional conference organised by its president.

That no country has responded to the ineffectiveness of the UN illustrates Edmund Burke's point referred to earlier. In a comprehensive and timely article, the journalist and author Con Coughlin concludes that 'the UN today finds itself at a crossroads. Either it undertakes wholesale reform to make it more relevant for dealing with the challenges of the modern age, or it becomes obsolete' [24]. If the president of the United States has his way and defunds most of the UN's activities, this will resolve itself.

So, there is nothing to stop Russia and its axis of evil (China, North Korea and Iran) from threatening the Free World. Its nations, led by the USA, have to do so on their own.

In this chapter, I have described in some detail the invasion of Ukraine by Russia and that of Israel by Hamas. While I am in the process of completing my task, Israel is about to sign a peace treaty with Hamas. But is a treaty with a terrorist organisation sustainable? Columnist Charles Moore also has his doubts [25]. To end World War 2, the Allies insisted that Germany sign an unconditional surrender (see earlier). Let us hope fervently that the Hamas–Israel agreement brings at least a temporary halt to bloodshed there. To end the wider conflict in the Middle East needs more than treaties with the likes of Hamas, Hezbollah and the Houthis. It requires that Iran, the sponsor of violence, be brought to heel.

There is also the possibility of a temporary peace treaty between Russia and Ukraine, though how this will lead to eventual peace in Eastern Europe is not clear. Sir Bill Browder, once the largest foreign investor in Russia, whose lawyer Sergei Magnitsky was murdered in prison when he exposed the theft of $230 million of state taxes by government officials (see earlier), understands the criminal mind of Vladimir Putin better than others (that includes the President of the United States). 'Putin needs war very specifically as a way to stay in power. If you look at the history of his presidency, every time his popularity has started to diminish, he started a war. ... This is straight out of Machiavelli. If you're worried about people being angry with you, you create a foreign enemy and you start a war'. John Bolton, Trump's national security adviser during his first presidency, considers his former master to be Putin's puppet: 'This is essentially surrendering to the Russian position, ... He (Putin) is as cold-blooded as it comes in pursuing Russia's national interests. ... Trump doesn't get it. He thinks he and Putin are friends' but 'this former KGB agent has been manipulating him for the last couple of weeks to get what he wants and Trump doesn't even realise' [26].

The final decade of the 20th century saw a relative peace descend upon the world. Thirty years on, the autocracies of China, Iran and Russia are threatening the free world: in the Far East, the Middle East and in Europe. The silent majority in those countries, plus Afghanistan and other Muslim-dominated states, as far as women are concerned, continue to suffer. For how long is a question only the autocrats themselves can answer.

Notes

1. Quoted by Bobbitt, p 436.
2. Jähner, Harald, tr Shaun Whiteside: *Vertigo* (London: W H Allen, 2024).

3. Julian Evans: 'Why the downfall of Weimar Germany should haunt us all' Sunday supplement in *Sunday Telegraph* 16 June 2024.
4. Beevor, Antony: The Second World War (London: Weidenfeld and Nicolson, 2012).
5. Lloyd, p 91.
6. *ibid*, p 99 and p 100.
7. *ibid*, p 105 and p 106.
8. *ibid*, p 23 and p 24.
9. *ibid*, p 115 and p 116.
10. *ibid*, p 121.
11. Dumbach and Newborn, p 203.
12. Spicer, pp 280–284.
13. Basil Liddell Hart, quoted in Fraser, p 77.
14. Fraser, pp 119, 266 and 320 resp.
15. Branigan, p 246.
16. Henry Bodkin: *Sunday Telegraph* 10 March 2024.
17. Iona Cleave: 'Organ harvest victim woke up chained to bed to find parts of liver and lungs stolen' *Daily Telegraph* 10 August 2024.
18. Tom Tugendhat, reviewing former Australian prime minister Kevin Rudd's book *On Xi Jinping*: *Sunday Telegraph* Supplement 12 January 2025.
19. Some of the more prominent of Putin's victims (Sweeney, pp 294 and 295) are listed below. In addition, more than 12,000 Ukrainian civilians have so far been killed in the illegal invasion of that country by the indicted war criminal.

Shortlist of Putin Critics, Adversaries Killed, When, Why and How

1998 Anatoly Levin-Utkin: was Putin corrupt? Beaten to death
2000 Artyom Borovik: was Putin a paedophile? Plane crash
2000 Antonio Russo: was Putin a paedophile? Crushed to death
2002 Nikolay Palenniy: protested corruption; strangled?
2003 Sergei Yushenkov: investigating September 1999 bombs; shot
2003 Yuri Shchekochikhin: investigating September 1999 bombs; poisoned
2004 Roman Tsepov: was Putin corrupt? Poisoned
2004 Lecha Islamov: investigating war crimes; poisoned, then shot
2006 Anna Politkovskaya: investigating war crimes; poisoned, then shot
2006 Alexander Litvinenko: was Putin a paedophile? Poisoned
2009 Stanislav Markelov: investigating neo-Nazi links to Kremlin; shot

2009 Anastasia Baburova: investigating neo-Nazi links to Kremlin; shot
2009 Natalia Estemirova: investigating war crimes; shot
2013 Boris Berezovsky: an irritant; hanged?
2014 Sergei Tsapok: an embarrassing murderer; poisoned?
2015 Boris Nemtsov: political opponent; shot
2018 Max Borodin: investigating Wagner Army deaths in Syria; 'fell out of a window'
2021 Dr Sergei Maksimishin: saved Navalny's life; 'heart attack'
2021 Dr Rustam Agishev: saved Navalny's life; 'stroke'
2023 Evgeny Prigozhin: mutiny; fireball
2024 Alexei Navalny: political opponent; murdered, method unknown
Missing from this list is Sergei Magnitsky, a lawyer who in 2009 uncovered a fraud of $230 million allegedly stolen by the government. He was sent to Butyrka prison where he developed gallstones, pancreatitis and other ailments. Denied medical treatment of any kind, he died within a year.

20. Sweeney, p 86.
21. *ibid*, p 134.
21a. Henry Bodkin: 'Hamas tortures Gaza people to silence protests' *Sunday Telegraph* 29 June 2025.
22. I am aware that some very level-headed persons find it unlikely that Mossad, one of the most effective spy agencies in the world, would have been unaware of the impending threat. Whether Prime Minister Benjamin Netanyahu was informed is not known.
23. Bobbitt, pp 425 and 435.
24. Con Coughlin: 'How the UN lost its moral authority' *Sunday Telegraph* 25 February 2024.
25. Charles Moore: *Daily Telegraph* 18 January 2025.
26. Melissa Lawford: 'Putin can't afford peace – his economy is hooked on war' *Sunday Telegraph* 2 March 2025.

Glossary

Cis-female: someone born female who identifies as a girl or woman.

Cis-male: someone born male who identifies as a boy or man.

LGBT: lesbian, gay, bisexual, transgender.

LGBTQ: lesbian, gay, bisexual, transgender, queer not heterosexual (i.e. homosexual) or questioning person.

Manshee: 'a man to female transsexual' (Urban Dictionary), i.e. trans-female.

TERF: trans exclusionary radical feminist.

Trans-female: someone born male who identifies as a girl or woman.

Transgender: a trans-female or trans-male person.

Trans-male: someone born female who identifies as a boy or man.

Transvestite: someone who wears clothes appropriate for the opposite sex; sometimes also used for those who live as one of the opposite sex.

Woke: 'Woke is an adjective derived from African-American Vernacular English (AAVE) meaning "alert to racial prejudice and discrimination". Beginning in the 2010s, it came to encompass a broader awareness of social inequalities such as sexism. ... By 2020, many on the political right and some in the center in several Western countries began using the term *woke* to insult various progressive or leftist movements and ideologies perceived as overzealous, performative, or insincere' (Wikipedia).

Wombman: trans-male (suggested by the author).

Bibliography

Agarwal, Pragya: *Sway: Unravelling Unconscious Bias* (London: Bloomsbury Sigma, 2020)

Anstey, Roger: *The Atlantic Slave Trade and British Abolition 1760–1810* (London: Macmillan Press, 1975)

Baker, John R: *Race* (London: Oxford University Press, 1974)

Berkowitz, Eric: *Dangerous Ideas: A Brief History of Censorship in the West from the Ancients to Fake News* (London: The Westbourne Press, 2021)

Biggar, Nigel: *What's Wrong with Rights?* (Oxford: Oxford University Press, 2020)

Biggar, Nigel: *Colonialism: A Moral Reckoning* (London: William Collins, 2023)

Blyden, Edward W: *Christianity, Islam and the Negro Race* (1887; 2nd edition Edinburgh: Edinburgh University Press, 1967)

Bobbitt, Philip: *The Shield of Achilles: War, Peace and the Course of History* (London: Penguin Books, 2003)

Branigan, Tania: *Red Memory: Living, Remembering and Forgetting China's Cultural Revolution* (London: Faber, 2023)

Browder, Bill: *Freezing Order: A True Story of Russian Money Laundering, Murder, and Surviving Vladimir Putin's Wrath* (New York: Simon and Schuster, 2022)

Browne, Anthony: *The Retreat of Reason: Political Correctness and the Corruption of Public Debate in Modern Britain* (2nd edition; London: Civitas, The Institute for the Study of Civil Society, 2006)

Diop, Sheikh Anta: *Precolonial Black Africa: A Comparative Study of the Political and Social Systems of Europe and Black Africa, from Antiquity to the Formation of Modern States* (translator Harold J Salemson; Brooklyn, NY: Lawrence Hill Books, 1987)

Douglas-Home, Charles: *Evelyn Baring: The Last Proconsul* (London: Collins, 1978)

Dumbach, Annette and Jud Newborn: *Sophie Scholl & The White Rose* (Oxford: Oneworld Publications, 2006)

Fish, Stanley: *There's No Such Thing as Free Speech and It's a Good Thing Too* (Oxford: Oxford University Press, 1994)

Frankopan, Peter: *The Earth Transformed: An Untold History* (London: Bloomsbury Publishing, 2023)

Fraser, David: *Knight's Cross: A Life of Field Marshal Erwin Rommel* (London: HarperCollins, 1993)

Furedi, Frank: *The War Against the Past: Why the West Must Fight for Its History* (Cambridge: Polity, 2024)

Glendinning, Victoria: *Vita: The Life of V. Sackville-West* (London: Weidenfeld and Nicolson, 1983)

Hughes, Geoffrey: *Political Correctness: A History of Semantics and Culture* (Chichester: Wiley-Blackwell, 2010)

Huxley, Aldous: *Brave New World* (London: Chatto and Windus, 1932)

Huxley, Aldous: *Brave New World Revisited* (London: Chatto and Windus, 1959)

Isaac, Benjamin: *The Invention of Racism in Classical Antiquity* (Princeton, NJ: Princeton University Press, 2004)

Joyce, Helen: *Trans: When Ideology Meets Reality* (London: Oneworld, 2021)

Lamb, David: *The Africans* (London: Bodley Head, 1983)

Levtzion, Nehemia: *Ancient Ghana and Mali* (London: Methuen, 1973)

Lloyd, Alexandra: *Defying Hitler: The White Rose Pamphlets* (Oxford: Bodleian Library Publishing, 2022)

McCarthy-Jones, Simon: *Free Thinking: Protecting Freedom of Thought Amidst the New Battle for the Mind* (London: Oneworld, 2023)

Macintyre, Ben: *Josiah the Great: The True Story of the Man Who Would Be King* (London: Harper Press, 2004)

Mounk, Yascha: *The Identity Trap: A Story of Ideas and Power in Our Time* (London: Allen Lane, 2023)

Niemietz, Kristian: *Imperial Measurement: A Cost–Benefit Analysis of Western Colonialism* (London: Institute of Economic Affairs, 2024)

Orwell, George: *Nineteen Eighty-Four* (Oxford: Oxford University Press, 2021)

Pakenham, Thomas: *The Scramble for Africa 1876–1912* (London: Weidenfeld and Nicolson, 1991)

Pasternak, Charles: *Africa South of the Sahara: Continued Failure or Delayed Success?* (Bicester, Oxon: Words by Design, 2018)

Pasternak, Charles: *Androcentrism: The Ascendancy of Man* (Singapore: World Scientific Publishing Co, 2022)

Peckham, Robert: *Fear: An Alternative History of the World* (London: Profile Books, 2023)

Roberts, Andrew: *George III: The Life and Reign of Britain's Most Misunderstood Monarch* (London: Allen Lane, 2021)

Rotberg, Robert I (with the collaboration of Miles F Shore): *The Founder: Cecil Rhodes and the Pursuit of Power* (Oxford: Oxford University Press, 1988)

Rovelli, Carlo: *Anaximander: And the Nature of Science* (copyright 2007; translator into English by Westholme Publishing, 2016; published by London: Allen Lane [Penguin Random House], 2023)

Ruse, Michael: *Homosexuality* (Oxford: Basil Blackwell, 1988)

Scruton, Roger: *Culture Counts* (New York: Encounter Books, 2007)

Segal, Ronald: *Black Slaves: The History of Africa's Other Black Diaspora* (London: Atlantic Books, 2001)

Sewell, Tony: *Black Success: The Surprising Truth* (London: Forum, 2024)

Spicer, Tim: *A Suspicion of Spies* (London: Barbreck Publishers, 2024)

Stock, Kathleen: *Material Girls: Why Reality Matters for Feminism* (London: Fleet, 2021)

Sweeney, John: *Murder in the Gulag: The Life and Death of Alexei Navalny* (London: Headline Press, 2024)

Talbot, David: *The Devil's Chessboard: Allen Dulles, the CIA, and the Rise of America's Secret Government* (London: William Collins, 2016)

Thesiger, Wilfred: *The Life of My Choice* (London: Collins, 1987)

Thompson, Lloyd A: *Romans and Blacks* (London: Routledge, 1989)

Truss, Liz: *Ten Years to Save the West* (London: Biteback Publishing, 2024)

van den Berghe: *The Ethnic Phenomenon* (New York: Elsevier Science Publishing Co, Inc, 1981)

Whitehouse, Senator Sheldon with Jennifer Mueller: *The Scheme: How the Right Wing Used Dark Money to Capture the Supreme Court* (New York: The New Press, 2022)

Young, Michael B: *James VI and I and the History of Homosexuality* (Basingstoke, Hants: Macmillan Press Ltd, 2000)

Young, Toby: *How to Lose Friends and Alienate People* (London: Little, Brown and Company, 2001)

Index

A
Achebe, Chinua, 52
Agarwal, Pragya, 17
agriculture, 11–12
Ai Weiwei, 139
Amodio, David, 18
Anglican Church, 40, 87, 121
Arab slave trade, 36–37
Atinuke, 30
Atlantic slave trade, 37–38

B
Badenoch, Kemi, 102, 111, 160, 162
Baker, John, 19
Baker, Josephine, 22
Balfour Declaration, 178
banks, 122–124
Baring, Evelyn (Lord Cromer), 46–47
Barry, James, 72, 160
BBC (British Broadcasting Corporation), 104–105
Beattie, James, 21
Bell, Derrick, 23
Berlin, Isiah, 162
bias, 17–18
Biggar, (Lord) Nigel, 43–44, 115

Birmingham City University, 71
Bismarck, Otto von, 52
Blair, Tony, 150, 161
Bliss, Rina, 18
Botswana (formerly Bechuanaland), 52
Boytchev, Hristio, 25
Bridges, Khiara, 23
Bronte Parsonage Museum, 118
Browne, Anthony, 95
Bruno, Giordano, 136
Burke, Edmond, 21, 120, 167, 181

C
Cambridge University, 127, 138
Cass report, 62–64, 85
Cherry Pickers, 106
Cicero, 98, 159
civil service, 84, 99–103
climate change, 6
Commission on Race and Ethnic Disparities, 26–29
Coutts Bank, 122
Crenshaw, Kimberlé, 23
critical race theory, 1, 23–24
Crusader squadron, 106

D
Darwin, Charles, 19–20
de Beauvoir, Simone, 4
Derby University, 110
Duke of Wellington, 39, 85
Dyer, General Reginald, 44

E
East India Company, 42–43
EDI (equity, diversity and inclusion), 12, 101, 105, 111–114, 127, 141, 163–164
Edinburgh University, 109
Egypt, 46–47
Einstein, Albert, 173
Elagabalus, emperor, 71–72
Essex University, 108
eurocentrism, 98

F
Fish, Stanley, 135
Fiske, Susan, 17
Forsyth, Frederick, 95
free thought, 151–153
Freud, Sigmund, 69–70
Furedi, Frank, 120, 137
Fourier, Joseph, 7

G
George III, 40
gender dysphoria, 60–61, 63, 71, 75, 81, 84–85
Gladstone, W E, 5, 39, 158
god, 10–11
Gould, Stephen Jay, 51
Graf, Jake and Hannah, 88, 160

Green Jackets, 106
GWR (Great Western Railway), 78

H
Hamas, 25, 178–179, 181–182
Hannan, Daniel, 41, 141
Harlan, Josiah, 45
hate speech, 138–139
Hitler, Adolf, 117, 167–169, 172, 179
homosexuality, 3–4, 13, 64–71
homosexuality in animals, 70
HS2 (High Speed 2), 103–104
Hughes, Geoffrey, 95
Hugo, Victor, 21
Hume, David, 7, 21
Huxley, Aldous, 2, 143

I
Ibadan University, 53
Iman, Inaya Folarin, 144
India, 42–46, 51
Isaac, Benjamin, 20–21

J
James I and VI, 65–66
Jefferson, Thomas, 12, 22
Jenner, Bruce, 80–81
Jensen, Arthur, 22
Joyce, Helen, 2, 85, 117, 138

K
King's College London, 109
Kinsey, Alfred, 70

L
Lancaster University, 109

Index

Leclerc, George-Louis, 7
Lefkovitz, Mary, 20
Leicester University, 109, 118
libraries, 116–118
Liverpool University, 108
Livingstone, David, 36
Lloyd's Bank, 124
Locke, John, 137
London Universities' Council for Academic Freedom, 149
Ludwig Maximilian University of Munich, 169, 171

M
Marsot, Afaf Lutfi Al-Sayyid, 47
McCarthy-Jones, Simon, 151–153
Medawar, Peter, 69
Moore, (Lord) Charles, 106, 150
Morris, James (later Jan), 73, 75, 84, 142, 160
museums and galleries, 118–119

N
National Trust, 124
Natural History Museum, 118
Navalny, Alexei, 175–177
Nelson, Admiral, 39
NHS (National Health Service), 12, 62, 85–86, 99, 106–109
Niemietz, Kristian, 40
Nicolson, Harold, 66–69
Nigeria, 52–53
non-crime hate incident, 141–143
Nottingham University, 110

O
O'Neill, Onora, 38
Open University, 83
Oxford University, 147

P
Pearson, Allison, 124, 141
Poitier, Sidney, 23
publishers, 114–116
Putin, Vladimir, 157, 173–174, 176–177, 182–183

R
race, 18–19
Ratcliff, Jessica, 42
religion, 9–11, 121–122
re-naming species, 125–127
Ridley, Matt, 8
Rhodes, Cecil, 48–51
Roberts, Andrew, 45
Rotberg, Robert, 50
Rousseau, Jean-Jacques, 34
Rowling, J K, 83
Roy, Tirthankar, 43

S
Sackville-West, Vita, 66–69
Scruton, Roger, 69, 115
sensitivity reader, 115–116, 158
Sewell, (Lord) Cleveland Anthony, 26–28, 38
Sheffield University, 109
Sigsworth, Tim, 164
Singh, Manmohan, 46
Smith, Adam, 44

South Africa, 47–51
Stock, Kathleen, 4, 61, 83, 108, 117, 138, 148, 159
Stonewall, 63, 84, 86, 108, 148
Strimpel, Zoe, 30, 112
Sturgeon, Nicola, 74
Supreme Court, 160
Sussex University, 4

T
Tate Gallery, 119
Tate Modern, 118
Tharoor, Shashi, 43, 45
The Key, 54
Thesiger, Wilfred, 18
Thompson, Lloyd, 21
Tombs, Robert, 159
transgender, 60–64, 71–88
Trevelyan, Laura, 39
Truss, Liz, 161

U
UN (United Nations), 180–181

W
Weimar Republic, 167
White Rose, 169–172
Williams, Eric, 40
Williams syndrome, 17–18
Woolf, Virginia, 68, 136

V
van den Berghe, 19, 33

X
Xi Jinping, 173–174

Y
York St John University, 117
Young, (Lord) Toby, 116, 139, 141, 145–147

www.ingramcontent.com/pod-product-compliance
Lightning Source LLC
Chambersburg PA
CBHW070309230426
43664CB00015B/2688